GUARDIAN

of
the

GOLDEN
GATE

Protecting the Line
Between Hope
and Despair

Praise for **Guardian of the Golden Gate**

"As a 30-year career suicidologist, I can say without hesitation that Kevin Briggs is one of my suicide prevention heroes. As a highway patrolman on the iconic Golden Gate Bridge, Kevin has literally talked hundreds of suicidal people back over the railing to live another day. This life-saving work was done with no formal clinical training as Kevin relied solely on his good judgment, plain-talk, a sense of humor, and his remarkable humanity. This book shares uncommon personal and professional wisdom from a public servant who 'worked the Bridge' offering us fresh perspectives about death and despair, challenges and opportunities, work and love, and what it means to care for others and truly be alive."

David A. Jobes, Ph.D.
Professor of Psychology, The Catholic University of America
Past-President of the American Association of Suicidology

"Kevin Briggs talks the talk and walks the walk. His real life personal and professional experiences helping people in distress give great insight into mental health, stress, and how to deal with life's mental and emotional challenges. It's practical and a must-read for anyone wanting to have a better quality of life."

Ron Barr
National Network Talk Show Host

"Sgt. Kevin Briggs is a man who cares for others passionately and who has the unparalleled experience to support his views on how to help those in crisis. His stories get the reader as close to the real thing as possible. As one who also has been in the position of talking to people who wanted to jump off of a bridge, I can honestly say Sgt. Briggs' account is truthful, respectful, forthright, and helpful to anyone who has tried to help someone contemplating suicide."

Dr. Andrew T. Young LPC-S, NCC
Professor in Behavioral Sciences, Lubbock Christian University
SWAT Negotiator, Lubbock Police Department

"In 1995, the very week I graduated with a 60-hour CACREP accredited Master's degree in Community Agency Counseling, I received a call from a 50-year-old man who attended my church. He reported he was calling to tell someone, anyone, goodbye as he was going to end his life with a shotgun. At that moment, I realized how unprepared I was to help. I would have gladly traded my diploma for the experiences and tools Kevin shares from his work as the Guardian of the Golden Gate Bridge. In this book, Sgt. Briggs talks about how he saved many lives standing on the other side of the rail, with a thin apron of bridge between them and suicide. No one should die alone and in despair, and Kevin and his team developed a strong model for compassionately relating, a framework that would benefit every reader invested in helping those in severe anguish hold on."

David Covington, LPC, MBA
President & CEO, Recovery Innovations, Inc.

"*Guardian of the Golden Gate* is a stunning portrait of courage, empathy, and the power of human compassion to save hundreds of lives. Sgt. Briggs writes with grace and humility about his experiences with suicide prevention during nearly two decades of working the Golden Gate Bridge. He also writes openly of his own battles with cancer and depression and how his struggles have deepened his ability to serve others during times of crisis. This is an intimate and haunting portrait of one of America's most iconic places. It reveals the truth that mental illness and suicide impact people of every demographic and that these deaths are preventable. *Guardian of the Golden Gate* has the power to continue Briggs' work of saving lives for many decades to come by making all of us better listeners [and] better gatekeepers for ourselves and others."

Meg Hutchinson
Singer/Songwriter
"Gatekeeper"

"Kevin's experience shines a bright light on a topic we have long sought to bring out of the dark. This book highlights the practical tools and skills that helped give hundreds of people a 'tomorrow,' sharing the immense power of connections and most importantly – that suicide can be prevented."

Linda Rosenberg
President & CEO, National Council for Behavioral Health

"Kevin Briggs is a true American hero and a champion for mental health, first as a member of the California Highway Patrol, where he helped prevent countless suicides, and now with his passion as a mental health advocate. Kevin works diligently to help break down the stigma of mental illness, which will continue to help reduce suicide. I have had the pleasure of working with Kevin at a suicide awareness conference, and his presentation was life-changing. You will not find a more genuine and compassionate man than Kevin Briggs."

Rick Strait, MS, LPC, CRDAC, CCDP, CCGC
IDDT Program Manager/Co-Occurring Therapist
Outpatient/Co-Occurring Division
Community Counseling Center, Central Methodist University

"In a crisis situation that involves life and death, a person needs honesty, sincerity, kindness, and empathy mixed together with just the right amount of each. Kevin Briggs taught me how to fine-tune the ingredients and reach people in the worst possible pivotal moment of their lives, help them grab the hope in their darkness and ask 'What's your plan for tomorrow?'"

Jamie S. Burton
CEO, Adanta Behavioral Health Services

GUARDIAN
of the GOLDEN GATE

*Protecting the Line
Between Hope
and Despair*

KEVIN BRIGGS
with SAM MELLINGER
Foreword by Meg Hutchinson
Afterword by Kevin Berthia

Requests for permission should be addressed to: Ascend Books, LLC, Attn: Rights and Permissions Department, 12710 Pflumm Road, Suite 200, Olathe, KS 66062

10 9 8 7 6 5 4 3 2 1

ISBN: print book 978-0-9904375-7-4
ISBN: e-book 978-0-9904375-8-1

Library of Congress Control Number 2015942744

Publisher: Bob Snodgrass
Publication Coordinator: Christine Drummond
Editor: Claire Reagan
Sales and Marketing: Lenny Cohen and Sandy Hipsh
Publicity: Bob Ibach
Dust Jacket and Book Design: Rob Peters

All photos courtesy of Kevin Briggs unless otherwise indicated.

www.ascendbooks.com

Contents

This book is dedicated to those who have been lost to suicide and their families, those who continue to suffer in silence, and those who have attempted suicide and survived.

Foreword by Meg Hutchinson

Kevin Briggs changed my life before we ever met.

It was 2003. I was 25 years old. My songwriting career was taking off, and to those around me, I appeared happy and successful – but I was falling apart inside. Nobody knew my struggles. I never mentioned them. I didn't even admit to myself that I had a problem.

Looking back, I was drinking and partying way too much. I was isolated – even while surrounded by friends. My highs and lows were getting worse.

That's when Kevin Briggs came into my life through an article in *The New Yorker* about the dark side of the Golden Gate Bridge. I read that when Kevin met someone on the Bridge and wasn't sure of their intentions, he would ask them simple and telling questions, like "How are you feeling today?" and "What's your plan for tomorrow?"

Those questions touched me deeply. They are so straightforward but, when asked with the right tone and sincerity, can bring out so much truth. After reading the article, I wrote a song called "Gatekeeper" and dedicated it to Kevin. Everywhere I played it, people were amazed that those ordinary questions could save lives.

When the day has grown too long
The hour's standing still
When you wonder if you could, if you will
With your toes upon the edge
With your eyes upon the sky
Tell me just these things before you fly
How are you feeling?
What are your plans for tomorrow?

I didn't tell anyone that the song was also about me. I had become a master at covering up what I was really feeling. I had always been the cheerful overachiever. I thought depression was a sign of weakness, so I worked hard to hide it. When I wrote the song, I had no way of knowing that Kevin's words and compassion would help save my life, too.

Looking back, the breakdown was inevitable. The longer I went untreated, the more extreme my highs and lows. Once you get used to hiding your true feelings from people, you can get good at it. You might be surprised how much pain and struggle you can keep from even your closest friends.

My breakdown came after a music tour in Europe. It was textbook. The changes in season, time zone, sleep pattern – combined with a crazy tour schedule and too much partying – made me higher than I'd ever been. When I returned home to Boston, I crashed.

My breaking point felt like what I imagine early Alzheimer's to be. I couldn't sleep. I had to write notes to myself when I fed the dog because I couldn't remember if I had. I got lost driving in my own neighborhood. I forgot how the washing machine worked.

I called my mom and told her something was wrong with my brain. I had to come home. My parents are former hippies, so for the first few days, we tried all the natural ways to heal. Nature walks, healthy food, Valerian root tea, salt baths. Nothing worked. I was plagued by insomnia. I was in a "mixed state" where I was both manic and depressed. I became acutely suicidal, so my sisters finally brought me to the hospital where I was diagnosed with bipolar disorder and spent 21 days in-patient.

In the hospital, I went back to Kevin's words. By that time, I'd been singing "Gatekeeper" for three years. The chorus cycled through my mind over and over again with those simple questions:

How are you feeling?

What are your plans for tomorrow?

I felt as though Kevin was standing there beside me, and I was astonished to find my life was saved, in part, by a complete stranger.

• • • •

Almost every 13 minutes someone kills themselves in the United States – and the numbers are rising. Suicide can be nearly impossible to understand. According to all who knew me, I was the least likely candidate for suicide. I came from a loving family. I'd been a straight-A student, a star athlete, a deeply optimistic person with a passion for life.

When I was at rock bottom, what gave me the deepest comfort was someone just sitting with me – not trying to fix me or change my experience – simply bearing witness to my pain.

This is what Kevin has given to hundreds of people on the Bridge.

Nine years after writing Kevin's song, I got an e-mail out of the blue. It began, "Hello, my name is Kevin Briggs..."

I was stunned. He had heard my song. We shared many letters in the following year, and in the spring of 2014, I flew to California. I was filming a feature-length documentary on mental health called *Pack Up Your Sorrows*.

Finally, we met.

I arrived a day before the film crew and drove to the Bridge alone at sunset. It was a beautiful spring evening and everything was bathed in golden light. I walked the length of the Bridge. Midway across, I paused at the railing and looked down. I felt a rush of vertigo. I thought of how fiercely I love my life and how profoundly grateful I am to have survived.

The following day, I stood there with Kevin and finally got the chance to say "Thank you."

"Thank you, Kevin, for the questions that helped me survive. Thank you for the hundreds of people who have been given a second chance because of your presence."

We want to believe that suicide happens to people who aren't like us. Maybe it helps us ignore the fact that over a hundred people are dying by suicide in the United States every day. More than a thousand of these deaths every year are college students.

Most people who commit suicide don't actually want to die. The few who have survived the 220 foot fall from the Golden Gate Bridge all agree that the moment they let go of the railing, they wanted to live. They would do anything to get back on that bridge.

People commit suicide because they are in agony. When a building is on fire, you might jump out the window to escape the pain of the flames. This is a more appropriate way to think of suicide. When there is someone like Kevin standing in that burning building beside you saying, "You don't have to jump. There is a way out of here," it can make all the difference.

Guardian of the Golden Gate has the power to continue Kevin's work by making all of us better listeners – better gatekeepers for ourselves and others. We must never underestimate the ability of a few ordinary questions to save a life.

1
I Work The Bridge

I work The Bridge.

The Marin Area of the California Highway Patrol (CHP) is responsible for law enforcement duties on the Golden Gate Bridge and most of the surrounding area. We also cover unincorporated cities, urban freeways, and rural mountain roads. For more than 17 years – and until I retired from the CHP in November 2013 – my professional career involved working directly on or supervising officers who also worked the Bridge. Even now, I still feel like I work the Bridge in a manner of speaking.

The CHP does cover a lot of ground, but my favorite place to work was always the Bridge. We all have our comfort zones, and the Bridge was surely mine. It was my job and my identity. It was how I fed my family and served the world. It was both rewarding and challenging. The Bridge could be bitterly cold and damp with fog one day and beautiful the next.

The same goes for the people you meet on it.

Tour companies bring groups from all over the world. One bus will be filled with people from China, the next Germany, and right after that, the Philippines.

Like I always say, I've loved and hated the Bridge, often in the same day. I've made new friends here and met up with old.

I've also seen people die here.

The Golden Gate Bridge is an American icon. It is one of the United States' greatest symbols of art and architecture: Standing at nearly 900,000 tons of steel and asphalt, of inspiration and ambition, it stirs awe in the millions of people that visit it each year.

You can talk about the Statue of Liberty and now the Freedom Tower in New York. Overseas, you have the Great Wall of China and the Eiffel Tower. Think about it, and you realize there is a short list of the most recognized and appreciated man-made structures in the world. It's hard for an inanimate object to make people *feel* something. But art does that. The Bridge does that. Me, I've come to think of the Bridge as something like an old friend. Sometimes, you get mad at your old friend. Sometimes, you're frustrated with your old friend. But, in the end, you have love. You have so much in common.

Ten million people come to the Bridge every year for reasons that have nothing to do with going over the Bay between San Francisco and Marin County. In this way, the Bridge is many different things to many different people.

It is the only realistic way for commuters across the Bay to get into San Francisco, so we divide the six lanes of traffic accordingly. Four lanes go south into the city in the morning and four lanes go north back to Marin County in the evening. For those workers, the Bridge serves mostly as a utility. It is a way to get from home to work and back again. Maybe in the morning they peek to the east at the skyline. Maybe in the evening they peek to the west at the ocean.

For many, many people, this landmark is a necessary part of their commute.

For millions of others, however, the Bridge is something more special. It is 1.7 miles long, so you can park at one end, jog to the other and back and have a nice workout.

There aren't a lot of places where you can get such an unencumbered view of the great city's skyline. You can see artists working on canvas or photographers waiting for the light to be just right. Thousands of pictures are taken every day on the Bridge and of the Bridge. Selfies, landscape photos, images of friends standing with a skyline in the background to send back home to jealous friends – memories made. Take a picture on the Bridge, and you don't have to tell people where you are.

The east walkway is where most of those pictures are taken. You can see Alcatraz, Angel, and Treasure Islands. You have to pick the right day, though. Fog is both famous and infamous on the Bridge. You can be looking out at the city one minute and the next be swallowed in a dark, mysterious haze. The Bridge can turn from a peaceful beauty to a rough and lonely foe in less time than a television commercial break.

When the weather is nice and the traffic not too heavy, it can feel invigorating to stand up there over the water looking out to the city. People get engaged on the Bridge. They plan their lives there.

A new and greatly improved gift shop opened a few years ago at the southeast parking lot of the Bridge, the part closest to the city. It is full of books and calendars and key chains and photographs and everything else you'd expect in a gift shop. They made sure to honor the Bridge's great history, too, so sometimes you'll see people browsing the information and pictures on the gift shop's walls.

Up on the Bridge, it sounds like hustle. Traffic is constant: You can hear conversations between old friends walking, horns from big trucks headed into the city, and every once in a while "On your left!" from a jogger coming from behind. In a rare quiet moment, you can hear the sea lions barking below or the birds squawking above. But there aren't many quiet moments. Cargo ships and the occasional cruise ship blare their arrival with horns that can be heard for a mile or more.

Go to the Bridge any time of day, any day of the week, and you'll probably see a bus loading or unloading a stream of tourists. There's something called the hop-on, hop-off bus in San Francisco, and the Bridge is one of its most popular spots. People can also pay $10 for ferry rides that leave from the city, head to the Bridge, and then back to land.

Walkways border the lanes of traffic on the Bridge. The walkway on the west is typically where we shepherd the bikers. Generally, only bicyclists are allowed to travel on the west sidewalk and only after iron workers and painters finish for the day. Honestly, in my opinion, bikers – at least those on the Bridge – can be a pain. They're fast, not always in control, and some of them can be quite rude. It's better for everyone when you can separate bikers and pedestrians.

From the top of the tower, you feel like you can see forever. I don't patrol the Bridge anymore – I'm retired from the CHP – but it will always be part of my life. My experiences here have shaped me forever.

I treat the Bridge with respect and caution. Sharks swim below, but the dangers are 220 feet above the water, right there amidst the steel and concrete. I know the secrets there, the things that politicians and tour guides don't want visitors to find out, the things that make this wonder of ingenuity and hard work a place of danger and tragedy.

I know that every ten days or so, someone walks on the Bridge and never comes back. I know that this Bridge, one of the most beautiful and iconic structures in the world, is something like a magnet for men and women who are tired of fighting their demons. I know that, even now, someone may be climbing over the rail contemplating the jump.

The Golden Gate Bridge is one of the top suicide destinations on the planet.

Most years, thirty to forty people come to the Bridge to make the last decision they'll ever make: whether to jump off the side and into the Bay, ending their lives. Most of them die on impact and eventually float back to the water's surface. What was a shattered life has been reduced to shattered bones, punctured organs, and broken hearts. The jump is an abrupt end for the victim and a bitter beginning for those left behind.

If only the fog was the lone danger.

. . . .

You can talk to twenty different people and get twenty different impressions of the Bridge. I like to think mine is more intimate, with both the beauty and the horrors of this place.

As an officer, my beat was not just the Bridge, but also the highways leading into San Francisco. My territory went down to Sausalito and north on U.S. 101 for several miles. The Bridge was always the busiest point for me, though. In an eight-and-a-half hour shift, I'd spend a quarter of that, often more, on the Bridge.

After the tragedies of September 11, 2001, security on the Bridge changed. It's such an iconic landmark that it is easy to imagine a terrorist group wanting to take a run at the Bridge. We bumped up our patrol and security from one officer to four to six officers patrolling the Bridge at any time.

We had security cameras on the Bridge before – and I have to be careful about how much I say here – but it's safe to assume that most every square foot of the Bridge is now under surveillance.

I also have to be careful about what I say about destructive attempts on the Bridge. We've had a lot of information about various plots or groups that might want to make a name for themselves with the Bridge. There was a time when we were required to use binoculars to track every plane that flew near the Bridge and record tail numbers.

The scariest thing for us was when a U-Haul truck would break down on the Bridge. That's happened a few times; it's the kind of thing that puts a real shake in you. You turn to one of your fellow officers, and it's like, "Okay, *you* take that call."

National security issues will always be part of what we deal with on the Bridge, but day-to-day, the far bigger concern is people who come to hurt themselves and the possibility of head on traffic collisions. The only things dividing the northbound and southbound lanes are round yellow traffic cones, about two feet tall – not even enough to stop a bicycle.

When you work the Bridge, you learn to read cues. The Bridge gives you signs. When it's rainy or foggy, there's a good chance you'll end up working a traffic accident at some point in your shift. When it's bright and sunny, there's a better chance you won't get a traffic call, but more people on the Bridge because of a beautiful day brings a different set of worries.

For me, it's always about safety and making sure traffic laws are obeyed. As a member of law enforcement, I need everyone to feel safe.

But working the Bridge means working the place where more people go to kill themselves than almost anywhere else in the world. Protecting life takes on a different meaning for those of us who work the Bridge.

I had no formal training on this type of protection when I took the job. Those who know me know that I can be rather emotional. I relied on this quality for quite some time, until I finally took a class in what we refer to as Crisis Intervention Training. Prior to this, most of what I learned about depression as well as suicide prevention and intervention was on the fly, either through real life experience or by reading articles about mental illness.

Most of the time, when I deal with someone in a true crisis state on the Bridge, I'm not seeing them climb over the rail. When I get to them, they're usually standing on what we call the chord, the 32-inch beam that parallels the Bridge and sits several feet below the walkway. It's used by maintenance staff and runs nearly the entire length of the Bridge.

Standing on the chord means literally standing between life and death. I've been fortunate enough to talk most of the people I've encountered back over, but it's always best if you can get to people before they climb over that rail.

When they're on our side of the rail, they're safe. When they're on the outside of the Bridge, anything can happen.

So you start to look for signs. In my line of work, everyone on the Bridge is a potential suicide call. You just never know what is really going on in someone's mind. You start to look for body language or any non-verbal expression that could signal someone has come to the Bridge to end their life.

There's a profile. People don't always fit profiles, obviously – there have been folks jogging with multiple people who suddenly just project themselves over the rail – but you work with the signs you can see.

If someone's alone, that's a marker. People don't typically decide to kill themselves when they're with friends. You also look at how they're walking. The slower the walk, the more you might be worried. You have to look for other visual clues, too. Is the person focused? Do they seem thoughtful or pensive? Do they look put together or like they've been up all night? Are they walking straight or appear to be under the influence with a meandering gait?

Sometimes, clothes can give away intentions. If they are not dressed for the weather, maybe that means they don't plan on being in it for long. If they're walking without much direction or never look in either direction – to the ocean on the west or one of America's great skylines on the east – maybe they have no direction.

These are just some of the signs that I have come to notice. Of course, none of this means a person is actually suicidal – the signs just raise suspicions. Watching for these cues is profiling in the purest sense, but it has nothing to do with race or gender. You learn quickly that depression and suicidal thoughts have no cultural bias; mental disease can affect anyone.

Now, when I see someone exhibiting any of these signs, I approach them gently and almost like a friend. I'm wearing the uniform and the Badge, so they know who I am. I don't have to flaunt it. I want to start a dialogue with them, ask how they're doing, maybe where they're from, or even something about the weather. I can get a good idea of where someone's mind is this way.

I ask questions like: "Hi, how are you?" or "Where are you from?"

One of my favorite questions is: "It's supposed to be nice tomorrow (or whatever the weather might be), what are you doing tomorrow?"

Nobody who's planning to actually kill themselves that day answers a question about tomorrow quickly. They're not planning on being around the next day. They're not thinking that far ahead.

I have found that even those who have planned everything to the last detail, written a suicide note dissolving friends and family from blame or guilt, given away belongings, made a will, and even sent a delayed email to friends with all of their passwords, do not think about answering a question like this just prior to the suicide act itself.

If a person has answered my questions in a manner that shows no indication of suicide intention or a plan to hurt others, I cannot legally detain them. They are free to go about their business. After all, I have a multitude of rules, regulations, and policies I must follow. I am granted a tremendous amount of authority, and I hold that authority sacred. If I don't have enough to legally detain a person, I won't do it. It's that simple. This, however, does not mean I go away.

If my intuition tells me otherwise, that the person may actually hurt themselves, I can unobtrusively watch from a distance and have Bridge Patrol watch them on camera. I don't do this to be a bother or watchdog; I do it because sometimes we all need to be protected – even from ourselves.

The best way to prevent suicide is to not let it get to the point where a person is over the railing, to the point where they're ready to pull the trigger, so to speak. This is referred to as reducing lethal means.

If we have any inkling that someone could jump but aren't sure, we always ask to walk them off the Bridge. Remember, the best way to prevent suicide is to not let it get to the point where they're over the railing. That is key.

• • • •

The Bridge's history of multiple suicides every year is about to change in a major way. They're going to build what everyone's calling a "suicide net" – which received approval in 2014. This is more than a decade in the making, and I have to say that for a long time I was among those who didn't want anything built.

I like the view.

Maybe that sounds strange coming from someone who did what I did for so long, but that's how I felt. It's a great view. You can't beat it. The freedom up there, the open air. I only changed my mind recently.

There's an organization called the Bridge Rail Foundation; they've been pushing for some sort of tangible suicide prevention for some time. The board is mostly made up of people who've lost loved ones on the Bridge, psychologists, and even a former Marin County Coroner.

Not too long ago, one of the board members saw me at a training session I attended. I actually worked his daughter's case years ago when she lost her life to suicide. The man recognized me and introduced himself. I did not get a chance to speak with his daughter on the Bridge. She jumped before anyone could reach her. Unfortunately, I did not remember the case very well. He spoke about meeting me that day and thanked me for being kind.

As we spoke, the topic of the suicide net came up. He asked me what I thought, and I wasn't going to lie to him.

"I really don't have much of an opinion on it, but if I had to choose, I would probably be against it," I answered. "I like to look out and see the view."

I explained my reasoning further: the extremely small number of suicide cases versus the number of people who visit the Bridge every year. I knew what I was saying and, understandably, expected to be blasted by this gentleman.

He was nice. He didn't get mad. He was actually quite calm.

"Kevin," he said. "Look at it like this..."

At this point, he put his palms out, like he was weighing something in each hand.

"You have the view, or life."

Shit.

How do you compete with that? In one brief second, his gesture made the issue totally clear.

My ignorance was changed that day. I'm very glad he approached me and spoke in the calm and collected manner he did. I'm now an advocate for the barrier. Sometimes in life, it's how an issue is presented that can make all the difference. It's all about perspective.

So, I'm glad they're going to build the net. When they call it "the suicide net," it's misleading – it is not a net as much as an iron apparatus that will sit about 20 feet below the Bridge. That's low enough that it won't block the view of the city or Alcatraz at all. If a person attempts to jump off the Bridge, they will still fall for a bit – and it'll hurt – but they will survive.

History tells us that when people jump off the Bridge, the first thing they feel is regret. They know they've made a mistake; of course, by then, it's too late. They're free-falling 22 stories to their deaths.

More than two thousand people have either been seen jumping or their bodies have been found in the water below. Nobody believes the actual number is that low. Whatever the real number of lives lost on the Bridge, it continues to grow every month. In hopes of helping those in dire distress, we've installed hotline phones along the walkway. Anything we can do to get someone contemplating the jump to think twice.

• • • •

The Golden Gate Bridge opened on a sunny morning in May 1937, as the largest suspension bridge ever constructed. Joseph Strauss was the

The California Highway Patrol put these phone stations on the Bridge some years ago to encourage people to seek help before it's too late.

The sign next to the phones. Hopefully, this will all be less of an issue once the suicide barrier is constructed. The barrier was finally approved on June 27, 2014.

chief engineer. Building something as grand as the Bridge is never one man's work, of course, but he's the one we've come to consider the father of this great American landmark.

Strauss came from an artistic family. His mother was an accomplished pianist until an accident ended her concert career. His father was a writer and painter.

While in college at the University of Cincinnati, Strauss was hospitalized in a room that overlooked the Roebling Bridge, which connects Cincinnati and Covington, Kentucky. That's where he became fascinated with bridges. After graduating college, he took a job with a firm that specialized in bridges.

Strauss was sharp and innovative. He came up with a cheaper alternative to the iron counterweights used at the time and went on to design bridges all over the continent, from Houston to Washington state and even Toronto. Despite having designed all those bridges, he will forever be remembered for his work on the Golden Gate Bridge.

At first, there were doubts about whether the project was even possible. Few bridges – if any – had spanned such a distance or reached as high into the sky. And then there were the forces of the ocean to contend with.

Although construction of the Bridge took more than four years, costing more than $35 million, Strauss was particularly proud that the project came in ahead of schedule and under budget.

Strauss was very concerned for the safety of those working to build his bridge. He developed a portable safety net that hung below the construction site and was credited with saving as many as 19 lives, men who called themselves members of the Halfway to Hell Club. Men did die in the project, though, most of them when the net gave out under the weight of a fallen scaffold.

The opening of the Bridge was such a big deal for the United States that President Roosevelt pushed a button in Washington D.C., which officially opened vehicle traffic. At the ceremony, Strauss remarked, "What Nature rent asunder long ago, man has joined today."

Strauss was also an avid poet and wrote a piece called "The Mighty Task is Done" for the occasion:

> *As harps for the winds of heaven,*
> *My web-like cables are spun,*
> *I offer my span for the traffic of man,*
> *At the gate of the setting sun.*

Reporters packed the event and – perhaps with the workers who weren't saved by the net in mind – asked about what would happen if someone jumped over the railing. Despite his idea with the safety net, Strauss was, at least in this crucial way, an artist first and an engineer second. He was justifiably proud of the Bridge's beauty and the views it gave.

"Why would anyone want to jump off the Golden Gate Bridge?" he asked in response.

Little did Strauss know that lots of people have reasons to jump off the Bridge.

In fact, just three months later, a 47-year-old man named Harold Wobber had a reason. He fought in World War I and, even eight years after the Great Depression, still couldn't find a job. He was in good company. The nation's unemployment rate was around 15 percent at the time.

The story goes that Wobber walked by himself to mid-span and said to a stranger behind him, "This is as far as I go," before he flung himself over the railing. His body was never found in the water below.

Wobber jumped close to what we call light pole 69. They're numbered, starting with 1 on the north end and going up to 128 at the edge of the south end. Even numbers on the ocean side, odd on the bay side. The point where Wobber jumped, light pole 69, is in the very middle of the Bridge, and if you look at a map of where people have jumped, the heaviest cluster is right there in the middle.

I don't know why that is. If you walk the Bridge, it crests in the middle. Maybe there's a sense of balance for people in that spot. Maybe that's where they figure it is highest. I don't know.

Over the years, suicide on the Bridge has somehow become romanticized. There's a myth that the water below will cleanse your soul. Some people believe that if they jump between the two towers – and light pole 69 is the midpoint of those towers – they will enter a different dimension.

These myths are completely made-up, of course. The reality is this: If a person jumps off the Bridge, they have a four or five second free-fall to their death. From that height, the water is more like concrete. Very few survive the fall: fewer than 2 percent – or 1 in 50. The people who do survive come back up with broken arms and ribs or a crushed spine. Most people drown because their bodies are wrecked and they can't keep their heads above water. Most of the ones lucky enough to make it out of the water alive die from their injuries within a few days.

Since Wobber, thousands of men and women have gone to the Bridge to end their lives. Most come primarily from the Bay Area and West Coast, but there have been many others who have made the trek from all over the country and even the world. There is no demographic untouched by the Bridge: old women and young men; Hispanic, Asian, African-American, and Caucasian; rich and poor; some homeless and others with five-bedroom mortgages.

Roy Raymond started a company called Victoria's Secret. In 1982, he sold it for $1 million. In 1993, that company became the country's largest lingerie retailer. He jumped off the Bridge that summer. In the same week, a presumably homeless black man jumped over the rail yelling at voices only he could hear. Nobody knew his name.

This is as real as it gets up here, but I don't want you to think it's all sad stories. As a matter of fact, the vast majority of my experiences with people who've reached their breaking points have ended happily.

On average, for every suicide, three to five people decide to give life another chance. I've been even more fortunate in my experience. I've talked to more than 200 people in that chaotic mental state of choosing to live or die, and I've helped all but two of them decide to live.

I always say it like that – I've *helped them* decide to live – because it's critical to think of it in that context. I suppose there's a self-sustaining tool here because if I can always remember that it is *their* decision about whether to live, it helps keep my mind where it should be – with them.

Also, it's important to empower the people you meet in these situations. This isn't some trick I'm using. It's the plain truth. It is, in every possible way, their decision. If they've gotten to the point where they're convinced that life isn't worth it anymore and all hope has vanished, there is little I can do. They're gone.

But, if I can play a small part in helping them realize what they have to live for and that life is worth living, even through the bad parts, then it's important that they know it was *their* decision as opposed to something I convinced them to do. I consider my work a conduit in their actions for self-preservation. I do not save people, as is listed in so many articles and news clippings. These people make up their own minds to save themselves. I'm just someone who is there to point out things that may not have crossed their mind in some time. That's one of many strategies that I and others like me have learned over the years from meeting people who find themselves living the worst moment of their lives.

Besides, if a person believes living was something they were talked into, then what was the point? And who will be there when they change their mind?

My job put me in front of people who were facing what can sometimes be the last stage of depression: when those demons have gone from merely suggesting suicide to forming a real plan and taking action. When a person gets to the point that a 22-story free-fall seems like the best option, we have to be delicate. Every move, every word, every moment counts.

I don't know that what I do is the best way. I just know that my years of experience have taught me certain ways to help people out of these potentially tragic moments. I'm not a psychiatrist. I'm not a counselor. I'm not a minister or a rabbi or a priest. I'm a sergeant in the California Highway Patrol. I'm a cop.

And I work *this* Bridge.

• • • •

Nobody wants to think of it this way, but the Bridge is a nightmare for those of us in law enforcement.

When I say this, I mean the events that occur on the Bridge and not the structure itself. Every time I drive or walk over it, I recall events that occurred in various locations. Sometimes, it is like I am still there, watching myself talking to someone over the rail.

I am fully aware that this is inconsequential to everyone outside of law enforcement, but it's worth understanding all the same. As I've said, the Bridge represents different things to so many. People are united by the Bridge – literally by connecting Marin County and San Francisco and figuratively as a meeting point and landmark example of American ingenuity. People are awed by the Bridge.

But those of us in law enforcement are often frustrated by the Bridge. As far as jurisdictions go, it's really difficult. Just as an example, if you're ever stopped for drugs or alcohol – not an uncommon thing at all on my beat – you should hope it's on the north side of the North Tower, closer to Marin County and Sausalito. If so, you would fall under the care of the Marin County Sheriff's Department. That's a pleasant group of officers, and their drunk tank is something like the beach resort of local jails. You can sober up and call your lawyer from relative comfort.

On the other hand, if you're unlucky and are stopped even a foot on the south side of that North Tower, well, then you're in the city of San Francisco's system. You have missed a relatively smooth criminal experience for the Seventh Street Jail, which is something like what you'd expect to see in a bad movie scene: dark, outdated, dirty, and overcrowded from the crime so common in cities like San Francisco and rare in more affluent suburbs like Marin County.

Another feature of the Bridge is that it has a group of wonderful and uniformed professionals in what is called the Golden Gate Bridge Highway and Transportation District. The CHP is tasked with security and police services on the Bridge and surrounding parking lots. After 9/11, the District hired patrol officers, referred to as Bridge Patrol. I was fortunate enough to be on a panel, as a CHP representative, in the hiring process of this new staff.

These men and women keep the Bridge running by looking out for problems, changing the lanes of traffic to better accommodate commuters, and monitoring everything that happens on the Bridge.

They are responsible for the day-to-day maintenance, toll collection, and security although they do not have the same authority as officers in the CHP or local police department. Because they can detain people until someone from the CHP responds, they are an extremely valuable asset in maintaining order and safety on the Bridge.

Bridge Patrol are also the first to arrive at traffic accidents, thefts, or other forms of disorderly conduct on the Bridge or its parking lots. From time to time, there will be a suspicious looking package left on the Bridge. The patrol officers will call it in and form a secure perimeter until help arrives. In other words, Bridge Patrol are usually the first eyes and ears on everything that happens on the Bridge. They are vital to the safety of people on it – including those who come to jump.

More often than not, they're the first eyes to see a potential jumper.

When that happens, they're the ones who call in a 10-31, which is cop talk for a potential suicide.

• • • •

One of those calls came in at 6 p.m. on February 11, 2013. The CHP went to 12 ½ hour work shifts several years prior. I'd started my shift at 5:45 a.m., so I was almost done for the day.

This particular day, I'm the supervisor and hear the call from my office. The Marin Area's new commander, Captain Tom Jenkins, is still in his office when the call comes in. I walk over to advise him of the call and that I'm going down there to help out if I can. I also tell him it will be on my own time and not to worry about me putting in for the overtime.

"I'll head down with you," he says.

The Captain was different than most commanders in that he insisted that I call him "Tom." Not Captain. Just plain old Tom. Being in the military years ago has had a lifelong affect on me in many ways. On duty, I would always refer to him as Captain. Off duty was another story.

We're not too different than the military; much of how we operate, how people speak to each other, and who does what is dictated by rank. Really, it impacts every part of life on this job. The titles mean something, so everyone respects them.

If your friend makes sergeant, he's no longer Mike to you. He is Sergeant, no matter if he's younger than you or anyone else.

Tom was different. It worked for him, too, because he had such an easy confidence about him that you could never forget who was in charge regardless of what you called him. There was no danger that anyone would take his informality as weakness, and if he wanted to go to the Bridge and see what happened, he was going to the Bridge to see what happened.

"Grab a jacket," I tell him. "It's cold down there."

If you live in the Bay Area for even a month, you quickly start to learn the idiosyncrasies of the weather. You could be sunbathing in the heat in Marin, but drive a short distance to the Bridge, and it might be 57 degrees with a mist that makes it feel colder.

If you're of a certain age, you might remember that law enforcement officers used to give "baseball cards" with their pictures on them to kids they'd run into while on patrol. Well, this was the picture on my baseball card. They were pretty cool. On the back, they'd have our names, how long we'd been on the job, our specialties, and some sort of message – "stay in school" or "just say no" for instance. We used them to make a connection between cops and kids, to build trust.

When we arrive, the sun is setting and the shadows from the towers are long. It's not a great evening for tourists. The water below hides behind the fog, but by now, I know the United States Coast Guard is down there. They get the same 10-31 calls we do and zoom out in a 40-foot boat to the Bridge, waiting for the all-clear from us or a body to fall. It's their job to locate and retrieve the body when someone can't be reached, when someone doesn't decide to give life another chance.

After a while, you sort of get used to the hum of city life as white noise in the background of someone's life-or-death decision. I can't tell you how many times I've been with a person on the edge and heard some jerk lean out the window of their car yelling: "JUMP you son of a bitch!" as they whiz by in their warm and cozy car with us standing there freezing.

When you're not intimately involved, it can be easy to forget how real and delicate these situations are. Arriving home a few minutes late from a commute can make some folks extremely agitated, but that's no excuse. All I can say to this type of behavior is, "Would you say crap like that if it was *your* family member over the rail? Probably not."

Anyway, the Captain and I head down to the Bridge. When we arrive 15 minutes later, we park the patrol car in the far right lane of northbound traffic.

Tom outranks me, but this is my wheelhouse. This is the part of the job for which I'd become known, my specific area of expertise. So, Tom wants to see how I work.

However, I don't ever drive down to the Bridge to take over the negotiations that have already started with another officer. Like I tell all the officers who work the Bridge: If you have any sort of ego, leave it at home. The Bridge and the work we do here is no place for that. Some people have these huge egos they must feed. Assisting someone at their darkest and weakest hour does not make you a hero.

"Are you going to talk?" Tom asks.

"Not unless I'm needed," I respond.

I see one of our officers – Officer Gonzalez – speaking with a man standing on the chord, which is where most people end up when they go over the rail. Jumpers often don't know about the chord and are surprised to find it. Sometimes, it can act as one last chance for them to change their minds, one last chance for us to help them decide to give life another try.

The natural reaction here is to rush to the scene. A life is literally in the balance, and you want to get there before it's too late. But, with experience, you learn rushing is the last thing you want to do. We always have to remember how we're perceived, and when someone with a badge and uniform comes rushing up, that can look aggressive. That can turn an already precarious situation into a tragic one. As an officer in uniform, we can greatly affect the mood here, and we always want to project calm.

The man on the chord is dressed in pants and a t-shirt. He wears a jacket. He's 45 or 50 years old. He doesn't look homeless, but he doesn't look freshly groomed either. He isn't looking at the officer, which is a bad sign. He isn't looking at the water either, which is a good sign. He is mostly just staring off into the distance.

I approach Officer Gonzalez. I tap him on the shoulder to let him know I am there and point to the Captain. I want him to know the Captain is there, too. As I do this, the man over the rail looks and me and asks, "You're the negotiator, aren't you?"

"No sir," I tell him. "I'm just here to assist however I can to safely get you back over the rail and get you some help."

The man then says, "You have three masters' degrees, don't you?"

I actually have no masters' degrees, but I agree with the man nonetheless. Anything I can do to keep the conversation going. Officer Gonzalez, observing this, steps to his left and introduces me. "This is Sergeant Briggs," presenting the perfect opportunity to pass this case over to me, which Officer Gonzalez does.

You see, negotiations are tough. They can really wear you down. It is difficult, taxing work. It's even harder when the boss is around. If I was the initial person on the scene and the man over the rail connected with another officer, I may have done the same thing as Officer Gonzalez.

I introduce myself as "Kevin" and ask him his name. He tells me it's Jim.

"Okay, Jim, what's going on today? What's got you out here?"

He doesn't say anything. I stay silent, too. If he wants to go slow, we can go slow. A minute goes by.

"Something has to be happening for you to be here," I say, prompting him to respond.

Again, he doesn't answer or even reply at all. Not at first, anyway. But I can see it starting. I can see his mind working, his mouth beginning to form the words before they come out loud.

"Nobody understands," he states.

This is a good sign because, even just a little bit, Jim is letting me in. He is offering a glimpse.

There is no set pattern to how these things go, no template you can use to handle someone at the brink of suicide. But there are certain commonalities, and I'd heard those words on the Bridge many times before.

My main goal is always to make the person feel comfortable, keep them calm, and get a conversation going. Building rapport is critical. The more I can do that, the better chance we have. If you get people talking, usually they'll tell you why they're here. It can be therapeutic for the person, too. The more someone bottles their feelings, the harder they are to get out.

With Jim, I can see a relief even after he says just those two words.

You can't expect someone to articulate all of their problems, especially not right there in that moment. If they were thinking clearly enough to do that, then they wouldn't be on the Bridge in the first place, inches from ending their life.

Jim struggles with talking about his feelings, too. He tells me that the people he cares about will be better off with him gone.

In my line of vision, the San Francisco skyline is in front of him. Jim must turn his head to speak with me.

It is dark out now and getting colder. I start to shiver, and I know that means Jim is freezing. I still don't want to rush things, but the elements are going to come into play.

It is my common practice to try and dress similar to the person I am talking to over the rail. If they have a jacket on, then I can wear mine. If they don't, then I don't. I want and need to feel what they feel. This is another way my empathy works. It's important to try and place myself in their shoes. See what they see and feel what they feel, so to speak. If you've ever been on the Bridge at night, you understand how bitter cold it can get.

Projecting that calm isn't easy, especially when the temperature drops. It's not natural. I take deep breaths, pausing, forcing myself to relax. It's best to have your heartbeat as slow as possible when you talk to someone on the edge.

As we speak, I get a sense that Jim has consumed a fair amount of alcohol. That doesn't mean he's on the chord only because of alcohol, but it's something we have to consider when we're up there. He tells me that he was a military veteran. Something about the Special Forces. I don't entirely believe him, but obviously this is neither the time nor place to challenge someone.

Instead, I try using that detail. I'd spent time in the military, too. Maybe that's a hook. Maybe we can talk about the military, no matter what his actual experience was. If nothing else, it's a connection that the two of us can make, something that I can hopefully use to pull his mind away from the Bridge and back into life.

Much of the rest of his story, unfortunately, is fairly common. He's recently lost his job and is struggling to make ends meet. He's borrowed money from friends and family and has no idea how he'll pay it back. He has also suffered from depression for years. I ask Jim if he has been prescribed medication for his depression. He says he's got medications from the Veteran's Hospital, but they weren't working, so he'd stopped taking them about a month prior.

"Wow, it really sounds like you're having a difficult time," I tell Jim.

I have seen this time and time again: A person stops taking their medication and several weeks later they're on the Bridge. This is the kind of sad story you hear frequently in my line of work. At some point, depending on how certain people are wired, they begin to wonder if jumping off the Bridge would end their pain and relieve what they perceive to be stress on people they care about.

I've wrestled with my own depression throughout my life. I think this helps me understand others and empathize with them. I can relate to deep pain. Even though I've never acted dangerously or put myself or others in harm's way, I know all too personally how daunting the battle with depression can be.

But I also know life can get better. That there is hope. Sometimes, the weight of depression and money struggles and failed relationships can feel overwhelming. I think of myself as an example of how you can make it out.

Empathy aside, I don't *ever* talk about my experiences unless asked about them. These situations are not "The Kevin Briggs Show," after all. It's about the person in need of help and how I can help them decide to climb back over the rail.

There's no magic formula, unfortunately. You do it in this moment and then the next moment and eventually this day and the next day. You have to create your own hope sometimes. It's earned as much as it's given.

Hope, even forced hope, is something that Jim and people like him need desperately in these moments of weaknesses.

Just enough hope to give the next day a chance.

This is all easier written in a book than said on a noisy bridge with traffic on one side and death on the other, however. The distance between us – about four feet, including a railing – means what should be an intimate conversation is similar to talking to someone in the middle of a concert. The experience of doing this has taught me how to project my voice in a way that can still be soothing and non-threatening while being heard over the noise.

I try to use those skills while talking with Jim.

"I can't promise you that if you come back over things will be better," I say to him. "The problems you have today will still be here. But I can promise you that there are people who care, people who will listen."

When I say this, it usually elicits the same response.

"Nobody listens," Jim says.

"I'll listen," I tell him, looking him in the eyes so he will know I mean it. "I'll listen to you as long as you like. All I'm asking is that you give it one more day."

Jim doesn't say anything for a moment. I don't either, giving him a chance to ponder what I had just said.

"I'm going to let you think for a minute, but I'm right here when you're ready to talk again."

I like to give people a couple of minutes from time to time to really think about what's going on, and what we have spoken about. During this time, I generally step several feet away. Before I do this, though, I get a verbal promise from them they will not do anything until I speak with them again.

I step back and stand by Tom, who's watching a few feet away.

"I don't know if this is going well," I tell him. "Get ready. If he goes over, you have to decide if you're going to watch him go down. If you do, just know that's something that'll be in your head forever."

Tom's face hardens. He doesn't say anything. I can see him thinking.

There is no set way that people think in these situations. Some people handle it better than others, officers included. But it changes everyone. You are watching someone kill themselves, so of course it changes you. You watch someone go over the rail, having given up on life, and you can count in your head the seconds until they hit the water and die. It's four seconds, which doesn't sound like a lot but, in the moment, feels like eternity. That experience stays with you forever.

I want Tom to be prepared.

I walk back over to Jim. Right away, I get a bad feeling. He's looking at me as I walk toward him. Then, he turns and looks down at the water. He starts breathing heavy, his muscles tighten.

This is usually what they look like right before they jump.

He's holding onto the cable on the ledge with his right hand, leaning as far out as possible. I have to do something. I'd heard of a technique to try when someone is at this stage.

I clap as loud as I can and scream: "HEY!"

Jim snaps up.

I re-engage conversation with him and find out he does have family in the area. I ask Jim how he thinks his family might feel if he jumps. He doesn't really come up with an answer. We speak for another twenty minutes or so, and I keep emphasizing the importance of family and the fact he has consumed a fair amount of alcohol.

"Jim," I tell him, "Don't you think if you were going to do this act, your last on Earth, you would at least like to do it sober, with your mind fully engaged?"

He thinks about this for a bit. I can see him turning it over in his clouded mind. Then, without saying a word, reaches for the pedestrian rail and then asks for help getting back over. You never know what will connect with someone.

On the car ride back, Tom and I sit in silence for a few moments, both of us thinking about what we'd seen.

After a while, he says "That was really cool what you did."

"What's that?"

"Well, when Jim really looked like he was going to jump, you clapped and yelled at him."

"Yeah, that was a technique I had heard about. I didn't know what was really going to happen, but it was worth a shot."

When contemplating suicide on the Bridge, people will sometimes go into a state of mind where they do a countdown of sorts, preparing themselves for what they feel they need to do. Some actually count down, others start breathing heavily (like people do before jumping off a high diving board or skydiving). Their minds are gearing up for the body to act. If we can break that train of thought, they will generally stop and we can then re-connect. That's why I clapped and yelled: to break Jim's countdown.

Captain Tom asks if I knew what happened when I did that. I have no idea, of course, so I ask what he's talking about.

"Well, for one, you scared the hell out of me," he pauses, turning to look me straight in the eye, "And two, Jim was not clenching the cable. His hand was flat. When you yelled and clapped, his hand really shook, and he almost fell off."

"Point well taken, Captain," I respond.

Like I've said before, there's no one way to do this. No "right" way to get everybody back over the rail to safety. I hadn't noticed where Jim's hand was when I clapped and yelled, and I'm happy this episode ended in smiles and relief.

As we drive back to the office, Captain Tom congratulates me on a job well done, pleased with the overall outcome of the day's events.

• • • •

Like I said earlier, I've helped more than 200 people off the Bridge. Not all of them were over the rail and not all of them have stories as dramatic as Jim teetering on the ledge, but these are more than 200 souls who had felt alone, lost hope, and thought about ending it all.

It's always been important to me to share these experiences, the ones where people don't jump, the ones where people decide to keep going, in hopes that others can be helped.

The media has taken to calling me "The Guardian of the Golden Gate Bridge." To be honest, I didn't like the name – especially not at first. There are a number of others who do the exact same thing. I don't believe it's fair that I get the attention and recognition. As time has gone by, I've realized that it provides me with a greater opportunity to reach out and help others, so I gladly take the name.

I hope this book can help people better understand the signs and dangers of depression as well as the warning signs people can look for to stop suicide before it happens.

I hope this book can inspire people to be that first line of defense in helping save a life.

I hope this book can save lives.

There is no magic here, just empathy and the ability to lend an ear and show compassion for your fellow man. And with that comes the power to prevent suicide.

2
Where I Come From

I grew up in Novato, California, a bedroom community about 25 miles north of San Francisco. It was a great place to be a kid. I had many friends who lived close by, and we spent many an hour playing touch football, hide-and-go-seek, and baseball on my street.

You could have made a TV show about my childhood. It would have been about a boy growing up in a loving, supportive family with role models who taught him the value of hard work, a good attitude, and a nice suit.

My father owned a printing shop in San Francisco, and my mother stayed home and took care of my three siblings and me as most mothers did in that day. We would have been considered an upper middle-income family, I suppose, and my father worked long and hard to keep it that way. Monday through Friday, he would leave the house at 6 a.m. and generally return around 5 p.m. My brother, two sisters, and I had it pretty easy thanks to the efforts of our parents.

Dad bought our home brand new in the late 60s. It had four bedrooms, but my dad wanted more for his growing family, so he had two more rooms added in the early 70s. That way, each of us kids had our own bedroom, plus one more for guests.

The house was painted cream with green trim – the trees, bushes, and lawn immaculately kept up by Dad. Every Sunday, he took us to church, paid the bills, and then spent hours mowing and trimming all the edges, making sure none of the shrubbery touched the driveway or house. After the yard work came shoe shining.

My dad in his natural environment when we were growing up. That's him on his favorite chair, with a glass of white wine, comfortable and relaxing but never allowing himself to look sloppy – notice the collared shirt tucked in.

Dad took great pride in his appearance, one of many traits he passed down to me. It was easy to see the "Type A" in him when it came to taking care of the home and of himself.

Mom was the oldest of four siblings. She grew up in McCloud, California, in the shadows of Mount Shasta. Back then, McCloud was a lumber town with a mill built in the late 1800s that supported the quiet community. Mount Shasta, or "White Mountain" as described by local Native Americans, rises to a height of 14,180 feet. It is a spectacular sight.

Growing up, we would travel five hours to McCloud to visit family every year; most years, we made the trip more than once, and we always went for Thanksgiving.

Five hours felt like a long time to be in a car with my brother and sisters. No DVD players or iPads back then. It must have felt even longer to my parents, the soundtrack of the drive being their children bickering and screaming, "Quit touching me!" in the back seat. We never felt like we had enough room in the car.

On our visits, we always stayed at Grandma and Grandpa's house – 505 Quincy. The whole family would be there – my cousins, aunts, uncles – everyone on my mother's side of the family. The men would play pinochle and the women would cook and chat in the kitchen. We kids would play outside until all hours of the night.

I have a cousin my age who lived in McCloud. As kids, we would meet up every time I visited, and we liked all the same things – fishing, hunting, and riding dirt bikes. He was a much better rider than I was, but it sure was fun trying to keep up riding all the logging trails in the area. There were miles and miles of them, seemingly endless. We would leave in the morning and come back just before dark, covered in the volcanic dust from Mount Shasta. Everyone would laugh when we came back. All you could see was the whites of our eyes and the smiles on our faces.

Like I said, I had a great childhood.

• • • •

Nearly everyone in McCloud worked at or supported the mill in one way or another. And, like most small towns, everyone knew everyone else and also knew their business.

Most homes had porches, and when you felt like visiting, you just sat on your porch and passing friends would stop by and chat. In the town's heyday, men worked long and hard in the woods, returning at dusk looking like coal miners. They would be covered in powdery ash that had spewed from Mount Shasta long ago, surrounding the landscape for hundreds of miles.

My maternal grandfather was an electrician in the town, a solid middle-class professional who did just well enough to keep his family fed and clothed. That is, until the accident.

On October 1st, 1947, two weeks before he turned 34, my grandfather was working on a high voltage power line in town. One story is that all of the town's power was supposed to be turned off, but it was controlled at the mill and mistakenly left on since school was letting out and folks needed electricity for washing and preparing supper. The message that the power line was still going to be "hot" was never relayed to my grandfather.

Another story is that my grandfather was advised that the particular line he was working on would be "dead," meaning the power had been shut down. He had complete faith in the people he worked with, so he didn't think twice about going to work on it. But, this day, that faith would cost him dearly.

Whatever the setup, as my grandfather began work on the line, he was immediately electrocuted. His muscles tensed uncontrollably, and he was knocked away from the lines. People think it's the electricity that propels you, but it's actually the extreme tensing of your muscles that does the work.

He was harnessed to the pole, near the top. Two or three men immediately climbed the pole, cut the straps that held my unconscious grandfather, and lowered him to the ground.

The men loaded him into a car nearby and drove him the short distance to the hospital. The medical personnel were able to save his life, but he suffered severe burns to his hands, arms, neck, and upper portion of his body.

He ended up losing his right arm up to the elbow, and his left hand was so badly damaged that the doctors could only save his pinky finger. They rebuilt flesh around where his other fingers would have been, but the result looked nothing like his original hand.

Grandfather spent a month and a half in the McCloud Hospital, then at Stanford Hospital off and on for several months over the next two years. He suffered severe pain, both mentally and physically, for the rest of his

This is the last picture my family has of my grandfather before the electrical accident that cost him his right arm and left hand. The kids are my mom, aunt, and uncle. The youngest boy had yet to be born.

life. Throughout the entire process, he would not allow his children to see him in the hospital. He didn't want them to feel scared or wonder if their father might die.

The fact that he didn't die at the scene was nothing short of a miracle. Losing an arm and a hand was tragic – hard luck to be sure – especially if you could no longer work in your profession. The way he saw it, it was no one else's problem and at least he still had his life.

Very little is actually known about all of his surgeries and what he actually went through. That's just the way it was. My grandparents did not speak of it. Their children weren't even in the loop. Later in life, children would ask my grandfather what happened to his arms. He would say, "I got run over by a train," and leave it at that. Even still, everyone knew something awful had occurred.

If any people deserved to fall into a depression or self-pity, it was my grandfather and his family. Instead, my grandfather reinvented himself. He was very civic-minded and believed everyone should contribute to society.

In April of 1949, the lumber company created a job for him in the town electrical shop as a clerk. While working there, he also began studying law. On June 6th, 1950, he was elected Justice of the Peace. He then furthered his education and was elected Judge of the Judicial District in 1952. Within a few years, he became one of the most popular judges ever in McCloud, a man known far and wide for his firm but fair justice. He was re-elected several times before retiring on December 31, 1976.

After law, at age 63, he took on a job as a night watchman at the mill. All the while, he and my grandmother raised two daughters and two sons and continued to live a rich life filled with friendship and love: the antithesis of depression. My grandfather died in 1987 at age 74 from complications due to a stroke and respiratory failure after a full and well-lived life.

My grandmother, who stayed at home taking care of the kids and my grandfather through all his struggles, was a saint herself. She was the grounding force for the whole family. She passed away at age 85 of cardiac arrest. Hers was another long life, well-lived.

They stuck together through the good times and bad. Both remain shining examples to me of how to live, how to fight through barriers, how to persevere knowing that better days are ahead.

To me, they are a guiding and eternal model of the power of hope to get through absolutely anything.

• • • •

My mother was a tomboy growing up. She didn't like dressing up or even running a brush through her hair.

Her family spent a lot of time at the McCloud Golf Course, a gathering point still today for those living in the area. She liked to fish, swim, bike – all the things a kid would do in a small town where life was simple and you could stay out past sunset without worry.

McCloud High School was a typical, small-town high school. Mom graduated in a class of about 28 kids. She was popular among her classmates. Like many small-town kids, she wanted to see the big city. She went to college for a bit and eventually moved to Oakland and worked as a secretary for a business in the financial district in San Francisco.

She met my father in Oakland, and it wasn't long before they married. Soon after, they moved to Novato to that cream-and-green house with the perfect lawn. I was their first kid, born in 1962. Then came my brother Darrin, followed by sisters Kim and Colleen– all of us in a span of just six years.

Mom began smoking around age 20 as many young people did back then. She smoked Marlboros, maybe half a pack a day. I remember that distinctive red and white package and the commercials with cowboys on the range portraying how cool it was to smoke. She would smoke first thing in the morning, throughout the day, and right before bed. She would smoke in any room in the house with all us kids around. Nobody knew about second-hand smoke back then or, really, about the dangers of smoking in general.

My mom and her siblings, taken one summer at my grandparents' house in McCloud. In the back row is my Uncle Donald and Aunt Barbara. On the front step is my mother Judy and my Uncle Rick. There was a festival in town every August; I'm sure that's when this picture was taken.

Mom was diagnosed with lung cancer when she was just 47. All that smoking had caught up with her.

We kids were all in our twenties when we found out the news. I remember my father first telling me about it. We were in the family room, just the two of us. It was a month or two after the initial diagnosis. The news struck me so hard that I had to sit down. We then spoke about treatments and what would be happening to her. Neither of us knew that the disease would eventually take Mom's life.

Early in her battle, I remember seeing her walking down the stairs one day. She was taking one stair at a time, planting both feet firmly on the same stair before she went down another. I'd never seen her do that before and asked what the matter was. She shrugged it off and said she hurt her knee, which we both knew wasn't true.

Initially, Mom had both radiation and chemotherapy. The radiation was a quick "zap," like a fast x-ray. She could never feel anything, and you didn't know if it was working until she saw her doctor for follow-ups. Chemotherapy was much different back then. She would take the "drip" and be okay for that day. But the following day was filled with violent non-stop vomiting, dizziness, head pounding, and itching.

The bottom of her feet and the top of her head would always itch. I think this was a combination of the chemotherapy, radiation, and medication that robbed her body of all of its hydration. She was unable to eat or drink anything for the first few days following the chemotherapy. The treatments ran their course: a few months for radiation and a few months for chemotherapy. I believe she had nine chemo sessions in all. She opted to stop the chemotherapy after that ninth course as she said it just wasn't worth it; her disease was not responding well to treatments, and she was simply too weak to fight.

As the cancer spread to her brain, the affect it had on her was much more visible and she began having seizures. Her first seizure took place upstairs in her bedroom. I was at work. My father and my sisters were with her. Kim could see something was different in Mom's eyes and had a feeling that something was going to happen.

In a split second, Mom's body began convulsing. Kim knew what was happening. For the few seconds it lasted, it felt like a lifetime. Like an earthquake, except for the human body. Colleen called 911, and Mom was taken to the hospital. This was my sisters' first time witnessing a seizure, and although it was unsettling, being there for the first one prepared them for more to come. All of her seizures were Grand mal seizures. They were just part of the "cancer" process that we were learning about as we lived through it each day.

Her second seizure was also in her bedroom. Mom felt that one coming, so she told Kim. My sister walked her through what was going to happen, reassuring her: "It will be fast, and it will be okay."

My mom told her, "Let's just get it over with."

Mom was okay, but there was a lot of pain. The pain would subside within a few long minutes, and once she caught her breath and was able to awaken a bit, they would talk about it. Mom was always very quick to have us tell the paramedics to keep their sirens off. Her third and final seizure was in the family room.

My sister, Kim, four years younger than me, was at her bedside night and day. She left college to take care of Mom. There was also a nurse, Norma O'Sullivan, who lived down the street, who visited frequently. She was a good friend of my mom's even before she got sick. They would chat about all sorts of subjects, which would take Mom's mind off the inevitable for a bit. Norma also provided us with information about medications and side effects.

Few stories regarding cancer patients are humorous, but I do remember one. The master bedroom was upstairs. Mom had not been downstairs in weeks. Kim tried everything she could to get her downstairs one day. Due to Mom's paralysis, even together they just couldn't do it. Then Kim came up with a great idea.

Kim decided to slide Mom down the stairs on a Monopoly game board. They tried it and got stuck at the very top of the stairs! They both laughed hysterically. It came to a point where they called my father at work. He told them to call the paramedics. Mom wouldn't have any of that, so my sister called me instead. I was at work at San Quentin on an overtime detail. I, of course, immediately left and headed home. When I got there, they were both sitting down at the top of the stairs, still laughing. It was nice to see Mom laugh again.

We finally got her down the stairs with me in the front, leading the way, making sure she didn't go down too fast, and my sister behind as support. My sister and I still laugh about that day.

As the cancer progressed, a hospital bed was brought into our home and placed in the living room. I remember working the graveyard shift at San Quentin and then coming home and making scrambled eggs, which Mom really loved. It became a sort of routine that we both looked forward to.

I didn't really notice much of a physical change on the outside, but that didn't matter since it was obvious the cancer was doing its damage on the inside. She would get angry at times, probably also because she knew she was dying, and would often mumble incoherently.

Toward the end, she was prescribed morphine shots for pain and also had oxygen tanks we would have to monitor constantly. Kind folks from hospice also came in for visits. All of our neighbors were fantastic during this period. They would visit and bring food, sneaking desserts to Mom.

On March 20, 1989, she slipped into a coma. She remained this way for about 24 hours before taking one last, shallow breath. The next day, Mom passed away. The whole family was at her bedside, including her mother. I was the one who closed her eyes after she took her last breath, a memory that continues to well inside me.

Maybe it's selfish, but the loneliness I felt immediately after her passing was almost overwhelming. A few days later, at her wake, we were all sitting in the front pew, with Mom's casket just a few feet in front of us. It was closed. Many family friends came to pay their respects. Near the end of the wake, the director at the funeral home announced that the casket would be opened for anyone in the family who wished to view the body. All my family stayed, but I couldn't handle it.

I thought about it deep and hard but decided I did not want to have my last recollection of my mother to be of her lying in a coffin. I still believe I did the right thing. People who did stay said she looked very good, peaceful.

She was cremated a few days later, and her ashes were buried in a cemetery in the city of Mount Shasta, next to my grandfather. She now has an eternal view of the great "White Mountain."

My mother never talked about her cancer with me, and I didn't have the courage to ask. At the time, I thought that if she really wanted me to know, she would tell me. I will live with the regret of not talking to her about it for the rest of my days.

I have other regrets as well. She would hug me more often than I hugged her and tell me she loved me. I also regret that Mom never got to see me graduate from the CHP academy, never got to cheer when I made sergeant, never got to meet my kids, and never got to know about the people I helped or the inroads we made on the Bridge.

The crippling grief I suffered when we lost her added another nugget of experience that I would use occasionally years later when others felt their lives were at an end. My memory of my mother and the inadequacy I struggled through during her final days helped me find the right words when I needed them most: when another life hung in the balance.

· · · ·

There were more than a few signs of depression on my father's side. His family knew the blues all too well. At the height of the Great Depression, when many other Americans suffered economic catastrophe, my paternal grandfather lost his life to suicide. He was a laborer in a sawmill near Scotia, California. He was just 32 years old at the time, and my father just three. He left behind my grandmother, my father, and my uncle, just three years older than my dad. He poisoned himself. Nobody knew his reasons.

Losing the man of the house at a young age was a much more common occurrence back then, but that didn't make it easier, especially during such bleak times. My dad's mother, Hazel, then hitchhiked with my dad and his brother all the way from Rio Dell to Livermore – some 300 miles! All they really had was the clothing on their backs and a few belongings. My great uncle, Rich Gandolfo, had a ranch there. They stayed there for a bit and then traveled the short distance to San Leandro, where they lived with my father's grandmother, who was a widow. My dad stayed there through high school and then attended college at the University of Santa Clara, staying on campus and graduating in 1954.

Tragedy struck again when my uncle – an extremely smart young man, an aeronautical engineer – died in a car accident at age 24, shortly before he was to be married. He sustained a severe head injury during the crash. My father, just 21 at the time, had his own head shaved so the mortician could make a wig to fit my uncle's head.

Heartbreak in the family occurred again years later when Hazel passed away at age 55 from colon cancer, my father being only 30 years old at the time.

Dad doesn't talk about his side of the family very often, but when he does, he tends to struggle to get through it. Like so many men of that generation, Dad was able to put those unspeakable horrors in a box, move on, and live a rich, productive life. After college, he owned a cocktail lounge in Oakland named Mocambo, and after that, he owned a neighborhood bar named New Mo.

In June of 1953, he married his high school sweetheart, Mary Patricia Coleman, and went on to have three children. Owning a bar was not the family setting he desired, so after eight years in the restaurant and bar business, he gave it up. Life went on, and as many couples do, my father and his wife grew apart. In 1961, they divorced. He moved to an apartment complex in Oakland by Lake Merrit, which is where he met my mother, Judy Claire Hanson. By 1962, they were married and had settled their growing family in Novato.

• • • •

Dad coached my Little League team. I can still hear him saying "C'Mon, Alice, hit the ball" – his way of "encouragement." He did so in a funny way though, not degrading or demeaning. Nowadays, kids are driven across the state for their sports. Weekends are no longer days off but are spent traveling for soccer, football, or whatever the sport may be. Back in my day, though, most of the games or practices were just a couple miles away at most, so we just rode our bikes. As they say: "Those were the days."

When my parents moved to Novato, that's where my father met Robert and MaryAnn Lehman. Robert sold printing presses for a living.

He and my father soon became good friends, and he introduced my father to Gordon Lindstrom, who was already in the printing business. My father and Gordon began a partnership, acquired a building at 1251 Folsom Street in San Francisco, and opened Golden State Embossing. At times, they would employ as many as 15 people, most of them running large Kluges or Heidelberg printing presses that made so much noise you needed earplugs.

Those machines were not your everyday copiers and printers that you see at your local copy shops, but huge, heavy, steel printing presses. His was a specialty trade shop, mostly foil embossing. He produced things like menus for cruise lines, foil embossed boxes for See's Candies, and wine labels for wineries such as Beringer and Gallo.

Gordon stayed as his partner for several years before moving on to open his own shop. My father continued running the business on his own. For 35 years, he commuted some 30 miles to San Francisco and back to Novato every week day. Even though it was just 30 or so miles, it would sometimes take him an hour and a half just to get home.

I would work for him in the summers occasionally, and when I got out of the Army, I worked as a deliveryman for almost a year. I would deliver jobs all over the Bay Area, passing by the San Francisco CHP Area office, located on 8th Street very close to my father's shop. Little did I know at the time that I would be cruising around in one of those cool patrol cars and eventually on a CHP motorcycle.

My father really loved the printing business. In 1980, he was awarded the highest award in the graphic arts industry: the Howard H. Hunt Award for exemplary service. Like most businesses, Golden State Embossing had its ups and downs. The downs took a toll on my father along with a lack of exercise and periodic martini lunches.

On June 18, 1998, he had symptoms of a heart attack: left arm pain and nausea. It was 3 a.m. He didn't want to disturb anyone, so he drove himself the 15 or so miles to Kaiser Hospital in San Rafael. Hospital staff immediately admitted him. The following day, he was transferred by ambulance to Kaiser Hospital in San Francisco and, the next day, had a quadruple bypass performed. I saw him just after the surgery. There were several monitors at his bedside and IVs in both arms.

Boy, did he look bad. He was extremely pale and weak. We were allowed to see him for only a few minutes. He didn't speak to us, but he opened his eyes and smiled just a little bit. I would be in a very similar situation years later – same hospitals and everything. This is one time the old saying "like father, like son" really sucks.

When home computers, copiers, scanners, and printers started becoming more popular, the printing industry really took a hit. Many folded. Dad sold his business, worked for a larger printing company for five years, and then retired. After four months, he decided retirement was not for him – that he just wasn't ready for it. While in high school, he had worked at a haberdashery shop and gained knowledge of men's clothing. He applied at Macy's and Nordstrom, and within a week both stores notified him that they would love to hire him. He chose Nordstrom.

After my mother passed away, my father led the single life for a while, occasionally dating. In 2001, twelve years after Mom passed, he was at a party and met Veronica Hallen, who is actually the sister of his first wife.

They had not seen each other in 30 years! He began dating her, and in 2002, they purchased a home in Roseville. They were married that same year and are to this day. I had no issues with my father dating or re-marrying as long as he was treated well and was happy, which he still is; he's over 80 and continues to work at Nordstrom, too!

My father put us all through Catholic school. I attended Our Lady of Loretto, where I had to wear black shoes, pepper pants, and a white shirt. We had no grass to play on, just an asphalt lot that was really just a parking lot for churchgoers. Our classes were small, maybe 25 kids for each grade. I went to this school from third through eighth grade. The friendships I built there have lasted decades and continue to this day.

After eighth grade, I went to a Catholic high school called Saint Vincent's in Petaluma. Each day, I would take the Golden Gate Bridge Highway and Transportation District bus from Novato to Petaluma, a journey of about 15 miles, and then walk a short distance to school. It was small, and as with most Catholic schools, nuns were the predominate teachers. I liked the school but also wanted to meet more people outside of the church, so after my freshman year, I transferred to San Marin High School, which was just about a mile from my home. I really enjoyed going to school even though I was just an average student. After all, it was where all the pretty girls were as well as my friends. I would spend the next three years there, graduating in 1981. I spent much of my freshman through senior year hunting and fishing with my buddies. I even traveled to Colorado on three occasions to hunt deer.

Although no one knows where their life will take them, it seems like my path to the CHP, to the Bridge, and to what I've done since I retired was laid out for me long before I realized it. Where I come from has definitely brought me to where I am.

3
Speed Bumps

My life has been mostly wonderful. I know that I am a very lucky man on a lot of levels. I have two healthy and generally happy kids, a career that I enjoyed, and the opportunity to make a positive difference in the world. And now, I'm able to share my experiences and knowledge with a much broader audience and am motivated every day that the message of hope and general suicide awareness can do some good for people.

That doesn't mean that my life or career have always been smooth and easy. And I'm not just talking about the struggle of losing someone on the Bridge, my divorce, or my own battle with depression.

• • • •

This is the military version of a school picture, the one we all take early on in basic training. Mine was at Fort Benning in Georgia, and this picture was taken shortly after I went into the service in August 1981.

I joined the Army almost immediately upon graduating from San Marin High School in 1981, in part because I appreciated the order and discipline of the service, but mainly because I knew that college wasn't for me.

My grades were average, and I just wasn't into the "studying thing," so the Army seemed like the right choice. More than that, I had every GI Joe there was as a kid and played Army games with my buddies, throwing rocks as grenades and holding sticks as rifles. So, I was ready to do it for real.

Infantry training and jump school put me in Fort Benning, Georgia, one of the hottest and most humid places I'd ever been. Basic training. Anyone who has been through it, no matter what branch of service, will never forget it. We were woken up at 4 a.m. by the frightening crash of a metal trash can hurled down the barracks from a screaming drill sergeant who couldn't care less about your sleep or your hunger.

If you enjoy a butt-kicking each and every day, join the Army. They're happy to comply.

From there, it was on to Fort Lewis, Washington – which is now Joint Base Lewis-McChord. A year later, I was deployed overseas to a little town outside Frankfurt, Germany – a place called Gelnhausen.

I arrived in Germany during the height of the Cold War when U.S. forces were ramping up short-range ballistic missile deployments on the edge of the Iron Curtain. The city of Frankfurt had almost as many American residents as Germans at that time, and most of them were uniformed servicemen.

I continued with my specialty – weapons. Small arms, explosives, and missiles that would blast through a tank like a BB through a soda can. Along

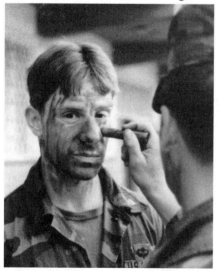

Getting ready for an infantry training mission in Germany. We caked that stuff on our faces all the time.

the way, I was also learning to speak a little German.

One day, while in the shower, I felt several nodules on my right testicle – sorry to just throw that out there. I had no idea what they were or could be, but I knew it wasn't right. I went to the infirmary, and a doctor told me to go get what I needed for a stay in the hospital. He didn't explain much after that, and with me being enlisted and he an officer, he didn't have to.

I had my first surgery in November 1983, in Frankfurt,

where they removed my right testicle. That's when I found out I had cancer. At the time, all I knew about cancer was that most people died from it. The news knocked me down. I was quickly shipped back to the States for treatment, including chemotherapy. I didn't know what chemo was, but the word scared the hell out of me.

I was transferred to Letterman Army Medical Center in San Francisco a few days later. I was sitting in the cargo hold of an Air Force jet with seats facing backward, holding a box that contained my own testicle. How degrading.

Just like that, I'd gone from thinking about a twenty-year career in the Army to wondering if I would live to see next Christmas.

Men don't talk about testicular cancer. At least, back then they didn't. It's a deadly disease, but because of where it is, it's like hemorrhoids or jock itch or any other "problem" affecting the male anatomy – the stuff of adolescent jokes, not serious conversation.

I arrived at Letterman Army Medical Center on December 5th, my 21st birthday. No party, no first legal alcoholic drink, just a hospital bed, blood tests, and the grand hospital food. I remember thinking, *at least if I die, I will die at home.*

On December 13th, which is my father's birthday, I had a lymphadenectomy. This is where a surgeon cuts you from your sternum to below your belly button and removes your lymph nodes. The doctor removed 45 of mine, all but eight of them cancerous. Bad news.

As I lay in my hospital bed awaiting the results of one more round of tests, a nine-inch incision in my abdomen stapled shut like a cardboard box, I wondered what my old high school pals would have made of my current state. I also wondered, as I stared at the sunrise through the small window in my hospital room, why I seemed to welcome this growing cloud of melancholy I'd been feeling since my initial diagnosis.

Four months of chemotherapy treatment dropped me from a stout 175 pounds to an emaciated 130. Even everyday tasks, like mowing the lawn or cleaning out the gutters, left me exhausted. I was living with my parents and getting paid by the government because my cancer occurred while I was enlisted in the Army. My most basic needs were being met, but I didn't want that to be my life.

I started slowly, taking walks at first. Small stuff. Then, I joined the local gym in Novato and worked up to going four times a week. At first, I managed just a few sets of lifts per body part. One or two sets of arm curls. One or two sets of squats. Like I said, small stuff. Before cancer, I was bench pressing 225 pounds. After, I started lifting 95 pounds. It took a year, but I worked back up to doing sets of ten with 225 pounds. Slow and steady.

It wasn't just physical, either. Yes, I needed to get my body back in shape, but I also needed to work out my mind. Cancer doesn't just attack your physical abilities; it also attacks your thoughts, your feelings. Or at least it did with me. The chemotherapy, the hair loss, the weight loss, losing a testicle – all of it made me feel inferior, weak.

Meanwhile, darkness continued its annex of my mind. The rules of depression grow clearer each day you play the game. But, at that time, the biggest rule was that you never talked about it.

This was the 1980s, when depression was still commonly viewed as a character flaw or a weakness of spirit. Only wussies or whiners sought counseling for anything so vague. The standard remedy was for a family member, co-worker, or friend to chew you out and tell you to buck up and carry your own water. Depression? Not a "real man's" struggle.

Since then, I had become accustomed to the routine arrival of despair. I didn't want to be depressed – although, if I had known what awaited me with the chemotherapy treatments, I might have become even more despondent. When the waves of anxiety came, I didn't fight them.

It took a full year before I was declared cancer-free. I eventually rebounded physically and emotionally, even though the scars from my battle with depression were as hard and fresh as those running from my sternum to my waist.

Despite having won that fight, my bout with cancer wouldn't be the last time I had to face the possibility of death.

• • • •

It was June 3rd, 2001. A Sunday. I was just off an overtime detail in Point Reyes, a rural town in West Marin. I was on my motorcycle (in law enforcement we just call them "motors") heading back to the office to complete paperwork and start my shift, which began at 1:45 p.m. I was on Point Reyes/Petaluma Road, a curvy country road with one lane of traffic in each direction and just a double yellow line between the lanes.

Beautiful country. Part of the reason I've always preferred the motor over the car was for moments like this: a pretty day, the wind in your face, and the feeling of the road underneath you.

Coming the other way was a fairly steady stream of traffic, including two motorcyclists on what we often call crotch rockets – those overly horse-powered motorcycles that are often driven way too fast by riders who think the road is their personal race track.

They both traveled over the double yellow lines, passing a couple of cars and then darting back into their lane as they approached me. I knew there was no way I would be able to make a U-turn and catch up to these guys, so as they neared me I turned on my emergency lights, just to scare them a bit. They both slowed dramatically, but just after passing me, I heard their engines accelerate and they were gone, disappearing into the curves in the road.

Their needless and dangerous race couldn't have been more different than my half of the highway. I had maybe four cars in front of me, four behind me, and not a care. I was in no hurry, so I was going with the pack about 45 miles per hour down the road when my life changed.

In the blink of an eye, another one of these crotch rockets came zooming around the corner.

You son of a...

I didn't even have time to finish the thought.

I saw him in front of me, far enough away that he looked about two inches tall, and then all of a sudden – *wham!* – he slammed into me. I remember him flying toward me, leaning far to his right, trying to make a turn, and that was it. He barely missed the car in front of me, and then hit me.

Later, they would tell me the man was traveling at about 65 miles per hour. I was going about 45, so that's more than 100 miles per hour of force. That split-second, you play it through your mind so many times. I see him coming toward me, leaning so far to his right that he's almost sliding. I see my handlebars, then, *boom*, and that was it.

The details are a bit foggy. I was so out of it. Since then, I've come to learn that the other guy on the motorcycle hit me basically head-on, right in my front wheel. Instantly, I was thrown from my motor and off the highway. Everything blew right out of my duty belt.

It may have been just a few minutes, but it seemed like an eternity. I blacked out again, and when I awoke, I was laying in a field. There were CHP officers and Sheriff Deputies all around me. I worked with all these guys and knew each of them. I remember hearing sirens and then some guys from the fire department cutting off my clothes. I was *just* coherent enough to think of my boots. Motorcycle boots, especially good ones, can cost $500. I may have been in a bad state, but I didn't want to have to buy another pair – if I was ever able to ride again.

The scene of my motorcycle crash in June of 2001. That's my motor there laying on its side, totaled. The people driving that convertible on the right made sure I was comfortable and safe before emergency personnel arrived on the scene.

"Don't cut the boots," I told them. "Don't cut the boots, don't cut the boots."

I have no idea what they thought of a grown man lying in the field after a head-on motorcycle crash telling them to preserve his footwear, but it worked. They left the boots on my feet.

The sun was beating into my eyes out there in that field. People are sometimes surprised to hear this, but I was completely numb. I couldn't feel a thing – my body's defense mechanism for what would've otherwise been nearly unbearable pain.

I remember hearing a helicopter and was so out of it, I thought: *Who'd they call the chopper for? That guy must really be hurt.*

I soon figured out the chopper was for me and then started to think about my own body. I got worried. I know they only call the choppers when someone is in truly awful shape. I asked one of my buddies who the chopper was for. He said it was for me. I asked him how bad I was. I knew that even if it was pretty bad, he'd tell me I was fine.

"You're good," he reassured me.

That's how it goes in these situations. You always want to calm the person in distress. As a highway patrolman, I'm used to being on the other side of this exchange. The one calming someone else, not the one being calmed.

"Oh, look at that. They brought you the *brand-new* helicopter," he said smiling.

The paramedic came out of the chopper, a woman.

"Wow," one of the guys told me, "she's really good looking. Lucky dog."

Obviously, I don't remember what she looked like, but I do remember she was very nice and caring and helpful. Everyone I encountered that day was so good to me in a moment when I really needed it.

It was about a twenty-minute ride to Santa Rosa Memorial Hospital. I was flat the whole time, receiving treatment, answering their questions as best I could. We landed on the roof of the hospital, and they rushed me around and into the emergency room.

As you can imagine, the impact of the crash wrecked my body. But I was incredibly lucky. I had no broken bones, somehow, just a horribly injured shoulder and a puncture wound on my right elbow. I had a lot of back pain, a lot of neck pain. My pants were torn up. My motorcycle helmet had a scrape two inches wide from my right eye back to behind my left ear. But there was very little blood.

The whole time – at the scene, in the helicopter, and in the emergency room – I kept thinking, *Okay, what's* really *wrong with me?* I was numb the entire time. In the emergency room, a doctor came and saw me very briefly, then they rushed me to x-ray.

It's strange what you remember from a near-death experience. I had to go to the bathroom. I mean, I *really* had to go to the bathroom. It was extremely uncomfortable. But I'm lying there, tied down in the emergency room, so what am I going to do?

In the x-ray room, I asked the technician if I could stand up just for a minute, but he wouldn't let me. Instead, he gave me a plastic container that I could use right there on the bed. I filled one up and needed another. The feeling of relief was almost euphoric. The technician laughed.

"Man, you really did have to go," he told me, chuckling.

After the x-rays, I was wheeled back to the emergency room. The doctor came back in and said he could see no broken bones. He asked if I recalled the collision. I told him what I remembered. He told me how incredibly lucky I was, and he wasn't talking about my bones. He was talking about me surviving. I felt lucky, too. I was so relieved to hear a doctor tell me I wasn't all busted up.

When you're injured on the job, the Department will go to your house and bring your family to the hospital. My dad was living in Novato with my wife at the time. Our little boy had just turned one. You can imagine how worried they were when they got to the hospital, so I tried to ease their concerns as much as I could. I was lucky, I told them, and really, I was.

When you ride a motor, you know you're going down. You just know it. The statistics say it's going to happen. It's just a matter of when and how bad it will be. I was in six, maybe eight, crashes in my time with CHP. That was the worst one, so I consider myself quite fortunate.

I took about three months off work. I wanted to get back, but my left shoulder was so bad I couldn't lift my arm more than six inches away from my body. Strangest thing. It wasn't painful, really, it just wouldn't move. It was two months before I could raise it above my head.

I'd go to the doctor, but they told me the only thing I could do was rest. So, I basically sat around the house for about three months. Officers would come over to visit, and I watched a lot of TV. The nice part of the time off, of course, was being around my son. It was fun seeing him all day, and with my shoulder the way it was, we were about on the same physical level!

The guy who hit me had a broken hand, but nothing more serious than that. He was very lucky he was wearing a full-face helmet and all leathers. I went to court and saw him with his attorney; he pled guilty to reckless driving causing injuries. He actually came up to me in court that day in tears. He apologized and said he would never ride a motorcycle again. I didn't have any anger toward him then, and I still don't. He made a mistake, and he was sorry for it. Hopefully, he doesn't put himself – or some other innocent person – in that kind of situation again.

After those three months, I was able to go in for some light duty. Basically office work, helping secretaries where you can, doing a lot of paperwork. Completely monotonous and boring. I was a road cop and needed to be on the streets. I did a couple weeks of that, which was about all I could take. I was still hurting, but I got my doctor to sign off that I was fit for duty.

People ask, and sometimes they're surprised to hear the answer, but I never felt like I shouldn't get back on the motor or like I didn't want to do this type of work anymore. I never entertained the thought of a patrol car over the motor.

I just like the motor so much more. There's more freedom and it's easier to patrol. Working the Bridge as much as I do, it's a lot easier to park and get around in tight spaces. You are assigned the motor, so you take it home after your shift. You save time and gas money.

Besides, being on the motor is a point of pride. It's sort of the CHP version of being a fighter pilot. They make you take a very difficult two-week course. They call it "motor school," but really, they're not there to teach. It's more of a test, and they make sure it's hard enough that there's a high dropout rate.

You may have ridden for years before going to "motor school," but you probably didn't ride the CHP way. There's a saying in the Patrol: There's a right way, a wrong way, and the CHP way.

They have cone patterns set up for detailed slow work, and mock city streets where you follow an instructor, keeping up as best you can. All the while, other instructors strategically place themselves in areas to watch your head and eye movement, how many fingers are covering the clutch, and a myriad of other tiny details. At first, you take the course at 25 miles per hour, then 35 miles per hour, then 45. They watch everything.

I've been fortunate that I haven't had a serious accident since. However, I haven't been so fortunate that the crash was my last health scare.

• • • •

The pain was minor. I kept telling myself that, anyway. But the pain also kept coming, from my upper chest, down my left arm, into my thumb.

I know how that sounds in hindsight, but at the time, I didn't think much of it – isn't that always how it is? It was a dull pain that affected only about a quarter inch of my left arm as it traveled down, kind of like if you hung a shoelace from your shoulder to your thumb.

This was September 2008, and I'd been training hard for a physical test we had at work. It was a voluntary test, but I'd just been promoted to sergeant and wanted to set an example for everyone else. So, I was training hard – maybe too hard. Maybe that's what was causing the pain.

The test came, and I did pretty well. Just like I was hoping. I beat most of the others doing the test, many of them much younger than me, but I must admit that I was sucking wind afterward. That struck me as a little odd, but again, maybe my old body just wasn't used to the aerobic activity.

Right about that time, I really wasn't sleeping well. I had this pain in my chest that was keeping me up at night. It felt like heartburn. One night of bad sleep turned into two. After the third bad night, my friend Mary talked me into going to the hospital. *Fine.*

They do an EKG and that comes out normal. No issues.

"We just want to run some blood work," the doctor tells me. "You should be out of here in about ten or fifteen minutes."

Well, ten or fifteen minutes later, he comes back in and tells me there's a problem.

"It's your heart," he says.

That hit me. Hard. I could feel the tears starting to form in my eyes. I was wondering if I was ever going to see my kids again. When you hear you have a bad heart, that's something you might not come back from.

They put IVs in me, a nitroglycerin patch on my chest, and a nitro pill under my tongue. The nurse told me I may get a headache from the nitro. I've never had headaches, but I sure got one within a few minutes of the nitro administration.

I was transferred to intensive care. Right away I got a bad feeling. I'd been in enough hospitals to know how these things often work. There's a subtle purpose to room assignments at hospitals. It's not one hundred percent certain, but I've come to think that the closer they put you to the nurses' station, the worse off they think you are. The further you are from the nurses' station, the longer it's going to take them to get to you.

They gave me the room right across from the nurses' station. I call that the "Death Room." I knew I must have been in bad shape.

I required what they call a cardiac catheterization, where they go through an artery to check on blockages. One of my arteries was 90 percent blocked. They put three stints in my heart and then released me the next day. I had been in the hospital for six days. Just a day later, I had more pain in my chest, so I had another stay in the ICU and another surgery on my heart. The doctors didn't find anything wrong, so I was again released.

After *that* I went home. You might think I'm crazy, but that's when I finally told my family what was going on. I didn't want any of them to worry, and I especially did not want my boys to see me in the hospital.

My wife and I were separated at the time, soon to be divorced. She and the rest of my family and friends were all shocked at first – and then mad at me. Obviously, I understood. I'd have been angry if the situation was reversed.

Throughout the entire ordeal, I was thinking of my kids. I couldn't bear the thought of them seeing their father lying in a hospital bed after surgery, hooked up to IVs and monitors. I knew the scary thoughts that would put in their minds, and I didn't want that for them. Instead, I called every day and said I was doing overtime or made up some other excuse as to why I couldn't come by.

Similarities in human behavior are fascinating to me. I didn't think about it at the time or use it as any sort of guidance, but my reluctance fell right in line with the history of my family. My mother and grandfather were the same way when going through their adversities – protect the children at any cost. Mom didn't talk to us about her lung cancer, even after it was obvious something was going wrong. My grandfather didn't want his kids seeing him in the hospital after his accident; he always brushed off questions about what happened.

I know that the way I handled the whole thing isn't how you're supposed to do it. The nurses let me know that from the beginning, actually. Those nurses were so nice and knowledgeable and helpful to me in there, but, boy, they sure let me have it about waiting to come in.

"You're so lucky and stupid!" I remember them saying to me. "We have people who die because they don't get checked right away, and you waited for *three days* of pain before coming in here?"

I knew they were right, of course, and if I had it to do again, I'd have been checked right away. It was just easy for me to think it was something else.

In hindsight, the motorcycle crash was obviously more dramatic, more gruesome, more instantly frightening. But for me, the heart problem was scarier. When I was lying in the field after the motor crash, I was numb, but I thought – or at least hoped – I'd be okay. With a bad heart, you just never know. You might not make it out.

When I was finally discharged, I remember it was a cool day, pretty clear, and I walked to the street corner and just stood there for a minute. I watched everyone around me going about their days: the smiles, the worries, or the appointments they had to get to. I thought, *Man, I'm alive again!*

It felt so good to be out in the fresh air. No more hospital bed. No more hospital food. Something like that resets you. It's a rebirth. Eventually, everyday life takes over and you still get angry when someone cuts you off in traffic. But you always have that memory. You always remember what it's like to get that second chance.

When I think about that day, it's similar to the feeling people must have when they come back to my side of the rail up on the Bridge. It's important for all of us to take advantage of that second chance, especially since not everyone gets that opportunity.

4

My Time at San Quentin

Once I got myself where I needed to be after my brush with cancer, the reality set in that I needed a job. Dad offered me one working for him at Golden State Embossing, which I happily accepted.

It was entry-level stuff – I was a gopher at the plant helping wherever I could, making deliveries, sweeping floors, and sometimes helping out the press operators. Regard;ess, it felt good to be active again. My grandfather felt it was important for each of us to contribute to society, and I feel the same way. A person's work is important.

I'd been working for my father for a time when my brother-in-law suggested I apply to the California Department of Corrections. He was an officer in the San Francisco Police Department and figured with my military background that law enforcement would be a good line of work for me.

Corrections was hiring quite a few people back then, and they were looking for men with military experience who were calm and sober, men who understood discipline but were also averse to the intoxicating lure of power. Few things are more dangerous than a short-fused corrections officer itching to exercise the authority he'd never had in any other aspect of his life. Having battled an enemy that was eating me from the inside out, the last thing I felt was entitled or power hungry – I was just grateful to have won the fight.

All I wanted, besides having my life back, was the chance to pursue the American Dream. Corrections seemed like a good place to start.

The application process was and is thorough, which is how it should be for the people hired to care for and control prisoners. There is a background and criminal history check as well as an investigator assigned to your case who looks at everything you submit. If you have anything relating to drugs, a DUI, a hit-and-run, or something similar, you're probably out.

Then, you go through an academy which, in my opinion, was tougher than the one for the CHP. At the time, Corrections Academy was six weeks – compared to six months for the CHP – but the physical training involved was more intense. The push-ups, sit-ups, and cardio stuff like running and burpies were harder and longer for sure.

Fortunately, I made it through, and my first assignment was at Soledad State Prison, near Salinas, California. I spent about a year there and then put in for a transfer, trying to get closer to home.

A job opened up just a few miles from Novato and a few yards from the San Francisco Bay. I was going to work at one of the most notorious prisons in the world: San Quentin State Prison.

Really, I only knew two things about San Quentin: it housed death row inmates and was close to home. The second part was important enough that the first never really bothered me.

• • • •

I started at San Quentin in 1988, when they were still redoing much of the prison. Old bunks with steel frames and steel springs were being replaced with metal, one-piece bed frames. This was because inmates had been taking apart the bedsprings, straightening the metal, and using them as makeshift weapons, like a shank or shiv.

Safety and security was the priority in all of the remodeling, as it should have been in such a dangerous place. My first impression was how thick the walls were. To me, it seemed like they were five feet or so. Old pipes ran along the walls on the inside, many of them leaky, with moss growing in places.

If you go there now, San Quentin has undergone another makeover. It's brighter, with a softened and modernized feel. In the late 80s and early 90s, however, it was like an ancient dungeon. Concrete and steel, the predominant color was gray with the occasional drab spots of tan. Gulls squawked above the yard and waves could be heard striking the rocky shore just a few paces away from the barbed wire and gun towers.

Were it not a state prison and the only place where criminals in California could be put to death by law, developers would have been fighting over the real estate with its views of the city and its private peninsula jutting into the Bay. Like Alcatraz before it, San Quentin had a natural barrier beyond its walls. Steep hills to the north, gates at the east and west with guards, and the south – well, any potential escapee would face frigid waters full of dangerous currents and inhospitable creatures.

Inside was even worse.

Inmates ran the gambit from young drug offenders to middle-aged car thieves to old convicted killers who had once been on the winning end of a knife fight. We also had the only gas chamber in California, which meant if you were awaiting execution, you did so in San Quentin. Executions stopped in 1967, but started back up in 1992. Nobody – neither inmate nor officer – spoke of executions. They were just there, part of the reality.

Tookie Williams, founder of the infamous Crips gang, was convicted of murdering four people in 1979 and spent his final days at San Quentin before being executed by lethal injection in 2005.

I worked "The Row" briefly. Most of these convicts generally went along with the program. They each had their own cell. When providing their meals to them, which was served in their cells, many of the inmates on Tookie's tier would request that their meals be passed along to Tookie.

"Give my eggs to Tookie," was a common refrain from the other black inmates.

Tookie was a very big guy, but he was not fat. He was big like a weightlifter. He started adding muscle while serving time in a juvenile prison, introduced to weightlifting by the facility's gym coach. Tookie used to tell the story about when he was released from the juvenile facility: He told the board that he planned on being the leader of the biggest gang in the world.

You can imagine how this type of background plays in prison. However, respect from some makes you a target for others. Shortly before I started working on what we called condemned row, an inmate attacked Tookie with a handmade shiv.

The attack happened during recreation time when the men were in the same yard. The attack wasn't successful, and after that, the offending inmate was designated as a "walk alone," which meant he had an exercise yard to himself, protecting him from other inmates – and protecting other inmates from him.

Tookie wasn't the only infamous resident of San Quentin. Randy Kraft was convicted in 1989, and remains on death row. He was convicted of the rape, torture, mutilation, and murder of at least 16 young men. He is suspected in 51 other murders.

Kraft's were heinous acts, even by San Quentin standards. His first known sexual assault was in 1970, the victim a 13-year-old boy. Kraft tricked him into coming back to his apartment where Kraft drugged and assaulted him. Most of Kraft's victims were in their late teens or early 20s, nearly all of them drugged, many of them found dead with gruesome bodily mutilation.

Another serial killer at San Quentin was Richard Ramirez, otherwise known as the "Night Stalker." He used guns, knives, a machete, a tire iron, and a hammer in various crimes. He claimed to be a Satanist, was sentenced to 13 death sentences, and never expressed any remorse for his actions.

The first known victim of Ramirez was a nine-year-old girl. She was found raped, beaten, stabbed to death, and hanging from a pipe. A judge described Ramirez's crimes as showing a "cruelty, callousness, and viciousness beyond any human understanding." Ramirez died of cancer while awaiting his execution.

Merle Haggard, the country music legend, was transferred to San Quentin after trying to escape from a jail where he was serving a sentence for attempted robbery. The story goes that Haggard was going to try escaping from San Quentin, too, but was talked out of it by other inmates. When he got out, the first song in what turned into a highly successful career was titled, "Skid Row." It is said that he got his initial inspiration from a Johnny Cash concert in January 1958, which led to Haggard joining the prison band.

The actor Danny Trejo, who often plays overly-masculine villains in movies like *Heat* and *Con Air*, also did a stretch in San Quentin and even became the inmate lightweight boxing champion while there.

• • • •

It's probably as true now as it was then that respect is the leading currency in prison. Everyone there thinks they have and deserve a little more of it than they do in reality. Prisoners are robbed of their freedom and ability to see their family and friends. Respect is all they're left with, so they guard it intimately.

Disrespect generally brings an "ass whooping" at least. Depending on the type of disrespect – "snitches get stitches" is old prison saying – you may find yourself shanked.

Basically, affiliations and status are everything.

Also, apologies don't cut it in prison, either. Instead of forgiveness, you're taught a lesson – the most popular teaching tool being a shiv to the back or chest.

A young inmate trying to make a name for himself may start a fight with an older or bigger inmate. Officers are targets, too, sometimes of physical attacks but definitely of constant verbal attacks to see how far an inmate can push the line. By whatever means, if an inmate gains respect, that inmate gains stature around the prison. That means he can walk places others can't without fear of retaliation for crossing a certain gang's turf.

So much of the prison life I observed was drawn down racial lines. Seldom did white, black, Asian,

Me in my uniform from my days at San Quentin. You might not think of it this way, but I couldn't have imagined a better place to learn human psychology.

or Hispanic inmates interact on a social level. They didn't eat together, sit together, or even talk when they were in a group setting.

When they were forced to work together, guards had to watch closely as someone was always jockeying for leadership. Everything was about machismo and who could gain an edge. As corrections officers, we understood that we worked on the precipice of anarchy.

Because of the delicate balance we had to maintain, I became an astute observer of human action and inaction. I actually learned more psychology and sociology in my two years at San Quentin than I would have with a standard formal education. How a man stood, how his facial muscles contracted, how he breathed or raised his eyebrows or moved his fingers: These were all subtleties that told us more about his intentions and state of mind than his words, especially in an environment where every movement was strictly controlled.

I could sense when a man lost the last vestiges of hope and welcomed the arrival of desperation and then depression. Finally, they would nestle into the basic instincts of all animals – survival by whatever means necessary.

The longer you're in a prison environment and the longer you're around specific inmates, the better you can read them and the better you know what to look for. An inmate who is continually scanning an area by moving his head from side to side is a "tell" that something may be going down.

Just like people on the outside, inmates have patterns. If a man who goes to the yard rain or shine suddenly declines one day, that's an indication a fight may be about to break out or someone is targeted to get shanked. I had to know who was in which gang because if I saw a number of Crips spread around the yard, watching officers, I knew I was about to see action.

Several of my fellow officers were shanked by inmates who perceived they were mistreated by that officer or who were trying to make a name for themselves amongst the other inmates.

One particular officer was a bodybuilder and, unfortunately, had an ego to match the muscles. This led to trouble. Once, he had some sort of argument with an inmate. A few days later, we let some prisoners out for various reasons – work, recreation, medical appointments, and the usual.

A prisoner got behind a wall and, as the officer passed, stuck a piece of metal into the right side of his neck. The gash was deep and six inches long with the skin left jagged – not straight like a razor cut. The officer nearly bled to death. He was taken to the hospital and the inmate was taken to the Security Housing Unit (SHU) to await trial for attempted murder.

The officer came back to work a couple weeks later. I remember going out to eat with him once after work. He was bragging about the scar to the waitress, like it was some badge of honor and not a mark from when he nearly died. Some people never learn.

When I first started, I was working the north block, which is five levels of 50 cells per level. The whole place was filled with cigarette smoke. It was loud and, honestly, intimidating. My first few nights' sleep there were interrupted with nightmares of getting shanked by an inmate on the top level with no help on the way. That's an awful way to wake up, especially in a prison.

I can't say I got used to it, at least not quickly, but after a while, I started to acclimate myself. Eventually, I was able to sleep normally.

I had no other choice, so it didn't take long for me to learn how to control my emotions. I had to be fair but firm, and I had to watch my back at all times.

After about a year at San Quentin, I was placed on what is referred to as "Vacation Relief." For the next six months or so, I would take the positions of officers who were on vacation or long-term injury. This meant changing work locations about every two weeks.

One afternoon when I was in the chow hall supervising a small group of inmates who clean the multitude of pots and pans, I saw two Hispanic inmates doing all the cleanup work while one large black inmate, who was the leader of the Muslim prison population, stood with his arms folded, not lifting a finger to help.

A couple of minutes later, I casually but firmly ordered, "Hey, you need to get in there and get to helping, please."

The man walked slowly and purposefully toward me and replied, "Don't you ever tell me what to do again." This guy was huge, probably

6 feet 5 inches, with 250 pounds of prison-built muscle and aggravation from years of being lock up. This was a test – one I responded to with a calm resolve.

If I took no action or showed weakness, he would not only continue with his behavior, but he'd also tell all his buddies about me. Word would spread that I was weak and easily manipulated. I would be a mark and useless as an officer.

I explained to this gentleman that not only would I continue to tell him what to do, but that he would, in fact, do it. To reinforce my point, I called over to his housing unit and asked the officers there to "toss his cell," which really means inspect every inch of it, making a mess of everything he has, to ensure that he wasn't hiding contraband or, more importantly, a weapon. My call that day hit the mark with the inmate, and we had no further discussions. Although he did just the minimal amount of work every day, I let it go at that.

Another job I had while on vacation relief was "escort detail." This is quite different from what most folks think of – there are no "ladies of the night" in this detail. It came as no surprise when I received orders to help with an escort detail in a section that was home to the high-profile and extremely dangerous inmates, the place for lifers who had nothing to lose but their badass reputations.

It was no place for carelessness. My senses were cranked to full-alert when we arrived. Our prisoner was an old man with black eyes and bad teeth, the kind of person you would walk past a hundred times on a street corner without noticing.

I don't remember his name or why he was in the SHU, but I do remember his neighbor. As we prepped our guy for the five-minute walk to the hospital, I heard a firm and inviting greeting.

"Hey, fellow, hey, why don't you take me with you."

I took one step back and looked his way, seeing what had to be the filthiest cell in San Quentin. Various flecks of trash had been there so long they stuck to the floor and walls like decorative paint and stains of human waste caked the sparse furniture and belongings.

Even the ceiling had a smudged look about it, although I knew the little man inside was too short to have left any handprints up there.

"Hello, Charlie," the other guard nodded at the man – it was Charles Manson.

"Hey, why don't you and me get out of here," Manson suggested to me as if he and I were drinking buddies or co-conspirators in some elaborate breakout scheme. "You know I'd be out of here anyway if it wasn't for that goddamn Jew lawyer. What do you say? They know me at the front gate. Let's you and me just walk outta here."

I ignored him, but that didn't deter Manson from jabbering on like some manic used car salesman desperate to make a new friend, jumping from one subject to the next without missing a beat. I glanced his way a couple of times, but only for a few seconds.

Manson's hair and beard were white and the famous swastika he had carved into his forehead for shock value looked like a silly affectation, lost in the ashen wrinkles of his sagging, leathery face. His eyes were still dark and crazy, and once they locked onto you, they never left.

After a few minutes of hearing him preach one nutty theory after another, I understood how this psychopath could persuade the young and feeble to his side. It was also a sad and sobering realization that such a guy still had a small but loyal cult following.

As we shackled our prisoner's feet and wrists for transport, Manson continued to spew gibberish, this time about life on the outside and how the entire legal system had been rigged against him. Then, he paused, which caught my attention. I could feel him staring at me like a wolf.

I looked his way again.

"All that stuff I just said, that's the devil talking," he muttered. "And your mama wouldn't want you to listen to the devil."

He stared and let a moment of silence hang in the air. Then, with total calm, he said, "If I ever get out of here, I'm going to cut your head off."

We moved our prisoner out of his cell, trying our best to ignore him.

Shortly after this encounter – though not because of it – I moved on to law enforcement.

5
The Dark Side of The Bridge

Before I transferred to the Marin Area, I had a four-year stint in Hayward in the East Bay. For whatever reason, that's a place where a lot of guys start out after the academy.

I knew I had some rough edges that needed to be smoothed. Because of my background, I had too much of what you might call the San Quentin mentality. It was sort of a "if you don't do what I say, we're going to wrestle, and I'm going to arrest you" mindset. That's how I got through in San Quentin, but it's not always the best approach on the streets.

There was one day early in my time at Hayward when I got a call to back up an officer on a vehicle stop in an unincorporated business area. There were four black males in the car, all around 17 or 18 years old. It was a basic stop, expired car registration. The fees were overdue enough that the car was going to be impounded. By the time I got there, two of the men in the car had left the scene. Only the driver and a man in the passenger seat remained.

The man in the passenger seat was what officers sometimes sarcastically call "a lawyer." He was talking about his rights, telling us what we could and could not do. I asked him to leave the scene, and he refused. He had baggy pants on with a long shirt that covered his pants, and I thought I could see some bulges. I didn't know what they were, so I told him if he was going to stay there, I was going to search him.

"No, you're not," he said.

"Yes, I am," I said.

"I'm not going anywhere."

So, I grabbed his arm, turned him around, and we started fighting. The driver stayed back, out of the altercation. The other officer did the same. We were wrestling on the ground for what must have been several minutes when, finally, I got him under control and the handcuffs on.

At that point, we took the man to jail for booking. The common procedure is that if there's a physical confrontation between an officer and a subject, we call in another officer to take the subject to booking. It's cleaner that way, and in a situation like that, you want emotions to be as even as possible – on both sides.

Shortly after, my commanding officer called me back to the office, which is highly unusual. For whatever reason, we never got along right from the beginning. I explained what happened with the traffic stop, the refusal for a search, and the wrestling match. She listened, then called Dispatch and had the other officer take the subject back to the scene of the stop or his house – his choice. According to my commanding officer, I didn't have the right to do what I'd done.

So, the guy got taken home, and the next day, I explained the story again at the office. My commanding officer didn't like that I put hands on the guy and arrested him. Combined with another incident – I was in a pursuit and skidded into another car, which was totally my fault since I was going too fast – I was suspended for three days.

The incident with the traffic stop eventually turned into a lawsuit. No further action against me was taken, but the case was settled out of court for $14,000. The attorneys working my case said I had done nothing wrong, but they decided not to leave that decision up to a jury.

Anyway, not too long after that, we got a new commander. He rode with me on his second day in charge, which was a little unusual for it to be that soon. He didn't say much to me that day, which, as it turned out, was a fairly typical day for me on the beat.

About a year later, he called me into his office. He asked if I remembered the ride-along. It had been a while, but of course I did. He explained that before the previous commander left, she told him about the good people in the Department and the bad people and the ones he would need to look out for. That's why he wanted to do the ride-along so soon after taking the job.

"I wanted to see for myself," he told me. "I found out where the actual problem was." He didn't have to say anything more.

We got along well, with a mutual respect for each other. He eventually became the commissioner of the CHP, and I had no punitive issues besides that suspension for the remainder of my career.

When you graduate from the highway patrol academy, they put you where they want to put you. Your placement is based on a lot of factors, but No. 1 is always the needs of the patrol. Even having a boss I got along with better, Hayward was not where I wanted to be.

It was 1994, and my fourth year in the CHP, a middle ground when I wasn't quite a veteran but wasn't tenured enough to garner a begrudging respect from the crustiest of colleagues.

This is a bit of a strange time for an officer, a bit awkward, not unlike adolescence. When you're a rookie, some guys – especially old timers – want nothing to do with you. That's not an exaggeration. They ignore you, treat you like you're invisible. You don't feel invisible, though. You feel like everyone's watching your every move, waiting for you to slip up.

For instance, as a rookie, you have to sit at the front of the room during briefings. You move back as you gain seniority, as older officers move on and younger ones are hired. It's very much like a classroom with assigned seating. If you're not where you're supposed to be, you will find yourself looking up at a senior officer telling you, "Rookie, you're in my seat."

Not long after I started at Hayward, there was a hiring freeze. I was stuck. Budget stuff and all. When they started hiring again, I was no longer near the bottom of the totem pole and had more of a choice on where I wanted to be – the Marin Area, closer to the Bay. I was so happy when I got my transfer, mostly because it would cut my commute down from a minimum of fifty minutes to around twenty. That's around an hour a day, sometimes more, that I got back.

Being in the Marin Area meant I'd be closer to friends and family and have time to meet for coffee or lunch more often – basically get back some of my life. I knew the Bridge as an international tourist destination, and thought it would be nice to interact with people from all over the world. That's why I wanted the transfer: something different every day, new faces, variety. I didn't really think about much else.

I didn't think about the Bridge itself.

In fact, nobody really talked about the Bridge. At least, they didn't talk about the Bridge's dark side.

• • • •

The Golden Gate Bridge is like a constant background to your life when you live here. You know it's beautiful, you know it's iconic, and you know it's a grand symbol for ingenuity and ambition and everything else, but somehow, it sort of blends into the background.

You don't actually *think* about it because it's always just sort of *there*.

Except for my time in the Army, I've lived in the Bay Area my whole life, which meant the Bridge was merely a backdrop to me.

Even after decades of living near the Bridge and then taking it on as part of my job with the CHP, I never knew how many people went there to end their lives. I never knew how many people walked onto the Bridge and don't walk off.

Obviously, I had no idea how much the Bridge would change my life.

Oh, don't get me wrong. I'd hear tidbits of information. I'd hear indirect references to it, and from living in the area, I knew that sometimes people jumped off the Bridge. But being aware and understanding are two different things.

You might think that an officer taking over a beat that included so many life-and-death negotiations would be given a heads up, but that's really not the case. Some of that is the culture of law enforcement. This is your job, so handle it. Period.

The rest of it, I have to think, is the same reason people in general don't like to talk about suicide. I hope that's starting to change.

Anyway, it wasn't long after I began working on the Bridge that I received my first call of a suicide. The man had jumped without warning or hesitation – a purposeful leap from someone who had no intention of backing out at the last minute.

What I discovered was that he probably hadn't looked down ahead of time. Whether it's vertigo or a fear of seeing their final destination, many jumpers either close their eyes or look up as they let go. Because of that, many of them have no idea where they are relative to the landscape – and they hit land rather than water.

Sometimes, they hit the brushy hillside near the North Tower. Other times, they hit the sandy area near the south end of the Bridge. Once in a while, people end up in the moat, an area of water surrounded by a concrete enclosure which encircles the South Tower. This circular barrier of concrete protects the tower from ships that may lose their way in the fog or go off course in the rough currents. Once, a person jumped from the Bridge and hit a metal railing that goes around the moat. This was years ago, but you can still see where they hit because the railing is bent. I don't know why that's never been fixed.

Regardless, hitting land from that height is a fall no one survives. This man jumped from the north end, just beyond Vista Point but well before reaching the North Tower, which meant he missed the water by a good hundred yards.

I reached the scene by driving down a winding road that leads under the Bridge. From there, I hiked down a steep hill to the mangled body. Several officers and a medical examiner were there.

The man jumped in the dark of night, so there's very little chance we'd have known where he was – or even that he had jumped – without a witness.

The witness, fortunately for us, not only called 911 but stayed and pointed us to where the man jumped. The witness was very shaken up, as you can imagine. These bystanders just happen to be in the wrong place at the wrong time and see things that not only affect their day, but may even impact the rest of their lives. It's a hard thing for officers, but we're trained to see tragedy and choose this profession knowing we'll see some difficult things. Witnesses, however, don't get to make that choice.

The jumper was a white man in his early 30s. He was dressed in slacks and button down shirt. The clothes were dark and so torn and bloody from the fall that it's hard to describe what he was wearing with any detail. Both of his arms were obviously broken, bent sideways or backward in ways that arms aren't supposed to bend.

His face was lifeless, and in his final expression, I saw a look of surprise. Along with the hopelessness that drives someone to jump, I imagine surprise is one of the last emotions he ever felt, maybe from hitting the land. His eyes were still open, which is always very eerie to me, no matter how many times this job puts me in front of death, no matter the circumstance.

Jumpers hit the ground instead of the water more often than you might think.

Now, obviously, most people who come to the Bridge to make their last and final decisions are not thinking clearly. When they arrive at the Bridge, they often don't look over the rail or, maybe, these people assume that once they're on the Bridge they're over the water.

I don't know the percentages, but there are a lot like this man who jump off over land and end up hitting the hard ground. This particular man bounded down the hillside, hitting rocks and brush and packed clay before stopping against a bush. If anyone thinks there is romanticism about suicide from the Bridge, they haven't seen one of these bodies.

Seeing him saddened my heart and soul. What could possibly be so bad in this man's life that he'd do this to himself? To think that the best thing to do is jump over the railing of a bridge to a gruesome death?

As a highway patrolman, you know going into this line of work you are going to see death. But death on the Bridge is different.

The natural acoustics around the area absorb sound. Noise from the Bridge is swept out to sea and the lapping currents and barking wildlife are muffled. Conversations sound like the soft tones of an NPR monologue. There are no screaming passengers, miles of blocked traffic, or news crews relentlessly nagging us for some grim message about the incident.

It is an intimate feel. No distractions. It's just me, a medical examiner, a few other officers, and death.

"Looks like he hit at least three times before landing here," the medical examiner speculated as we all looked up the hillside at the various impact points.

"Any way of knowing which one killed him?" one of the other officers asked.

Now, in practical terms, the answer to that question is completely irrelevant. What does it matter which hit killed him? The man is dead, after all. But we cops know the kinds of things that family members might want to know about their loved one, which is why we ask these questions. They might ask us. If there are answers, it would be nice to be prepared for that brutally difficult conversation.

The medical examiner shook his head.

"If he hit his head, it could have been the first one," he answered.

We all looked at the body in silence. For this man's sake, I hoped that was the case – death on the first impact instead of the third.

As officers, we really like to think that none of this stuff affects us. It's just part of the job, so we deal with it and move on. To some extent, that's true. But we're also human beings, and seeing a dead body leaves a lasting impression, makes a permanent impact – I don't care who you are, you can never un-see it.

• • • •

There is something I've come to call "cop humor." We use it in these situations where what we see or experience is so stressful or gruesome or otherwise saddening that a lot of us turn to dark humor or a snarky remark.

If you're not one of us, it might come off as detached, unaffected, or inappropriate. I understand that. But, from time to time, we use this dark humor as a coping mechanism because we see some awful things.

Once, when I was a supervisor, I was called to the scene where a woman was hit in traffic. This was in Fremont, and apparently, she had just walked out in front of heavy traffic. It was dark at that hour in the morning, so maybe the cars had a hard time seeing her. However it happened, she was struck by anywhere from four to six cars.

It was pretty ugly. I don't think there was a piece of her body that was even the size of a frisbee. She was obliterated. We found a shoe and a driver's license. That was it. The rest of her was just kind of there.

An accident like that, we call them "a hundred-foot pedestrian."

Again, we mean no disrespect to the deceased or the situation. But, like I said earlier, we're human beings, and taking ourselves out of the immediate reality of what we're seeing and experiencing can be a helpful. That's especially true in law enforcement, which largely has a "macho" culture where people often don't feel comfortable opening up about what they're seeing or feeling.

Same goes when you work the Bridge. What you see there can be every bit as sad and shaking as a hundred-foot pedestrian.

Sometimes, people think that hitting the water is somehow soft, like jumping off a diving board. That couldn't be further from the gruesome reality. There is a myth in some circles that jumping from the Bridge is a peaceful way to go, but the truth is so much worse.

Those who jump at mid-span hit the water at speeds over 70 miles per hour with a force of 1,500 pounds per square inch. That's highway speed, and from that height – remember, the Bridge is about 22 stories above the Bay – the water is more like concrete than a swimming pool. The whole thing takes about four seconds, which doesn't sound like much but has been shown by research to be much longer than jumpers expect. One survivor remembers thinking, *I must be about to hit*, three times.

The actual cause of death for people who jump off the Bridge is usually a blunt-force trauma, most often with the ribs snapping and turning into blades that puncture lungs, kidneys, hearts, and other vital organs. Spines snap, and quite often the livers rupture.

If a person hits head first, their necks break and their skulls fracture under the force. Some actually survive that initial impact, but their bodies plunge too deep into the water. They can't recover, inhaling once submerged and drowning as their lungs fill with sea water. If they're lucky enough to come back to the surface, they usually have so many broken bones they can't remain afloat.

Some bodies get caught in a sort of undercurrent that's intensified by the Bridge's enormous stone piers and moat. Bodies have been found as far as 30 miles away and are sometimes ravaged by sharks and crabs. I don't know how or why this myth about a calm, peaceful way to go began, but it is completely wrong.

In reality, jumping off the Golden Gate Bridge is an awful, excruciating way to die.

• • • •

The first person I dealt with over the rail was a woman, a drug user and probably homeless. She was white, and at least in my memory, her sandy blonde hair came to a swoop at the end.

I met this woman at her darkest moment, and I did almost everything wrong. I ran up to the rail, shouted at her to come back over, talked too much, and told her that it couldn't be that bad. It's a wonder she didn't jump just to get away from me.

Thankfully, another officer and I were able to help her decide to come back over, but for weeks afterward, I worried about how quickly things could have gone the other way. *This is why so many officers don't want to work the Bridge beat,* I often thought to myself.

I quickly saw my job on the Bridge and my own personal history of depression as signs that this was what I was supposed to do with my life. This was something I could be good at, something I could use to serve people, something I could do to help.

But, first, I needed to educate myself. After my experience with the sandy blonde haired woman, I had to make sure I didn't make the same mistakes over again. I had to make sure I was prepared and comfortable for the next meeting on the Bridge.

My first step was going to the library. Simple, right?

Well, I didn't know anything about negotiations, much less anything clinical or any research on mental illness. I didn't know what psychosis was and didn't know all the ways that depression could start and manifest itself. I wasn't looking for self-help books, but rather research that could help explain what some of these desperate people were going through.

That's the chord we often refer to, the spot over the railing where people often stand when we're trying to get them back. This was a young woman who, for some reason, took her shoes off when she got to the chord. I was the on-duty supervisor that day, and we were fortunate enough to get her back.

I wish I could say I had a turning point, that some book I read or workshop I attended or speech I heard or negotiation I facilitated showed me the light and gave me all the information I'd ever need. But it didn't work like that for me.

As you progress in life, hopefully, you're paying attention, trying to get better and notice things. You start to see pain in people's faces. You see it, and you acknowledge it. That's how it's worked for me, anyway.

One thing I did right with that first woman: I told her I could see that she was in pain. I know that sounds like such a simple, obvious thing, perhaps even too simple and too obvious to say. But I've found that saying the simplest thing helps.

Sometimes, when a person experiences that – another human being looking at them, validating and acknowledging their pain – they can feel better. They can feel like you care and that, maybe, there's help out there for them. Just being acknowledged can be all a person needs. Maybe it sounds silly to say to a person that you can see they're in pain, but one of the reasons I do it is because I know there was a time in my life when that would've helped me. That fundamental human interaction and understanding can feel so good.

We helped her, that first woman, back over the railing, and that experience stuck with me. The fear of what might've happened because of my mistakes up there shook me. I could've lost her because I was too eager, too loud, too sporadic.

This fear and doubt weighed on me. *What could I have done differently? What could I have said that would have made a difference?* I often wondered.

I thought about the guilt I would have carried if she'd ended up jumping. And, most of all, I thought about what I could do to better prepare myself for the next person on the railing because when you work the Bridge, the only certainty is that there will be a next person.

One advantage I have is that I have been depressed. I haven't thought about hurting myself or someone else, and I certainly haven't been motivated to go somewhere like the Bridge to end it all, but having been depressed gives me a better understanding of and empathy for what these people are going through. I know what it's like, which allows me to better communicate and listen.

Simply put: Depression sucks. You don't think you can feel better. For me, I always thought it was important to focus on the good things. No matter how bad it got, I would have some good days. It could be something as grand as the birth of your kids to see the potential of human life, as temporary as a vacation to Lake Tahoe to see the beauty of nature, as simple as a nice conversation at the coffee shop with a friend. Whatever it was, I always tried to focus on the good.

Which is why, sometimes, up on the Bridge and talking with someone who wants to end it all, I ask them to look around. There is so much beauty around the Bridge. There's the human accomplishment and ambition of the San Francisco skyline and the natural beauty of the Bay and the hills and the ocean.

"Look around you," I'll say. "Could a world this beautiful be all bad?"

• • • •

I was promoted to the rank of Sergeant in 2008. It was quite a rigorous testing process. If I had not passed, I would have required myself to seriously consider attempting the test again.

There were 125 names on the promotion list, and I was a ways down. It's difficult to promote from the road. It's usually the people with administrative jobs that are at the top of the list.

When the list got to my name, I decided I would take anything in the San Francisco Bay Area just to get the promotion and start my seniority as a sergeant. Probation would be a full year, and then I could put in a transfer back to the Marin Area, my home. The Hayward Area had a position for a sergeant, so I jumped at the opportunity. When I was promoted into Hayward, I found myself the only sergeant on the graveyard shift from Friday through Monday morning.

In fact, I was the only graveyard sergeant on duty for a while, and when you're the graveyard sergeant, you're alone until the next morning. On the weekends, there's never a lieutenant or captain on duty. That's a lot of pressure, a lot of stress, and even if I was mellow and would ask someone to go out for coffee or something, nobody wanted to go out with the boss.

Once, there was an officer who came in my office and we talked for about an hour. It wasn't about work, but life. I enjoyed that conversation so much. When it was over, I was surprised how much I enjoyed it, which made me realize that I needed to get out and talk to people more often. It was that human contact I was missing.

When I was working at night in isolation, I also slept through the days, meaning I was isolated from most people by my work schedule as well as isolated from people at work by my rank. That's a lonely place.

However, all of that time on the graveyard shift did provide me the opportunity to learn as much about suicide and what drives a person to consider it as I possibly could. After all, every life event can have a lesson or purpose, even if those directly involved have no idea what that purpose is.

I felt as though my feelings of loneliness and desperation – as overwhelming as they were at times – are what led me to work the Bridge and, in turn, confront suicide.

Again, my depression had never taken me to the point where I thought about ending my own life, but when you experience those unrelenting feelings of sadness for no reason, the vacuum of energy, and difficulty of even getting out of bed in the morning, you have a different understanding of the issues many people face.

It's a hard thing. You see people playing outside, working, accomplishing things with their lives, and you just want to sit inside and stay in bed. I don't wish that experience on anyone, but I think going through it helped me to see how mental illness can wreak havoc on a person.

For starters, warning signs almost always exist. Whether or not people notice them is a different question, but there can be changes in mood and behavior, changes in appearance, or maybe a sudden disinterest in old hobbies, personal hygiene, or interaction with friends and family.

But noticing those changes and acting on them are not the same thing. Nobody wants to admit there is a problem because it's a lot easier if there isn't one. Besides, how do you approach someone you suspect might be suffering from mental illness? What do you say? What do you ask?

I know that, many times, we tend to dismiss the signs we notice as a job for mental health professionals, but there are more than 800,000 suicides every year worldwide. This job is bigger than just the mental health community. Talking about this problem is critical – talking about it can save lives.

There is no magic here, no routine formula to follow. I've helped many people off the edge of the Bridge, and sometimes, when I give speeches, people ask when I started to feel comfortable up there. The truth is I don't think I ever felt comfortable up there. There are too many moving parts, too many unknowns, too many things that are completely out of my control.

You know, I think I like it that way, actually. Maybe that sounds strange. But I like that this is something I can't ever feel like I've mastered. Not knowing what to do or exactly how something will play out keeps me on my toes, keeps me motivated to keep learning, keeps my mind open to finding new ways to help people.

Suicide prevention isn't something that can be scripted. To help people see their way to the other side and past the darkness requires vigilance, thoughtfulness, and a willingness to adapt.

The dark side of the Bridge is much too important to approach it any differently.

6
Out of Nowhere

An officer named Julie was on bike patrol for what she now refers to as the worst day of her professional life.

Nothing was particularly memorable about that morning. Not rainy, not foggy. A little overcast. It was a normal, pleasant day, the kind that Julie had put in her transfer for about six years earlier.

She was something like a Highway Patrol lifer, on the job for 21 years already. Something about the uniform, the image, the idea of being outside and not behind a desk, or doing a job people don't think of as "typical" for women – something about the whole law enforcement thing had always appealed to her since she was a little girl.

She grew up in Southern California, in Orange County, and actually had two run-ins with the CHP as a kid. The first was in the second grade; she decided to take a shortcut to the candy store and ended up running along the shoulder of a freeway when a patrol officer found her and brought her back to her house. She got grounded for a week, but remembered the officer.

The next time, she was 17. She was driving in the carpool/HOV lane by herself in Huntington Beach. The officer who pulled her over was a woman, which Julie thought was cool. Even after getting a ticket, she decided that's what she wanted to do for a living. She served three years in the Army before she applied for CHP once she hit the minimum age requirement.

Julie worked in Santa Cruz for about 14 years, but like a lot of things in life, that got old after a while. Traffic accidents, stolen cars…she wanted something different. She knew a few people in the Marin Area office, and the change really appealed to her – she could work on a bike and away from the monotony she was growing tired of on the central coast.

She knew enough to know that working the Bridge would mean working with some individuals who wanted to hurt themselves, but looking back, she didn't know the full extent of it. At first, it was good. It's rewarding to be able to help someone in that situation, and being a sort of crisis counselor was new and engaging, a welcome change.

Julie couldn't have imagined how that day would end.

Some iron workers saw an Asian woman, around 35 years old, 5 feet 6 inches, about 120 pounds – we'll call her Kathy. She just had a bad look about her, so the workers called Bridge Patrol.

Kathy was on the Bridge for hours, walking back and forth, which doesn't necessarily mean anything suspicious – some people are just in awe of the Bridge and view. But there was something about Kathy's body

Bridge Patrol are often the ones to make initial contact with people who go over the rail or look suspicious. They have the safety of all visitors to the Bridge in mind. They called in Julie after they didn't have enough to detain Kathy. Something just didn't seem right.

language that looked off. She was walking around, holding her purse, setting her purse down, standing in one spot for a long time. That's when Bridge Patrol first made contact with her, but they didn't have enough to detain her, which was where Julie came in.

It was about 11 a.m. when Julie asked Kathy for identification, which she provided. As an officer, the purpose of this is to see if anyone has filed a missing person's report or if there is any other concrete reason to be suspicious that something is wrong. Kathy was clean.

She said she drove, that her car was in the east parking lot. Julie asked if Kathy had her keys. She did. That can be a sign, not having their keys, because people who plan on jumping will sometimes leave their keys in the car to make it easier on those they leave behind. At that point, there was nothing Julie could use to justify detaining Kathy, and the situation was made more difficult by Kathy's skittishness at the questioning.

At one point, Julie asked directly if Kathy was planning on hurting herself. You might be surprised how many people will admit when asked, but Kathy denied it. Not just that, but she was using words like "harassment" and said she felt embarrassed to be talking to officers out in the public like this when she hadn't broken any laws.

Legally, Julie could not violate Kathy's civil rights by handcuffing or otherwise detaining her. But Julie still didn't feel right about what was in front of her, so she offered to walk Kathy off the Bridge. Kathy agreed.

Julie was still on her bike, riding slowly along with Kathy and another Bridge Patrol officer.

"Man," the patrol officer told Julie. "I don't have a good feeling about this. I think she's going to go."

They got to the point where they were no longer over water, which made Julie feel good, but then they hit a bit of an open spot on the Bridge. The suspension cables that hold up the Bridge road and sidewalks are secured in part by massive concrete blocks, called pylons. There are two of these concrete pylons on each side of the Bridge. The cables run through these pylons. Between them stands a tall cyclone fence just on the other side of the pedestrian rail.

As soon as Kathy walked past the pylon, she took off toward the railing. Julie was half-anticipating this and might have been able to stop Kathy, but there was no hesitation on Kathy's part. Most people who jump take the railing slowly, or at least step on the bottom part of the railing before swinging themselves over. Not Kathy.

Out of nowhere, she ran toward the railing and vaulted over, like a gymnast. Straight to her death.

It was a chaotic scene there on the Bridge. A woman was coming the other way on a bicycle and was maybe ten feet from where Kathy went over the rail. The woman screamed, stopped, and fell over.

Kathy landed some 200 feet below, at Fort Point, which is the old military site that protected the San Francisco harbor from Confederate and foreign attack during and after the Civil War.

Julie was shocked. Devastated. She had already been wrestling herself all morning about what to do with Kathy, weighing a bad gut feeling against the reality that there was no tangible or ethical reason to detain this woman. Then, right when she started to feel good – *finally, we're no longer above water* – Kathy leapt over the edge to her death.

Watching that rocked Julie's world. She'd seen people driven to desperation jump to their deaths before and had come to accept that was an unfortunate part of the job. But Kathy was different. Much different.

Just to the left of the pylon in the left photo, that's where Kathy jumped, out of nowhere, and in Julie's words, "like a gymnast." At the bottom of the right photo, you can see Fort Point, where Kathy landed, dying on impact.

This was the first time she felt like she could've done something to prevent a person from jumping – like she *should've* done something to prevent Kathy from jumping.

Was there *really* nothing Julie could've done? Should she have been more or less direct? What if, instead of riding on her bike, she'd walked alongside Kathy on the way back to the parking lot?

Truthfully, Julie just wanted to cry. To get away from it all and just be by herself, away from the nightmare. But there's a mode officers get in sometimes, sort of like autopilot, where we compartmentalize our feelings and do what needs to be done. She called Dispatch, reported what happened, talked to witnesses, and began to put together the information needed for the report.

All the while second-guessing herself on what was now the first day of the rest of her career.

I was the on-duty supervisor that day and was at my desk. When I heard Julie's call over the radio, I got on my motorcycle and traveled the eight or so miles to the east lot. When I arrived, other officers told me Julie was in the trailer we have in the east lot, which we use as a satellite office.

When I walked into the trailer, it was Julie and two other officers. Those guys were not trained in crisis negotiations, and they were oblivious. We have this term we use, *smoking and joking*. They weren't literally smoking, but joking around, not acknowledging what had happened. They meant no disrespect to Julie. This is a way officers sometimes cope with traumatic events.

Immediately, I could tell that Julie was upset, so I quickly kicked those two out of the trailer. Just as soon as the door shut, Julie broke down. We talked for a while. She told me the story, and I explained to her it was my opinion that she did what she legally could and the woman's death was not in any way her fault. I could tell she felt guilty, but there was nothing in that situation she should have or could have done differently.

I told her to go home. She didn't want to. I said, "Well, at least take a break for a while. Go into the city or Sausalito. Get some coffee. Take a few hours. Take your mind off the events of the day."

So, Julie rode with another officer into the city where they had lunch. The whole time she was running through the case and what she wanted to do next. Did she want to take a few days off, like I suggested? Did she want to go right back to work? Did she want to see a counselor?

• • • •

Eventually, she decided she wanted to come right back, so that afternoon – by this time, it was about three o'clock – she was on the same area of the Bridge where Kathy had jumped.

Julie saw a tall black man, just standing there, looking down to where Kathy landed. Julie walked up to him, and the man told her he saw Kathy jump. Julie got a vibe from the guy, so she engaged him in conversation. He said he was at Fort Point when Kathy jumped; he'd seen her land or seen the reaction of people who saw her land.

"I just don't understand how people can take their own lives," Julie shook her head.

The man focused.

"I do," he muttered. "I understand."

The man went on to say that his mother had committed suicide and that, in fact, he had taken a bus in from Monterey that day to kill himself.

Julie was floored. The man's statement hit her hard. She has come to think of this moment as something like instant therapy, like an immediate chance to make sure that watching Kathy jump was not the only thing she remembered from that day.

"I'm glad you didn't jump," Julie said. "I'm here to help."

They ended up talking for a while. The man opened up to Julie, not just about his mother's suicide but also about what had driven him to this point. The man asked Julie questions, too. Julie told him what it was like to lose Kathy, how upset it made her, and that she was sorry the man had to see it.

Although Julie never asked the man specifically if seeing Kathy jump kept him from following through with his plan, maybe seeing Kathy jump and then talking to Julie about it somehow kept him from doing the same. It might have helped, but then again, research shows that exposure to suicide often leads to more suicide, which is why many newspapers and other news outlets won't list the cause of death when reporting on people who kill themselves.

Regardless, the man was entirely pleasant. He offered no resistance. More often than not, this is how it goes. He made it relatively easy. He wanted help and knew he needed it. Julie called him in on what we call a 5150, which is cop-code for an involuntary hold for a psychiatric evaluation.

It was a job well done for Julie and a much-needed chance to feel good about something after what had happened with Kathy earlier that day.

But that didn't mean Julie went home feeling good.

The lasting effects of that day were just beginning.

• • • •

Even after two years, Julie has a hard time talking about Kathy without tearing up.

"I don't think I'll ever stop second-guessing," she says. "I just didn't know. I wish I would've."

The facts haven't changed, and Julie knows she didn't do anything wrong. She's run through it in her head a thousand times, and using only the facts she knew at the time, she would have done the exact same thing.

This was just such a strange case. A lot of people who go to the Bridge looking to hurt themselves are obvious. You see people outwardly weeping, obviously depressed. These cases are never easy, but at least many of them are straightforward. With Kathy, she was cold and detached, and that can be a red flag, but there were no obvious signs. Kathy denied being in need of assistance when asked directly. She got defensive, even.

In hindsight, Julie thinks she would have been a little more forceful about getting Kathy off the Bridge. But we can't operate in hindsight even if it is 20/20.

If she could somehow remove herself and experience this story not as the officer on the Bridge that day but as an unbiased and unaffected bystander, Julie knows she would realize that there had been no mistake made, no protocol that wasn't followed, no opportunity to detain Kathy that wasn't taken.

That's not how it happened, of course, and Julie is living in the aftermath, living in hindsight.

She has flashbacks on occasion. Like, seeing an Asian female on the Bridge. Sometimes, it doesn't even have to be that specific. A flashback could be triggered by seeing someone wandering on the Bridge by themselves.

Julie is glad she went back to work that day, but after she went home, she realized she needed some time. I called to check on her, and she asked if she could have some time off. I said, "Absolutely." I told my lieutenant and captain, who both agreed with my decision. Julie took about a week and spent that time thinking about everything.

We have what we call the Employee Assistance Program (EAP), which allows officers to see a counselor or other professional therapist up to seven times per year. Julie took advantage of that, trying to process everything that happened and her role in it. Still, two years later, she goes to talk to someone every once in a while.

This "healing" is an important part of what we do because it's an acknowledgement on CHP's part that what officers see and deal with in their daily work lives can affect them away from the job, out of the uniform. It's recognition of the importance of mental health in general as well as its upkeep. There is no shame in needing to talk to someone, and there is no glory in refusing help. Mental health issues can affect anyone, after all.

If we didn't have the EAP, who knows, maybe Julie wouldn't have felt comfortable or wouldn't have had the opportunity to speak with someone. Most importantly, this event could have permanently affected her mental health and, as a secondary result, could have taken away a very good officer from the CHP.

• • • •

Julie's experience from that day has stuck with her, and she admits to doing her job a little differently now. She says she takes more time when talking with potential 5150 cases and is more deliberate in separating people from the railing. The biggest change for her is asking more questions.

We all have our own life experiences that we bring with us to our jobs, and if we're conscientious and trying to improve ourselves, we all try to figure out how we can learn and be better in the future.

Julie has done that with her experience with Kathy, but that's a very different thing than picking through mistakes. Julie didn't do anything wrong, and she knows that. The sad truth is that if someone is truly determined to kill themselves, they are going to find a way, regardless of any help that's offered. They have to make the decision. You can't make it for them.

We can and should work very hard to do the best we can to provide hope and an alternative. But, this is part of why I always say – and I stress this point when talking to others – in a crisis negotiation like we encounter on the Bridge, we have to remember that ultimately the decision is up to the other person.

I believe that keeps me in the right frame of mind, both in empowering the other person and in not growing so egotistical that I think I can control the result. An ancillary benefit is that, in those unfortunate times when we lose someone, we can remember whose choice it was.

That's a small consolation in a case like this, of course. And if Julie weren't the type of person to run back through her interaction with Kathy to see if she'd missed something, she probably wouldn't be the kind of person CHP would want on the Bridge. She'll never forget that day. But, for what it's worth, she's a better officer because it's stayed with her.

For me, it's an important reminder of a few things critical to this job and to suicide prevention.

First, you can do everything right and still lose someone if they're truly determined to hurt themselves. Second, with regard to law enforcement and negotiations, resilience is of paramount importance because you never know when the next crisis is coming – Julie's immediate ability to help the man that afternoon proves this.

Third, and perhaps most importantly, it's crucial to remember that those left behind can be affected and may also need our help. Our job doesn't stop on the Bridge.

7

"It will get the job done."

It was July 22, 2013, an average Monday by any indication.

Heavy commuter traffic with plenty of minor damage collision calls. It was about 5:45 in the evening. Peak commuter time. I had a fair amount of officers working that day and was buried in the monotonous mounds of paperwork that state agencies produce.

I was actually going to "hit the road," as we say, and go for a ride on my motor. This is what a CHP sergeant should be doing – field supervision. It was a great day outside, so I headed out to assist the officers, get coffee, just get out of the office for a bit. But, at about 6:15 p.m., Dispatch put out a call of a man over the rail on the Bridge, east side, near midspan. Instead of going for a ride, I immediately headed toward the Bridge to see if the officers responding needed any assistance.

The nice part about being a motor rider is the time it saves responding to incidents. I can work my way through traffic easily, and while on the Bridge, I can utilize the sidewalks. I arrived midspan at about 6:30 p.m. There was a Bridge Patrol officer already speaking with the man – Elpidio Rocha, a well-seasoned veteran. Elpidio, in his 50s, is the perfect person for this kind of work. He is smart, compassionate, reads people well, and can de-escalate most situations that come his way.

Perfect, I thought. *Elpidio is here.*

Bridge Patrol were already beginning to set up a perimeter, having unfortunately done this too many times to count. We were lucky this was a Monday and pedestrian traffic was minimal. For the most part, people can be very compassionate, but I have seen a few from time and time again who get as close as possible to take pictures of an individual over the rail.

I cautiously walked over to Elpidio to let him know I was there. He introduced me to Jason Garber, from New Jersey. Jason was on the chord.

When speaking to people who are in a crisis state, it does no good to be above them. Subliminally, it shows domination. I don't care if it is on the Bridge, in a classroom, or at a dining room table, in order to even begin to try and establish rapport, you need to try and be at eye level, or better yet, slightly below.

Since Jason was actually sitting on the chord, Elpidio had to almost lay down to get to head level with Jason.

Many of those who go over the rail have had years of neglect, abuse, depression, abandonment, drug use, the list goes on. Whether they are a congressman, radio announcer, philanthropist, or street sweeper, they have issues that have become too much for them to cope with. Our job is to simply listen, provide comfort and, if at all possible, *hope*. Give them a sense of control, of options, and the time to tell their story. Elpidio knew this well, and he was trying his best to do just those things.

Elpidio recognized Jason from a previous contact, so we knew that this was not something he had just woken up and decided to do. Also, Jason had activated the emergency phone at midspan, so we knew he wanted us there.

Jason was 32 years old, calm, sober, cordial, and controlled in his manner and speech. We could tell right away that there was something different about him. A very smart man.

Since it appeared rapport was established with Jason, my main job was to stay out of Elpidio's way and let him work. After that, it was my responsibility to assist Elpidio with whatever he may have needed. I wouldn't interject unless asked. I did, however, take turns with Elpidio on occasion in hopes that, between the two of us, we could help Jason to decide come back over the rail.

Elpidio asked Jason questions requiring him to answer with more than a simple yes or no. This provided us with more information about Jason and also helped stretch out the time. Generally, it is very difficult for human beings to remain extremely emotional for elongated periods of time. By stretching the time with conversation, a person will usually calm down. This is where a more calm and rational mind will hopefully take over.

But this technique proved to be very difficult as Jason was already calm – calm and determined. He was intelligent, funny, very neat, and well versed in mythology, religion, politics, and sports. He actually even apologized for what he was about to do.

At one point, I asked Jason why he had chosen this particular bridge.

"It will get the job done," was all he said.

Jason had left a bag on the sidewalk. He described its contents and told Elpidio his phone passcode and that numbers were in it to reach his family. Things were not looking good. Jason had given this a tremendous amount of thought, had planned this in every detail, and was now just going through the motions.

Jason seemed peaceful, absent of any momentary impulses. He was so calm, in fact, Elpidio told him that he should be on our side of the rail, talking to folks contemplating suicide. Jason just chuckled a bit.

As time passed, it was getting colder and colder. Elpidio handed his uniform jacket to Jason, which he took and put on. That's a good sign, wishing to be warm. Jason reminded us that he had come before to the Bridge but that "doubts" had changed his mind. This time, he had no doubts. He said several times that, emotionally, he wanted to come back over. But, mentally, he needed to end it.

The conversation turned to sports and the New Jersey Devils hockey team. Another Bridge Patrol officer, "Smitty," was at the scene, assisting with whatever we needed as well as pedestrian control. Smitty, who is an avid hockey fan, spoke to Jason for several minutes, which gave Elpidio a break.

Jason talked about trades the Devils had made, both good and bad, and their chances to win the division. As Smitty and Jason conversed, I kept thinking, *Maybe we have a chance here.* My emotions were on a roller coaster ride during this entire time, my mind swirling, *Maybe Jason will come back. We can't lose him. This guy has a lot to offer the world.*

After talking sports for a bit, Elpidio returned and Smitty stepped back to resume his watch. The conversation then turned to hope.

I don't generally talk about myself during these ordeals, but a story about my own life just seemed to fit at the time. Since Jason had brought up the topic, I thought it appropriate to tell a story about myself and hope. I told him about being 21 years old and told I had cancer.

I told him how difficult that cancer fight was and how each day I woke up just hoping for one more day. The view from a window in the hospital overlooking the Bay and the Bridge was part of my hope; it meant a lot to me and was a large part of my recovery, at least emotionally. After telling this story to Jason, he looked at me and just smiled for a bit.

He then asked us if we knew the story of Pandora's Box. We both nodded that we did, though I was a little hazy on the details until Jason told the story. In Greek mythology, Zeus created Pandora and sent her down to Earth with a box. Zeus advised Pandora to never, under any circumstances, open the box. Well, curiosity got the best of Pandora one day, and she did open the box. Out flew plagues, sorrows, and all sorts of evils against man. The only good thing to come out of the box was Hope.

Jason looked at us and then said something that caught us both completely off guard.

"What if hope is the greatest evil of them all?"

We didn't know what to say. This was a story that Jason had done a lot of thinking about, as we would later learn. And Jason's question completely caught me by surprise. Elpidio, too. We were all quiet for a brief time.

Then, Jason began to take off Elpidio's jacket, which caused Elpidio to become quite emotional, almost begging Jason to leave the jacket on.

We all knew what this meant. Jason was preparing himself. As Jason handed the jacket back to Elpidio, Elpidio made a grab for Jason's arm. Jason jerked back, instantly pulling away from Elpidio. No words were exchanged. It was as if both Elpidio and Jason knew each had a job to do.

We were silent for several seconds, trying to come up with something encouraging or positive to say. Jason smiled at us briefly then turned his head to face forward, looking toward the North Tower.

I could see a tear come from his right eye. He straightened his body, leaned to his right, and was gone.

Elpidio stepped back, obviously shaken by what had just occurred. I looked over the rail and observed Jason's fall. He struck the water several seconds later. I could not see Jason for a brief time because the impact into the water enveloped him with what looked white foam.

When Jason emerged, he was lying on his stomach, a large pool of blood surrounding him. I have had the misfortune of witnessing numerous jumps, but this was the first time I had seen blood surround a person. Both Elpidio and I were stunned, to say the least.

I thought I could reasonably tell when someone was going to jump.

I remember asking myself: *What the hell just happened?*

I have since realized why he used the emergency phone. It wasn't so that we would come and talk him off. It was so we would know who he was, could find his body, and then contact his family.

Before we ever got there, Jason knew he was going to jump. There was nothing we could have done. He'd already made his decision.

• • • •

The Coast Guard had positioned their boat a couple hundred feet east of the Bridge in the event Jason did jump.

I regained my composure quickly, as I was the on-scene commander. I had to "keep it together" for everyone else. Years of training, mental conditioning ... I don't know, it's just what I've had to do.

I asked Bridge Patrol to throw out a flare marker. Even though the Coast Guard was on scene, the water below the Bridge is treacherous and a body is lost easily. They responded quickly and retrieved Jason. From my view, I observed no signs of life.

We all seemed to just stare at each other for a bit with looks on our faces of pain, loss, and a feeling that we failed.

While we stood there, a man came running up to me yelling, "Officer, Officer, there's a body in the water."

I have worked many years at trying to control my emotions under such stressful situations, but this angered me. I barked at him – "What the hell do you think I have been doing for the past hour?" – with my best, pissed off cop stare.

What he said next hit me like a brick to the head. "No, there's a body in the water over *there*," pointing toward the North Tower.

I thought to myself, *Crap, another one.* There was no time to be lost, since the currents can take a body in minutes, sometimes never to be found.

I got on my motor and hurriedly headed where the man had pointed. When I got there, several people pointed out a body in the water to me. I asked Bridge Patrol to immediately throw out another flare marker, and I radioed for the Coast Guard to respond back. The body, which appeared to be a male, lying on his stomach, showed no signs of life and was approximately 100 yards east of the Bridge now, floating in the Bay.

There had been no actual witness to the jump (at least no one came forward), and only two people who happened to be looking over the rail spotted the man in the water. I continued to watch the body, hoping the Coast Guard would respond quickly and recover it.

As I watched the body drift, an extremely large container ship was heading right for it, traveling in the shipping channel. I knew that due to its massive size, there would be no way that ship would be able to even turn in time, much less stop.

The Coast Guard was still handling Jason Garber's body as I watched the flare marker and body disappear in the wake of the huge ship. I remember saying "Damn it" very loud. I advised Dispatch of what occurred and still requested the Coast Guard and air support to look for the second body.

It was never located.

• • • •

As I rode back the eight miles to my office, I had so many emotions going through my head. I was disappointed in the outcome…and in myself.

I had moments of being angry at Jason for what he had done, coupled with compassion. I felt horrible for all the officers and witnesses involved and about the fact we'd lost another person all together, without ever getting to speak with him.

All this was nothing, though, compared with what I felt I needed to do next – notify Jason's parents. I knew the Marin County Coroner would not make notification to Jason's family that evening. This is in part due to the fact they require absolute proof, a positive identification of the body through fingerprints, dental records, photographs, to name a few.

To make a mistake and notify the wrong family would be absolutely horrible. But I had Jason's New Jersey driver license, his cell phone, and we had been speaking with him for at least an hour, confirming his identity and address. Jason also advised us of his parents' names, Marvin and Barbara. It was my sincere belief this truly was Jason Garber from Marlboro, New Jersey.

Arriving at my office, I closed the door and sat at my desk for several minutes, trying to clear my head in preparation for what was to come. I needed to now be there for Jason's parents.

I'd lost someone I barely knew; they'd lost a son. I still cannot imagine the agony.

I knew getting the information to them as quickly as possible was the right thing to do, though.

If he were my son, I would have wanted to know immediately.

• • • •

Three thousand miles away in a police department across the country, an officer scooted a chair behind Marvin Garber. The worst news imaginable has a way of knocking people off their feet.

An email from Jason's phone had gone to out his pastor, saying that Jason would probably be dead by the time this was read. A friend who met Jason through the church called the Garbers. Marvin doesn't remember everything he heard on the phone, but he remembers the friend quoting the email: "by the time you read this there is a 98 percent chance I'll be dead."

That's what Jason meant when he said the Bridge would "get the job done."

Marvin and Barbara were already frantic that day. They couldn't get a hold of Jason, which by itself isn't all that rare, but parents have a way of knowing things, and this day felt different.

Marvin went to the police department to report Jason as a missing person. Every second that went by drained his hope that missing was all Jason was.

He took a picture of Jason, one from a 5K race he ran. He was smiling in the picture, his beard trimmed, his hair flowing. Runner's tag No. 226. Running helped him. It eased his pain. He was proud that he'd run more than a thousand miles one year. He was also proud that he'd run some half-marathons and finally completed one in less than two hours.

The police officers were professional. Marvin found out later that a friend who works as an officer was supposed to be on duty that night. He was off for some reason and apologized to the Garbers when he found

out what happened. He felt like he should have been there to help them. Marvin later told me he was glad his friend was off because a family friend didn't need that burden.

Marvin told the officers all about Jason. He was such a smart man. Sometimes too smart. He worked on various novels. One was about two friends. He started that in high school. He also spent two years researching the war in Iraq for a non-fiction book, which he'd hoped would be the definitive work on the country. Jason had a wide range of interests in that way.

This is Jason Garber at a 5K race in Freehold Township near his home in New Jersey, in 2007. He got into running on the advice of his therapist; it helped him and really eased his pain. Jason being Jason, he got really into running – one year he ran more than a thousand miles.

This is the picture Marvin took to the police station to fill out the missing person's report, but his worst fears were confirmed when police told him that Jason had jumped off the Bridge and died.

Everyone says their kid is smart, but Jason was different. The Garbers played games in the car, like a lot of families. One of Marvin's favorites was to give

Jason math problems. This was when Jason was a little boy, so Barbara used to scoff at some of the problems Marvin would give him, only to hear Jason come up with the right answer in his head.

Jason wanted to join the military at one point. Special Ops. He took a test that included problem solving a completely made-up language based on patterns and clues. Jason's score was off the charts, quite possibly the highest mark in New Jersey history, but he didn't finish the application process because he knew that disclosing the medications he'd been taking would mean not being accepted.

A lot of people lie about that kind of thing, and Jason had been told that if he didn't disclose the information on the application, nobody would be the wiser. But Jason was a very principled man, too.

Anyway, Marvin loved to talk about his son. The police officers there at the Marlboro station listened and took notes. The conversations all happened there in the lobby.

It was about this time that I reached the officers in Marlboro. I told them what had happened, and they told me that Marvin was there in the Department. That's when they called him into the office.

Marvin was trying to process what he knew in his heart but hadn't yet heard out loud. Then, a cop pushed a chair behind him, and Marvin knew. There was no reason for a chair to be pushed behind him unless the officers thought their news would shake him off his feet.

After a brief exchange, Marvin remembers hearing, "You're right. Jason did go to San Francisco, and he did go to the Bridge."

Then a pause. The officer didn't say anything. For a second, Marvin got hopeful again. Maybe they talked him off. Maybe Marvin was about to hear that Jason changed his mind, that everything was going to be fine again. Maybe he jumped, but survived. That happens, you know. Not a lot, but it happens. Maybe, maybe, maybe. Marvin was clinging to maybe when the officer finally spoke again.

"I'm sorry for your loss," was all he said.

That's when Marvin lost it.

• • • •

They wouldn't let Marvin leave. They told him the worst thing a parent can hear, and the first thing he wanted to do was go home to tell his wife, but they wouldn't let him leave.

They wouldn't let him drive, and maybe he could understand that, but they wouldn't even let him get a ride or take a cab or leave the police station until he met with a rabbi. Wasn't even his rabbi, either, the one he'd known for ten years. The police had a rabbi who served as the chaplain in cases like this, and with it being one o'clock in the morning, it took a while for him to get to the station.

Marvin met this other rabbi, answered some questions, cried some more tears, and was finally allowed to go home. To his wife. To the worst conversation of his life.

But they still wouldn't let him drive there. They would not budge on this. The rabbi and a police officer had to take him home. Marvin thought hard. He kept thinking about Barbara. He knew she was wide-awake. He knew she had the same awful, certain thoughts about their son all day long but hadn't yet heard those terrible words out loud.

Barbara deserved to hear those words, but she didn't deserve to hear them from a stranger.

"Let me tell you how it's going to happen," Marvin told the cop. "You will drive my car. You will drive onto my driveway. Then, you will get out, you and the rabbi will get out and go stand over to the side. I will open the garage door. I will drive into the garage. Because as soon as my wife hears the garage door she's going to come to the laundry room door and open it, and I'll be damned if I'm going to let her see a police officer driving my car.

"I will tell her, and then you can come in."

They agreed. The Garbers live a mile from the police station. The drive is three or four minutes. Marvin didn't have a lot of time to think about how he would tell his wife that their son was gone. The car pulled into the driveway at the gray and red ranch on the corner.

The cop and the rabbi got out. Marvin got in the drivers seat. He hit the button on the garage door opener, pulled in, and saw his wife open the laundry room door even before he put the car in park.

"Let's go inside," he told her, and right then she knew.

They went into the den. Marvin told her what happened. They hugged. They cried. After a few minutes, Marvin went to let the cop and rabbi inside.

The rabbi and I spoke on the phone that night. I did my best to project strength and calm, but I must've done a lousy job because the next day the rabbi called to check in on me.

I spoke with the Garbers directly, too. I told them everything I could remember. Every detail. I told them that Jason was different than the people I normally see on the Bridge. Clean cut. Well groomed. Sober. I told them about our conversation, how Jason talked about his family, especially his sister, and about God and the church and hockey. I told them about the Pandora's Box story, and the tear running down his cheek, and how Jason leaned to the right. I told them about how Jason's intelligence was obvious and striking, and at some point, I broke down crying because the world really lost something. Jason had so much to offer, and of course, his family knew that.

Before we got off the phone, I made sure they had my cell phone number. I wanted them to call me any time, day or night, if they ever thought I could help. I can only hope I brought them some small bit of clarity about what happened on the Bridge.

Suicide ends one life, and it affects so many others. Jason ended his pain on July 22, 2013. He didn't intend it this way, but the pain for his parents was just beginning.

"My life is shattered," his father says. "My father died when I was seven months old. I grew up without a father. I set the bar really low. I had one goal in life, to be a good father. A father's job is to protect their child, and I failed. So, I set the bar so low, and I couldn't even achieve that. I'm angry at myself because I couldn't help him. I'm angry because I feel like I gave him permission with that last talk. I'm angry I didn't call sooner."

Barbara is sitting across the living room when Marvin says this. She wipes her eyes with a tissue.

"It's horrible," she says. "I can't tell you. This is the last thing Jason would want, for us to be miserable. That I know. And I think Marv knows that, too."

• • • •

Jason died on a Monday night. Marvin couldn't sleep, of course, the grief and pain and anger and heartbreak too much to allow rest. By Tuesday night, he had been up for 40 hours and didn't know how he would ever sleep again.

The funeral was coming up. Marvin was due for the hardest thing imaginable, eulogizing his own son. How do you even begin such a thing? Marvin didn't know how, but he also knew he had to try. He wasn't sleeping that night, that much he knew, so he sat down in front of the computer and started typing.

Marvin isn't completely comfortable writing. Jason was always the writer in the family. He was such a good writer, even if he never finished those books. The essay for his college application was so good that it helped him get into every school he applied to. Some even quoted it in their acceptance letter for him, saying they just had to meet the man who wrote it.

Marvin didn't know how to wrap up 32 years of such brilliant life into a few hundred words. He started by writing about how special his son was. Jason didn't like it when people said things like that. He would argue with anyone who complimented him, really. Well, anyone but his Nan and Pop.

But Marvin thought the world of his son, and he wrote the eulogy from his heart.

"The words I'm going to say will probably anger him, but I saw him very differently than he saw himself," Marvin wrote. "Jason knew he was brilliant, and that was his gift and his burden. He felt that because he was so smart, he should have made more money and achieved great things. In truth, he didn't make a lot of money. But we differ on the definition of achieving great things."

Marvin wrote about the Jason he knew. He mentioned the Challenger Baseball League, which is a local program for challenged kids. Most of the people who work there are parents with kids in the program. When the league got volunteers like Jason, without children to pull them through, most of them don't last even one season. Jason did it two years.

The kids grew to love Jason. They hugged him with such joy. They knew he cared for them, which made them care for him.

Jason volunteered at a soup kitchen. He spent many Wednesday nights at a homeless shelter playing board games with the men. He took people to the hospital when needed and was there for them after their procedures. Marvin wanted people to know that Jason was the kind of man who would do anything for anybody. All you had to do was ask, and sometimes, you didn't even have to do that.

He read so much. His apartment and the house had stacks and stacks of books, the vast majority of them with worn out spines and bookmarked pages. His Kindle had 375 books downloaded.

Running seemed to help his mind, seemed to tilt the battle against the demons in his favor.

Marvin had so much joy seeing his son happy. The problem was what always seemed to come after his son felt happy.

"Whenever things started going good, the demons in his head would drag him down," Marvin wrote. "He fought them for decades, much longer than he thought he could. He always said he was a fighter. But, after numerous attempts at quelling them, they finally wore him down. He was tired of fighting every day of his life for all of those years, and he yearned for peace."

This is how Marvin and Barbara want to remember their son. It's how they hope others will remember him, too. Not for the last decision he ever made, the one that left so many people asking so many questions that still have no answers.

But for the life he lived before that, the tireless search for information, the unrelenting willingness to help strangers through the church and other means.

"We loved you when you were born, we loved you through your way too short life," Marvin wrote. "And we will continue to love you for the rest of our lives and into eternity. Anyone who achieves that kind of love is a huge success. We love ya boss."

That last sentence is what Jason always said to his parents before leaving. "Love ya boss" is on his stone, too.

About an hour and a half after starting, Marvin read through the words one last time. The words had come in bursts and then stops.

He'd had the unfortunate experience of eulogizing his father-in-law, so the process was not completely foreign to him. He tweaked a few things here and there, but for the most part, he felt good that people at the service would know Jason the way he knew him. This is what Jason meant to Marvin, and this is what he wanted others to remember about him.

Marvin turned the computer off, and finally, after 40 hours, he went to bed. He laid down and felt a light. He describes it as bright, like the sunlight coming in when the shade isn't drawn, only purer and white. He lifted his head, opened his eyes, and the room was pitch black.

He laid back down, and here came that white light again. It was brighter and bigger this time, and Marvin didn't open his eyes. He just laid there, letting the warm light envelop him. He relaxed and went to sleep.

He and Barbara are convinced this was Jason, approving of what Marvin had written.

. . . .

Marvin can't help it. He thinks about his son's last moments all the time. I've talked with him and told him about the whole thing. How we talked for an hour or so. How he was calm, well-dressed, looked good. How we talked about his family, the Devils, the church. How I thought we were going to get him back over that rail right up until he told us the story about Pandora's Box, let that tear go down his cheek, and leaned over the side of the Bridge.

I've told Marvin everything. About how I watched his son fall and about how I saw his body float back to the surface.

Marvin wants to know everything. He thinks about everything. He can't stop thinking about it. He thinks about things I can't possibly know, things that nobody can possibly know. Did Jason keep his eyes open? Marvin thinks they were closed. What was Jason thinking as he fell? Marvin thinks he was talking to himself. Jason always liked the 23rd Psalm.

"The Lord is my shepherd; I shall not want..."

They shipped the body to New Jersey, but Marvin and Barbara weren't allowed to see their son until minutes before the service. Marvin wanted to kiss his son goodbye, but the coffin was on a cart, and it was too high for him to reach over. Some guy told Marvin to kiss his fingers and touch his face that way. Like that would be the same.

There are no little things when a parent is forced to bury their son. Marvin read in an email from Jason that he wanted to be buried as a Christian. Marvin had his rabbi and Jason's pastor speak, and they decided on a joint service. The pastor for Jason, and the rabbi for Jason's family.

Jason's conversion to Christianity was such an important part of his life. He had originally kept it a secret from his parents, and Jason thought Marvin would be angry when he made the decision. But, when Jason broke the news, Marvin told him, "I'd rather have you alive and Christian than dead and Jewish."

They talked for hours when Jason told Marvin what he did. That conversation meant a lot to both of them, and the conversion gave Jason what his parents think of as four or five more years of life – and good years, too.

Religion was very important to Jason. At one point, he wanted to become a minister. Just like everything else in his life, Jason inhaled all the information he could find about Christianity. It wasn't long before he knew more about the religion than many who had been Christian their entire lives.

Once, two good friends of his got him involved in a Bible study group. The group was already full, but Jason's friends just asked that the rest of the group give him a chance. Let him come once, and you'll see. So, the group met him, and not only wanted him part of the group, but they eventually made him co-leader.

He worked for the church, too, particularly putting free sermons on their website and participating in a lot of community outreach – really helping people. That's what Jason loved to do, and the church gave him so much joy in that way. His parents had never seen him as happy as when he was involved in the church, so of course the service would recognize his conversion.

Marvin got Jason's Bible – he didn't take much with him to the Bridge, but he took his Bible – to put in the coffin. Marvin also put a pad and pens in there because Jason was always taking notes. And a Devils' calendar, so he'd know when his team was playing. The coffin had the Star of David on it because of the Jewish funeral home they used. Jason had told his parents he felt more Jewish than ever before after his conversion.

No father should have to think about his son's coffin. No parent should have to plan their child's funeral. They didn't know what to do. What was right, what was wrong. At first, they wanted to invite only the immediate family. Jason was a private man. He loved his family and he had friends, but in his heart, he was private. Marvin and Barbara thought he would want a small service.

But, then, Jason sent a delayed email to some three dozen friends telling them what he was doing. They must have meant a lot to him, more than his parents realized. So, they invited everyone on the email list and some others, too. Barbara had some reservations about this, at least at first. She worried about gossip spreading or people who didn't really know Jason coming for such an important event. But more than a hundred people came, many of them telling the Garbers that Jason was their best friend. There was so much they didn't realize.

A lot of the ceremony dealt with the question about whether Jason's last decision would prevent him from resting with God. It's a brutal question, but one that any Christian struggles with after a suicide. Jason opened this question when he converted, and it's something he knew would be talked about after his final decision. Nobody has a definitive answer, of course.

"God gets the final word," Jason's Pastor said at the service.

The ceremony was at a beautiful mausoleum four miles from the Garber house. Jason's grandparents are there, too. That's important to Marvin so that, in his words, "Jason isn't alone."

Jason loved his grandparents so much. On the den wall in the Garbers' house is a black and white picture of Jason's grandparents on their wedding night. The man Jason knew as Pop held the woman he knew as Nan in his arms. Before going to the Bridge for the last time, Jason used his cell phone to take a picture of that picture. Marvin and Barbara think it's one of the last things he looked at. That makes them feel a little better.

Barbara calls that first week "very tortuous," and the truth is she could be describing any day after Jason died. She and Marvin drove to see Jason at the mausoleum every day in the beginning. Then, it became a couple times a week. Then, once a week. Now, they go whenever the pain draws them there. They pray for him every night and talk to him before they go to bed.

They think about him constantly. Life moves on, of course, but for the Garbers, it sometimes feels like only temporary distractions before thinking about Jason again. They try to think about the good times, but usually their minds go back to why he's no longer here. Is there something they could've done? Something they should've done? Why could no one reach him? They always knew he was so brave, very courageous, for fighting those demons as long as he did.

They know why he gave up the fight. He was tired and wanted peace. He held out as long as he felt he could, but that doesn't make it any easier for his parents.

It's a Jewish custom to leave a rock when visiting a tombstone. It symbolizes your visit and shows that you were there. Jason happens to be at the bottom corner of the mausoleum, but if you wanted to visit him, you wouldn't need to know that.

Just look for the biggest collection of stones.

• • • •

Jason's room is the same as the day he left. He is gone. The demons won. Others carry the fight now. Marvin and Barbara walk by his room every day, at least twice, down the hall and out into the world in the morning and then back for bed at night.

That room is always there. If there was ever a moment where Marvin or Barbara were thinking happier thoughts, getting on with the business of living, walking by that room would jolt them back.

The whole house is like that. They bought this house in 1979, about a year and a half before Jason was born. Marvin had this vision in college that his life would be like this – a house on the corner, a dark-haired wife, and a happy marriage, raising two beautiful children and a dog. Marvin talked about this vision in a way that made it feel less like a dream and more like a certainty, like this is how his life would always go.

There are so many memories in that house. They used to have a swing set out back. Jason had a routine with each swing. If something stopped him in the middle, he would go back to where he left off. He was so logical and ordered.

This is the house where Jason lived the happiest years of his life, especially those first 11 or 12 years when he was just a tireless child who never stopped moving and never stopped learning.

The pictures are everywhere, too. They haven't changed any of the pictures. It's like a tangible slide show of Jason's life on the walls, a hundred four-by-sixes telling the story of a mom and a dad and a son and a daughter growing up together. Jason's happiest pictures are with his grandparents. Or maybe at his sister's wedding.

Marvin and Barbara look at those pictures all the time.

"This house is a constant reminder," Marvin says. "The bedrooms are all down that hall. You have to walk past Jason's room to get to ours. We have pictures all over the place. Memories. It's good, and it's bad. It's painful, and yet, it's comforting. It's a whole mix."

It's more good than bad for Barbara. According to Barbara, being home "is just tortuous." Marvin is angry and, in many real ways, lost. He doesn't work. Barbara is a second-grade teacher, and it's good that she works. It gives her a release, something to do. Every part of her life will never be the same, of course, but when she's at school, it's the same as before. The mind needs a break.

Jason at his sister Caryn's wedding. It's one of many photos his parents have of him on the walls of the house where he grew up.

Coming home is sometimes the hardest part of her day.

"I don't have a place to put the feelings when I'm here because I'm always concerned because my husband is doing badly," she says. "I just wish I had some sign from Jason that he's doing okay. That would make me feel so much better. People tell me they feel things and all of this, but I guess I'm not spiritual, or I'm not in tune. I don't feel things. That's something I would die for, to have some connection."

They've thought about moving. In a lot of ways, they think it would be good for them. Start something new. They'll never forget Jason and will never love him any less or miss him any less. But sometimes being in that house can be overwhelming.

They've done some things to get out. They went to Chicago for a few days in an effort to make some good memories. Ocean City, Maryland, to their daughter's for a few weekends. When they're engaged for a day or a couple days, they can be happy. Happier, anyway. The sadness of Jason's death is always there, but it helps to be busy.

They've talked about moving closer to their daughter, who lives in Maryland near the Delaware state line. Their relationship with their daughter is strong, and they'd like to see her and her husband more often. Hopefully soon, that will include a grandchild or two.

But moving also means giving something up, which is part of why they haven't done it yet. It means giving up the house they've lived in for so long. It means giving up some memories, or at least such a close connection to some memories. They also have a lot of friends, a good support system.

But staying means something, too. It means the same pain, the same empty feeling. They called a realtor. Someone came out to the house, even.

One of the first things the realtor told them was that they had to take the pictures off the wall to sell the house.

They can't take those pictures off the wall. Not yet.

• • • •

There is no one way out of the fog from losing someone you love to suicide. Some people who have tried will tell you there is *no* way out of that fog.

You start to replay so many things in your mind. Conversations. Words you said, words you didn't say. After Jason died, Marvin went through his son's cell phone. He found some 30,000 emails. He went through all of them, and it took months.

He found a draft of an email Jason had written but never sent. It was, in effect, a suicide note. From his mind, an explanation. Jason addressed it to his dad and attempted to tell Marvin how he felt. Why he needed to do what he planned on doing. The pain, the frustration, the demons. They were too much. The draft was last saved on June 22. Jason was in San Francisco then, and when his parents found out he was there the next day, Marvin called Jason in hysterics. He left a message, breaking down and begging his son to reconsider. Jason got on a plane and came back home. Marvin convinced him. As it turned out, that phone call gave him and Barbara one more month with their son.

On that phone, Marvin saw other notes that Jason had written. Reasons to believe in God, and reasons not to believe in God. He saw email after note after email after note of his son's exhausting battle with the demons that nobody could see.

That brain of his was his gift and his burden, like Marvin wrote in the eulogy. Jason had no emotional connection to the Golden Gate Bridge. He had no mythical draw to it, and there is nothing to suggest he bought at all into that silliness about entering another dimension.

He chose the Bridge not for its beauty or stature, but for its utility: He had read that 98 percent of people who jump die. In Jason's mind, those were good odds.

He had considered the small chance that he would survive and decided that if he would be the exception in that 98 percent, he'd be okay with that, too. Surviving would almost certainly mean being handicapped physically in some substantial way. Jason had come to think of his problems as crippling, and if his body were to be crippled, well, at least then people on the outside would see him the way he saw himself.

For those left behind after suicide, the questions can feel endless. The regret. The night before Jason died, he and Marvin had a long talk. This was after a great weekend. Jason had moved out of his apartment in Manhattan and brought all his stuff home. They felt like his whole attitude toward them changed.

There are signs they now feel they should have seen, but that in the moment just felt...nice. They ordered pizza, for instance. For as long as Marvin can remember, whenever they ordered pizza, they got half cheese, half cheesesteak. Marvin loves cheesesteak pizza. Well, on this night, Jason told Marvin to just order the whole thing cheesesteak.

"I'm like, 'Great, you're finally into the good stuff,'" Marvin says now.

They watched *Life of Pi*, which Jason loved. They watched *Ray Donovan*, a show on Showtime. They played Simpsons' Monopoly. Everyone had a great time. At some point, Jason and Marvin started talking hockey. The Devils were said to be interested in Jaromir Jagr. Marvin was teasing his son. What do they want with an old man who can't even finish a shift before needing rest?

That night, Marvin and Jason had a talk. They'd had talks like this before, Jason talking about suicide. Jason was particular. He kept saying he wanted his dad to understand. Marvin told his son he understood how tired he was, that he needed peace.

"But you have to understand," Marvin remembers saying, "I can never say it's okay."

He talked to his son about hope. Hope can be the greatest thing. You have to hold onto hope. There is always a chance. Why do people play the lottery? Because there's a chance. You never know if there will be another drug that might help, or maybe you'll find the right doctor. Whatever. There is always hope, and you have to fight for that hope.

This goes back to why he told us the Pandora's Box story back on the Bridge. Jason felt like he had given hope all the time he could. In Jason's mind, the worst always came right after the best.

"I can't deal with possibilities," Jason told Marvin. "I need probabilities."

Marvin remembers it as a good talk. They'd talked like this many times before. The conversations were always respectful. They never screamed. Never yelled. Just spoke to each other. Jason seemed at peace that night, like he felt his dad understood his feelings more than in the past.

At some point that night, Jason walked into his parents' bedroom. Barbara was lying in bed.

"I really love you, Mom," he told her.

That gave Barbara a bad feeling, like something was about to happen. The next morning, Jason was getting ready for his day with a particular level of detail. He put on nice jeans, a nice shirt. He trimmed his beard. For a moment, Marvin had the same bad thoughts as his wife.

"I said to myself, 'Is he getting ready to kill himself?'" Marvin recalls. "Then I'm like, 'What the hell is wrong with me?'"

When Jason walked out of the house, he was carrying only a bag he slung over his shoulder with his Bible, his Kindle, and pen and paper. No change of clothes. His parents had no tangible reason to suspect he'd be flying across the country again to kill himself.

In the middle of the day, Marvin saw somewhere that the Devils had, in fact, signed Jagr. He reached for the phone to call his son, but then figured he'd see him later that night.

By then, Jason was on a plane across the country. This time, he made no hotel reservation. He made no backup plan. He would go straight from the airport to the Bridge.

"I didn't call until it was too late," Marvin regrets. "I will never forgive myself for that."

The people who loved Jason will never stop thinking about him. They'll never stop wondering what they could have done. What they should have done.

"The shame is you know all this after the fact," Barbara says. "After the fact, we feel this."

• • • •

Marvin was working in debt settlement when Jason died. It was a fine enough job. Paid the bills.

Marvin took two weeks off – the week it all happened and then one more week sitting shiva, the Jewish grieving period. When he went back to work, he was, in his words, "a shell." He just didn't do much. Didn't care about much. Before, he could make 300 or 400 calls a day in his sales job.

After, maybe half of that. He was fine when he got someone on the phone but was mostly just going through the motions.

After three months, his bosses let him go. Marvin doesn't have much hope that he can find something. Doesn't have much desire to look, either.

"I still don't give a shit about anything," Marvin asserts. "You're not supposed to bury your child. I don't look at things the same way. I don't care about things. I stopped watching sports. The only thing I still do to keep my sanity is I still play free fantasy sports.

"The purpose, the point, you live your whole life for your children. And now, I know I still have a daughter. I love her very much. She means the world to me, and we might move to be closer to her. But it's not the way it's supposed to be. You're not supposed to eulogize your child."

Marvin's sadness and anger have been hard on the marriage, too. It's possible he hasn't had a good night of sleep since that first Tuesday night when he felt that warm light and considered it a sign from Jason.

He doesn't go to sleep until two o'clock in the morning at the earliest. A lot of nights it's three, sometimes even four. He just can't sleep. Can't get into bed unless he's nearly unconscious, unless he knows he is so overwhelmingly tired that he will pass out immediately. Otherwise, he lays in bed and just starts thinking. He can't sleep when he's thinking.

He has to collapse into bed, which is hard because now he and his wife are on two different schedules. She gets up at six to get to work, and he's in bed by four.

"That creates problems," Marvin admits. "But that's how I have to be."

Mourning has changed their lives. It many ways, it's taken over their lives. Barbara would like to get on. Working is good for her, and she wishes Marvin could find something to occupy his mind. He can't, which creates more problems.

They used to go to shows on Broadway. That was one of their favorite things to do together. They didn't take a lot of vacations, but they loved going to those shows. They've gone to a few since Jason died, each time hopeful that the night will be good for them, but it's not the same.

"I'm not angry that he's angry," she says. "I'm not angry at him. But it's not helping me, and it's not helping him. I feel it's never going to help him get better. He's not going to miss Jason any less if he's not angry, if he's less miserable. But everybody has to mourn the way they are."

Marvin hears his wife say this. He's heard her say it before, and he knows she has a point.

He wishes he could move on. He's tried, in his own ways. Nothing has worked.

"My pact with God was that he could throw on me whatever he wanted, but my children would be happy and successful," Marvin states flatly. "So God and I are not on very good terms. God dumped plenty on me over my life. And God didn't live up to his bargain.

"Am I angry? Yes, I'm angry at God. Jason died in July, and September is the High Holy Days. We go to temple, and we always sit on the aisle so when they walk around with the Torah we can kiss it. When the Torah came past me, I turned my back. So do I have anger? Yeah."

When people think about killing themselves, they usually are thinking only of their own pain. That's understandable. But the impact of those decisions stretch long after.

· · · ·

Barbara has come to see her son's last act as something he felt he had to do.

"He didn't think he had any control over it, but I look at it as a choice he made," she says. "I'm not angry at God because I feel like the five years he was in the church, that really comforted him. But, in the end, man has free will, and he made a choice. He may have felt like he had no choice, that this was the only way to end his suffering. I see it from his point of view, but I do feel he made a choice."

Marvin explains that his anger is not aimed at his son. Barbara is not angry at Jason, either.

"He definitely didn't do it to hurt anyone else," Barbara states. "He delayed doing it so many times."

Jason talked about suicide enough that neither parent was shocked, but there was a sense among them that he wouldn't actually do it. As much as they had talked to him and tried to help him, they did not fully grasp the depth of his demons. Jason wanted it that way. He was very good at hiding things.

"I think he wanted to protect people," Barbara says. "That's what he said. By hiding it, he protected everyone."

Suicide is such an under-appreciated problem in our country, and one of the things people often miss about it is how far the pain stretches.

Jason's father lost his job. His parents' marriage is strained, though they've always had their disagreements and both have a very deep love for each other. They want to move out of the house they've lived in for more than three decades, but struggle to find the strength.

There isn't a day that goes by that Marvin and Barbara don't both think about how they could've better helped their son. Depression and suicidal thoughts are so dangerous in large part because they can be invisible.

Jason was very good at hiding his pain. He was diagnosed with several different forms of mental illness, but never anything that fit. He was hard to classify. That ability to hide pain is common among the millions of Americans who suffer from depression. There are red flags, but you have to look for them, and not just that, you have to be willing to see them.

The consequences are enormous and, in a lot of real ways, never-ending.

"Don't give up hope," Marvin urges.

"When you have teens," Barbara reflects, "they can be so frustrating at times, but you can't ever give up. It's not a tangible thing, but you have to keep fighting. You have to keep at it. You have to fight."

Marvin and Barbara are living through the aftermath of a suicide, like far too many other Americans. They are sharing their story here publicly for the first time with the hope that talking about it will help erode the stigma that's clung to suicide for too long.

Suicide isn't something that only happens to soldiers returning from war, or drug addicts, or people who find themselves in financial or relationship problems. It happens to smart, kind-hearted people like Jason. One of the things his parents cherish the most about his life is his desire to help people.

I join Marvin and Barbara in hopes that sharing their story can help someone, too.

My younger brother, Darrin, and me always up to something. A casual pose on the left and all dressed up with nowhere to go on the right. We had a great childhood, worry free and full of fun.

One of my baseball teams as a kid. That's me, bottom row, second from the left. My dad was one of our coaches. He's on the left, behind me.

Haven't changed that much, have I? These pictures always make me smile, thinking back on a very active and happy childhood.

A family trip to Hawaii one summer. That's me in the red, Darrin in the blue, and our mom between us.

Me and my parents. I was about 16 or 17 at the time, just starting to figure out what I wanted to do with my life.

At my grandparents' house in McCloud. I probably caught that fish at Lakin Dam, and I'm almost certain we would've had it for dinner. You know what's funny? Looking back at this picture from so long ago, the kitchen of that house still looks exactly the same now.

Before I got my cancer diagnosis, my dad had made plans to go on this fishing trip to Cabo San Lucas, Mexico. The trip was going to be in the midst of my treatments, so dad thought it would be fun if we went anyway, as sort of a celebration or at least a break. The doctors cleared it even though I was weighing in at about 130 pounds. That fish I'm holding is the only thing we caught the entire trip. Funny thing is, it weighed about 150 pounds or so, 20 more than I did! They let me real it in, which was a heck of an experience.

Fishing trips with my dad were always fun. This was from a salmon trip to Half Moon Bay when I was about 17 years old. We took my friend Kevin Fleak.

In June 2014, I gave myself a retirement gift. I went salmon fishing in Alaska with my good friend Jim.

U.S. Army Jump School in November 1981. Can you tell I had pneumonia?

Army buddies. Jungle Warfare School in Panama, September 1982. The bigger guy, to my right, is Tim. We became close during the time we served. My experiences with the military taught me so many lessons about sacrifice and discipline that I continue to use in my everyday life. Don't be fooled – we had fun, too!

Kevin Jr. and me at the beach in Hawaii. This was Kevin's first trip to the ocean. He was so excited to be in the water that when I put him down, a wave knocked him off his feet and started pulling him out to sea. I had to jump in between the wave and the beach to catch him as he was being swept away. He was so scared of the water after that he only wanted to swim at the hotel swimming pool.

My son Travis on his way to Aikido practice. It's important to me that my kids retain their maternal Japanese culture as well as strengthen themselves physically and mentally.

Here I am with my friend, Mary, who later became my girlfriend. It was Mary who talked me into going to the hospital for chest pains. In the end, she gave me really good advice.

Here is Travis, riding his bike home from school with a "police escort." Whenever I had a free moment and was in the area, I would ride along side him. These little moments are among my favorite memories from my time with the CHP.

THE GUARDIAN

On the staff picture board at the Marin CHP office before I retired. You can say my fellow officers jokingly started calling me "The Guardian" after my public interviews began. The media caught on, and what started as a joke has developed into a very important campaign for mental health and suicide awareness.

I make sure to spend lots of quality time with my kids. Here we are having fun on Shasta Lake in August 2012.

I had the opportunity to do a protective services detail when Vice President Al Gore came to the Bay Area for a fundraising event in October 1996.

April 2002, Officer of the Year award presented to me by Bill Walsh, then San Francisco 49ers head coach. Such an honor.

At the American Foundation for Suicide Prevention awards banquet where Kevin Berthia said he was "saved" for the second time. That's Kevin standing to my left with Capt. Shon Harris, my Marin Area Commander, to my right.

One happy motor sergeant.

Courtesy John Storey / San Francisco Chronicle / Polaris

This picture was in the San Francisco Chronicle *and shared around the world – you can see why. I was so happy we were able to help Kevin Berthia back over the railing that day. At the time, I had no idea what would come of his life or how much of an impact he would have on mine.*

Courtesy Todd Trumbull/San Francisco Chronicle/Polaris

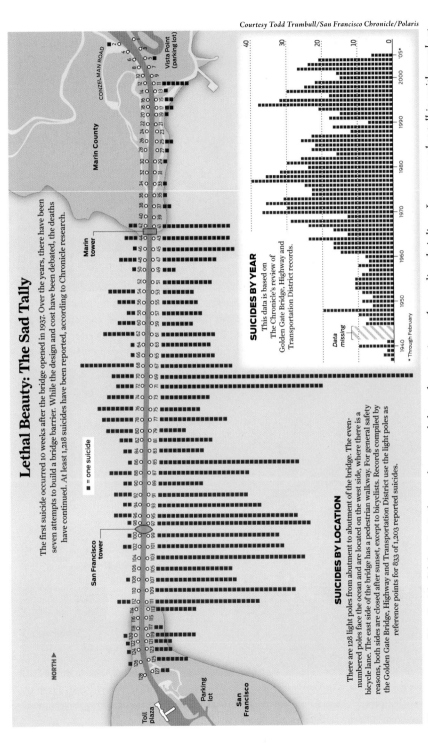

Lethal Beauty: The Sad Tally

The first suicide occurred 10 weeks after the bridge opened in 1937. Over the years, there have been seven attempts to build a bridge barrier. While the design and cost have been debated, the deaths have continued. At least 1,218 suicides have been reported, according to Chronicle research.

■ = one suicide

San Francisco tower

Marin tower

NORTH ▶

Toll plaza

Parking lot

San Francisco

Marin County

CONZELMAN ROAD

Vista Point (parking lot)

SUICIDES BY YEAR

This data is based on The Chronicle's review of Golden Gate Bridge, Highway and Transportation District records.

Data missing

* Through February

40   30   20   10   0

1940   1950   1960   1970   1980   1990   2000   '05*

SUICIDES BY LOCATION

There are 128 light poles from abutment to abutment of the bridge. The even-numbered poles face the ocean and are located on the west side, where there is a bicycle lane. The east side of the bridge has a pedestrian walkway. For general safety reasons, both sides are closed after sunset, except for bicyclists. Records compiled by the Golden Gate Bridge, Highway and Transportation District use the light poles as reference points for 833 of 1,203 reported suicides.

This map is something I wish didn't exist. It shows where people have chosen to jump, thus ending their lives. I can remember talking with people at almost every point on the Bridge. In the future, I hope charts like this one won't exist now that the BridgeRail Foundation is constructing "the net."

My very last ride on the bike, on my last day before retirement. Riding the bike was a pain in a lot of ways; you had to go through a rigorous class to be authorized, and you never felt like you could relax the way you could in a car. But I loved it. The bike was more fun and so much easier to maneuver. In fact, the only time I didn't want to be on the bike was in the rain.

My last day of work at California Highway Patrol – Nov. 22, 2013, at Fort Point. From the left, that's Dan Ruiz, Andy Civin, me, Angie Cost, and Darren Bruestle. True professionals, it was an honor to work with them all.

Here am I conducting a presentation for some area Cub Scouts at the Marin Area office. Part of what we do is demonstrate the tools we use in law enforcement, including the Taser. Like a lot of boys, they love the guns and sirens and handcuffs and batons. But, when we tell them about all the paperwork involved, they tend to look disappointed and a bit overwhelmed.

Me taking part in an FBI crisis negotiation class. What a great opportunity to improve the skills we all might need in law enforcement. I try to use what I learned whenever possible, to better myself and enhance my skillset.

Me with Meg Hutchinson, a wonderful person and talented songwriter and artist. She wrote the song "Gatekeeper" after reading an article in The New Yorker where I was featured. It was such an honor when I heard that song that I reached out to her to say, "Thanks." We've met a few times and have since become friends. The song has reached a lot of people and, I think, furthered our cause.

At a charity event for EMQ FamiliesFirst, a non-profit that helps children and families. EMQ is one of the largest, most comprehensive mental health treatment programs in California. It's a privilege to join them in their mission.

The best part of these conferences is the people you meet. When I did La Ciudad de las Ideas — it's basically Mexico's TED Talks — I had the opportunity to meet a Harvard professor named Amy Chua, best known for her book Tiger Mom.

I was fortunate to have the opportunity to do some speaking in Australia and New Zealand in 2015. This was one of my favorite parts of the trip, holding a koala named Princess. She actually fell asleep in my arms.

I attended a Mexican cultural event in San Francisco at Yerba Buena Gardens on July 31, 2014. On my left is José Antonio Meade Kuribreña, Secretary of Foreign Affairs for Mexico, and on my right is my good friend Andrés Roemer, Consul General of Mexico, San Francisco Office.

March 2015, in a small Outback town called Barcaldine in Australia. Spreading awareness of mental illness and suicide prevention. Barcaldine is regarded as the birthplace of the Australian Labor Party because it was the headquarters of the 1891 Australian shearers' strike. In the background is the Tree of Knowledge, a 200-year-old Corymbia aparrerinja – or Ghost Gum.

I had the chance to talk to about 400 high school students about suicide awareness in Elmira, NY. I was surprised and honored when they were wearing t-shirts that welcomed me, with the message: "If I had my wishes about a legacy I could leave, it would be one of helping others at their darkest times."

8
On The Bridge

There have been some extremely sad moments that I've had to deal with on the Bridge. There are, however, some atypical stories, some lighthearted, others just strange. The life of a highway patrolman has no shortage of bizarre and often humorous incidents which always bring a chuckle, a smile, or at least a shake of the head.

The Wyatt Wrestling Match

One call involved an intoxicated and belligerent passenger named Walter Wyatt on one of the Golden Gate Bridge Highway & Transportation District buses. These buses carry thousands of passengers to and from San Francisco to the North Bay communities every day. It was a particularly nice Friday evening when I received this radio call. I was actually taking a break at one of my favorite delis in the city – Marina Deli at the corner of Chestnut and Scott Street. I had ordered my favorite, a chicken breast sandwich. This is one of those places, and one of those sandwiches to be quite honest, that you would actually drive a distance to get.

Sitting by the large bay window, I could eat and do some people watching, one of my favorite pastimes. You just never know who could walk by. This is San Francisco, home to every type of person under the sun. I had just finished my sandwich when the call came through.

The call blared to me in that restaurant:

"34-20, Golden Gate, Golden Gate Bridge is requesting a unit for a 647(F) disturbing passengers on a bus. They're stopped at the northbound bus pad at the Toll Plaza."

Most everyone has heard of "beats" that cops have. Mine was beat 20, basically freeways leading into and from San Francisco to the Golden Gate Bridge and a few miles past that on U.S. 101. The "34" is the nomenclature given to the Marin Area of the CHP. "Golden Gate" after 34-20 refers to who is addressing me, in this case it is our dispatch center. The 647(F) is the California Penal Code for Public Intoxication.

By the time I arrived to the south entrance of the Bridge near the toll plaza, the bus was stopped at the curb. Two Bridge Patrol officers were speaking with Wyatt outside of the bus. The man was about 6 feet 4 inches tall and weighed a solid 240 pounds. He might have been mistaken for an NFL linebacker.

As I stopped behind the bus, I could see him arguing with the officers. Upon seeing me, the arguing stopped and he took off running. Well, it was more like weaving. It was quite apparent he had consumed more than his share of alcohol. I charged after him and grabbed him before he could get far. Knowing that he had the upper hand physically, I attempted to take him to the ground by knocking his feet out from under him with a swift kick. You know the move I'm talking about, where you knock one foot of someone who's running, which causes them to trip and fall to the ground – it worked wonderfully! As he fell, he grabbed me, and we both hit the ground on a steep grassy hill between the highway and a parking lot near the Golden Gate Gift Shop. Then, the struggle really began.

A buddy in the Army first introduced me to the saying, "Never wrestle with a pig. You both get muddy and the pig likes it." I could say the same for large, agitated drunks. My wrestling partner and I tumbled down the hillside through grass that had just been watered, rolling in mud and crashing through scrub bushes and rocks along the way. We grappled like a couple of mud wrestlers. Neither of us could get the upper hand due to all the mud, grass, and shrubbery.

When we landed in the parking lot, I was on top of him, straddling his chest and sitting on his arms. We were both covered in mud and brush debris. I could feel he was trying to grab my gun – an officer's nightmare: to be shot with your own weapon. This was cause for deadly force.

With my left hand, I grabbed his throat and squeezed with all my might. My right hand pressed firmly against his left hand, which was on my weapon. I was pressing down with everything I had, trying desperately to keep him from pulling my weapon from its holster. This seemed like an eternity but, in reality, was probably 20 seconds or so. Wyatt continued struggling and tried several times to bounce me off his chest by arching his back and kicking.

"No way," I kept telling him.

I had him pretty good and was not about to let him up again if at all possible. The pressure on his throat must have done the job. His eyes started to roll back into his head. His grip loosened on my weapon. Immediately, I tried to roll him over so I could handcuff him, but as I did so, he regained his composure and struggled once more. This time, I pulled out my pepper spray and filled his face with it. He instantly started spitting at me and screaming obscenities. I was getting very tired and could not afford to let this guy get the upper hand. His intentions were clear: do whatever he had to do to get away, even if that meant taking me out all together. The pepper spray did the trick, and he writhed in pain.

As I was trying to secure his arms behind his back, one of the Bridge Patrol officers came running up to me, gasping for air. He used his knees to help secure Wyatt's arms.

"Where were you?" I asked, annoyed and exhausted but still riding an adrenaline high.

"I was running after you," he huffed.

It was obvious he did not take the path I did, or he would have been full of brush debris. He'd run around the entire lot, avoiding the brush and grass. He caught his breath and straightened up.

"I didn't want to get my uniform muddy," he said pointing to the stains on my shirt and pants.

"Thanks," I responded.

That's when I heard the clicks. I looked up and saw two-dozen tourists snapping photos. They were all around me in the parking lot. When I made eye contact with one of the tourists, he gave a thumbs-up and shouted something in a language I did not understand. I could only assume he was suggesting I "say cheese," so I smiled and let them snap away.

Due to the use of the pepper spray and possible injuries incurred to Wyatt while we were fighting, I called for an ambulance. During the fifteen minutes or so that we waited for the paramedics, we were entertained by every swear word you could possibly imagine, over and over.

I tried to assist Wyatt by pouring some water on his face to dilute the pepper spray, but he wanted nothing to do with it. He continued with his onslaught of obscenities and even spit at me, striking me right on my chest. He also swore up and down he would get me and he was also going to sue me for everything I was worth. We had to place a spit sock on his face, a device which covers a subject's head to limit where spit may travel while still allowing for normal breathing – kind of like a cheesecloth.

Due to Wyatt's attitude and struggling, we were forced to hog tie him. We bound his feet, bent his knees backwards and latched them to his handcuffs. This is only used in cases like this, where a person is adamant about fighting, resisting, or escaping.

When the ambulance arrived, it took four of us to load him, and then an officer rode in the ambulance to San Francisco General Hospital. After Wyatt was medically cleared, he was transported by patrol car to jail, where he remained for some time.

I did not go along with Wyatt but, instead, went back to my office. When I showered, I looked for cuts and ticks, then started with the report and Wyatt's criminal history check. Unlike the TV show *CHiPs*, the one with Erik Estrada and the catchy theme song where they're always out on patrol and never at the station, we spend a great majority of our time writing reports. Despite being a bit corny, the show brought a tremendous amount of positive attention for the CHP.

Anyway, Wyatt had the longest criminal history I had ever seen. It included burglary, auto theft, selling drugs, public intoxication, fighting, and even attempted murder of a police officer. I stood on a chair and held the printout up. The record went all the way to the ground. This man needed to do some serious detox and time away from the community.

I never went to trial on Wyatt and never heard from or about him again. But I'll never forget our wrestling match.

The Iced Tea Lady

A decade into my career, I received a call for a woman over the rail.

I was on another call at the time, at Marin General Hospital admitting another person for attempting to end their life by leaping from the Bridge. Thankfully, I was just about through with the admissions paperwork. I spoke to the woman I had detained and explained I needed to go. I told her "I'm so very glad you are still with us."

As I was opening the door to leave, I heard, "Thank you and God Bless." I turned around, smiled, and kept going. Over the radio, I heard that two other officers were responding. I completed my assignment quickly and headed to the Bridge.

When I got there, I saw that the woman was standing over the rail, leaning out, and holding onto a vertical support cable with one hand. She was in the throes of a psychotic episode, screaming and swatting at people who were not there. I was advised by one of the officers that the woman had stopped her car in the northbound traffic lane. When they arrived, she locked the doors and refused to come out.

As they were attempting to reason with her, she was injecting herself with iced tea, pouring the liquid in the cap with one hand and filling a hypodermic needle with the other. I have no idea what she thought she was doing, injecting iced tea, and I really don't think she did either. If there is an affect that iced tea can have on the body when injected, I haven't heard of it.

When the officers tried to reason with her, she threatened them with the needle, wielding it like a butcher knife. She was not talking coherently, rambling on different subjects and, with every other word, cursing.

After a brief time, she got out of her vehicle and would not allow anyone near her. She kept swinging the needle at them. She managed to get to the sidewalk and then climb over the pedestrian rail, which is when I showed up.

The two officers had tried their best to prevent her from getting to the rail, but they weren't about to get stuck themselves, and since the woman was not charging them or attempting to do anyone else harm, deadly force was not justified. It seems like it would be a relatively easy task for two officers to overpower and subdue a woman who was 5 feet 4 inches, around 115 pounds, and it generally would be – except for that damn needle she was wielding.

Who knows what may be waiting for them in that syringe, what pathogens could be entering their bodies? Maybe it was just iced tea, or it could be HIV, hepatitis C, or a host of other diseases that could make the rest of our lives miserable. Given this circumstance, where no one else could be injured, it was best to stay back, contain the threat, and let the situation play out.

We all tried talking to her, attempting to get her to calm down and talk with us. She was too far gone. She kept swinging her arm at us, trying to stab us with the needle if we even reached out for her, all the while screaming at us incoherently and swearing like a sailor. After a few minutes, she made one more threatening wave with the needle, then let go of the cable.

I watched her travel all the way down and strike the water. A spray of white foam enveloped her. After several seconds, her lifeless body floated to the top. I worked the scene, coordinating with the Coast Guard and the medical examiner, but I couldn't shake the feeling that this wasn't a suicide in the classic sense. No one will ever convince me that she had any knowledge of what she was doing. There was no note or other sign that she had been planning to kill herself. Maybe she thought she could fly or believed she could jump off, land softly, and swim away. I don't know.

Courage

There is a moment I think about often, especially with the scary episodes I've lived through in my personal life and the dark hours I've tried to assist strangers with on the Bridge.

It was a normal day for me, going through the routine of what we call "showing the paint." I patrolled the Bridge and surrounding areas, took short breaks at local coffee shops, handling and returning what were typical calls for a patrolman.

When we talk about "showing the paint," that's cop talk for driving around in your black and white patrol car or motorcycle. There is value in people seeing you out there on the road. Value in both potential criminals and law-abiding citizens seeing the badge. This is active patrol, and I bet even if you never do anything worse than commit a minor traffic violation, you know this kind of thing can be effective.

Drivers pay more attention to the rules of the road, making full stops at intersections and being careful not to speed. Would-be thieves keep walking down the street, instead of taking advantage of the briefcase you left on the front seat of your car.

I was on my motorcycle riding around, watching for traffic violations while checking my beat. Like I said, it was a normal day for me. I had no way of knowing it would be one I'd remember forever when I pulled into the Vista Point area.

I worked my way slowly around the parking lot, smiling at the tourists while looking for the scum who would take advantage of them. There are always those who pray on the naïve, innocent, or just plain unlucky. The parking lots around the Bridge are no exception.

Criminals will pose as tourists, waiting with lookouts for sightseers to put their valuables in the trunks of their cars and walk away.

Then, they casually walk over, punch the door lock with a screwdriver, open the door ,and access the trunk and passenger area. The whole thing takes seconds, and then they're gone, leaving a damaged rental vehicle and its passengers without their purses, computers, gifts, and passports. The crappy thing is there are signs in the lots advising people to lock their valuables in their trunks.

I rode to the southern most part of the Vista Point lot, where most people go to view the Bridge, the Bay, and San Francisco. You ride in, stop, and just look around. Most everyone has either seen or at least heard of the *CHiPs* TV series, so people all over the parking area tend to stare at you.

Anyway, for a couple minutes, no one approaches. People can be shy. But, after one person approaches, it sort of signals to everyone else to do the same. People see its okay to talk to the cop on the motor. We don't bite. We won't scream at you. So then a line starts. Young, old, families. Some ask questions ("How fast does your bike go?"), some want to share stories ("My cousin is a cop, and he says..."). Many just want their picture taken.

"Of course," I always say.

It's a cool thing for kids. I'll get off the motor and let a child climb on, showing him or her how to grip the handlebars, all the while the parents taking as many photos as they can. It's fun for them, and fun for me, too.

On this particular day, I was probably there for 15 or 20 minutes when two older women approached. They asked if they could each have a picture with me, which of course was fine. They took turns, one posing and the other snapping the camera.

After a bit, one of the women asked where the restrooms were. I pointed her in the direction, and she began walking that way. The other woman stayed, and we began talking. She told me her friend had been diagnosed with brain cancer a short time ago. The doctors said it was terminal. Nothing they could do.

So these two women – best friends for years – decided to use the time they had together to travel all over the world as much as possible while they still could.

My heart sank. Having had cancer and having watched my mother die of cancer, this hit me in a very personal way. Like a lot of people, I know how fragile life can be and how fast it can be taken away.

I remembered how sick I was while battling cancer. Those treatments are brutal, and mine came with a depression from the disease. When I was in that state, there was no way I could have or would have traveled. No way I'd have grabbed my best friend and had anything approaching a good time. I was worried whether I was going to live. Looking back, I know this wasn't the healthiest approach, but I didn't tell anyone what I was feeling emotionally. I kept it all inside, which made it worse, that sadness locked within my own head.

I looked at this woman in a whole new light. With a whole new respect. Here she was, knowing fully that she would soon be bedridden and then dead, smiling and traveling the world. It was humbling just to be around someone like that. Humbling to think back at how I'd emotionally dealt with my cancer, and then seeing how this woman approached hers. It was refreshing and inspiring.

Those are the times you realize that so many little things you think are important really don't matter. They are irrelevant. I think we probably all get wake up calls like this from time to time. Who knows? When I had cancer, maybe that was someone else's wake up call. I hope so, but if that was the case it certainly wasn't because I was fighting my disease with as much energy as this woman.

When the woman was walking back to us, her friend asked me not to mention her cancer. Her friend did not want anyone to know. I asked them if they were in town for a bit. I thought I could maybe get them a tower trip.

Very few people get a chance to go to the top of one of the Bridge towers. It would be up to Bridge Patrol, but I could at least make the request.

Unfortunately for me, they were leaving on a plane soon and did not have the time. They had more sights to see.

I think of my encounter with this woman from time to time. She is sure to have passed by now, but she made a difference to me that day and many days since.

9
A Dog Story

All of us bring life experiences to the job. But it is our dark and troubled episodes, those hard moments in our past that we regret or wish had never happened that forge our compassion and empathy – those moments sharpen our ability to teach and assist others as we age. I'm no philosopher, but I think Nietzsche's observation that "what doesn't kill you makes you stronger," is incomplete.

The hard things in life can make you stronger and wiser, but in my opinion, they also make you more humble and humane.

I discovered this in nuggets, as most people do, picking up the lessons of my youth like minerals in a sandy river and putting them away for later examination. As they were happening, I gave no more than a passing thought to the quiet days I spent hunting with friends, but those moments alone on the hillsides, swamps, and by the streams honed my instincts.

Waking up at three o'clock in the morning and walking into the darkness with my decoys on my back, I learned to read my surroundings, to become one with the sounds, smells, and movements of my environment, and to adjust to almost imperceptible changes around me. A slight shift in wind and the hunter couldn't be more exposed if he were streaking naked. When stalking deer, a change in temperature as the sun climbs on the morning horizon and the prey will vanish as if they were never there.

These and hundreds of other tiny lessons were self-taught from a childhood that many would consider old fashioned or downright weird today. But this is what we did back then, in a world mostly void of cell phones, Xbox consoles, and home computers.

That's Linda on the left, the schnauzer is Ulla. This was taken around 1979 I sure loved those dogs.

I also learned at an early age never to be careless in matters of life and death.

During one weekend duck hunt, around 1981, I brought along my black Labrador retriever, Linda, to fetch any ducks I might kill. The two of us trudged through mud and muck until I found a spot to wait for first light. Where I hunted ducks, the best place to be was in the water, which was generally 2-3 feet deep. I'd brought along a bucket as a stool, and Linda, as I had trained her to do, sat beside me.

A couple hours in, I noticed her shivering. After a bit, she acted like she had gone mad. She would not sit still. All I really noticed was that she was screwing up my hunt even though her behavior should have struck me as odd. I kept yelling at her to sit and stay. Linda tried her best and then suddenly passed out, sinking into the water.

I immediately picked her up and yelled for my buddies to assist me. I had no idea what had happened. I carried her as I walked the mile back to my truck. I still had my gun and was wearing waders. It was all I could do to remain upright with all this gear, walking through mud.

When I finally neared my truck, another hunter came over and asked, "What's going on with your dog?" I explained what happened. He quickly replied, "Your dog has hypothermia. You need to wrap her in a blanket, rub her, and hope she warms up or she'll die."

This scared the hell out of me. Linda was like my best friend, my compadre, and I did this to her.

After about 20 minutes of being wrapped in a sleeping bag and me gently rubbing her body, she opened her eyes a tad and let out a little whine. I cursed myself for being so wrapped up in finding the right hunting spot, so absorbed in my own interests that I'd almost killed my companion, a cherished partner who wanted nothing more than to be with me.

That morning changed me. From that day forward, I vowed to remain vigilant in my quest to protect those in my care, human or otherwise.

Fortunately, there is a funny little ending to this story. When Linda seemed like she was going to make it, I left her in the back of my pick-up, not wanting her to get cold again, and locked the camper shell. One of my buddies had brought frog legs for us to try later. I was really looking forward to them, having never tried that "delicacy." Well, when we all returned to the truck a few hours later, my dog was up, tail wagging. She'd eaten all of our sandwiches, cakes, and, of course, the frog legs.

We all couldn't help but laugh. Hours ago, she was near death. Now here she was, enjoying what must have been a real treat.

10
A Life Saved – Twice

Kevin Berthia is smart, energetic, loving, and well-liked. He is a former college soccer player and was a three-sport athlete in high school. He is caring, conscientious, selfless, and quick to smile.

He is a reminder that suicidal thoughts and attempts can happen to anyone.

There are a lot of reasons Kevin doesn't fit what people tend to think of as a suicide risk. He grew up with two loving parents and a lot of ambition. He was an active and healthy kid.

In some ways, that layer of so-called "normalcy" is part of what kept him from getting help. Nobody knew Kevin was suffering from all these life-threatening problems.

Not even those closest to Kevin.

Heck, not even Kevin.

Kevin's story sounds implausible. He had a lot of friends and a bright future, so why suicide? Why would he put a knife to his throat in front of his family? Why was he unable to fully escape his demons even after trying to get well? Why, in his confused state, would he feel this almost gravitational pull to the Bridge, a spot he didn't realize had attracted so many others, a spot he knew so little about that he had to ask for directions?

How in the world could a man without a drug problem, without any other visible problems for that matter, who has a family and a house and a car and people who love him, wake up one morning and decide to kill himself?

There is so much to Kevin's story that sounds like the exception. Unfortunately, the sad truth is that there is so much to Kevin's story that's common in the millions of Americans who battle depression and suicidal thoughts.

• • • •

Kevin grew up in Oakland. His is not a story about the streets or avoiding gangs or drugs or any of those other sad urban clichés. His is a story about a kid growing up in a place where nobody wants to hear about your problems because nobody thinks to ask.

Kevin liked it that way, although later he would see this as denial. He would see this as living his life in a sort of disguise. But, back then, as a kid growing up in the 80s and 90s, you would've just called it normal.

Kevin was adopted at six months old. His mother didn't mean to get pregnant and didn't think his father would be much help. She made it clear she had no intention of raising this baby, so she made what she thought was the best decision for herself and Kevin: She put him up for adoption.

One of Kevin's earliest memories is finding out he was adopted. His mom and dad, or at least the people he called mom and dad, told him. He loved them very much and knew that they loved him, too. His was a good childhood. He can't complain about that. But something about knowing his parents weren't his *real* parents and that his birth mother – the person who's supposed to love him without condition or end – gave birth to him, kissed him, and then gave him away...well, it shook Kevin's world in a very real way.

For one thing, he didn't look like anyone in his family, and when he was in the fourth grade, a girl in his class made fun of him for it. That's the only time he remembers being picked on because of being adopted. He doesn't even remember what the girl said, but he does remember how it made him feel. Isolated. Weird. Rejected. Unworthy.

Something about that experience triggered a change in Kevin. He began thinking more and more about his birth mother. *Why didn't she want him? Didn't she care? Was it something about* him *that wasn't good enough? Why wasn't he good enough?*

Kevin had good friends and a good relationship with both of the parents who raised him. They talked about a lot, but never about these fears and disappointments and insecurities that shook him. Kevin didn't want to talk, told himself he didn't need to talk, that there was no reason to feel down or confused.

This overwhelming sadness was a sign of weakness, he decided, and even if he didn't understand where it came from, he had it in his head that he needed to just get over it, to push it down and out of the way. When he couldn't, he would feel more sad, and the cycle would feed on itself.

He dealt with these issues through sports. Lots of sports. Constant sports. He played six sports growing up – soccer, basketball, football, baseball, and he also ran track and swam. Anything to stay busy.

His days were school, then practice, then another practice, then he'd go home, and then have a third practice at night. The weekends revolved around games or meets. He didn't know it then, but sports were his escape, and not in a good way. He knew he felt different at night, especially late at night, when life slowed down and he ran out of things to do. He didn't like it when life slowed down. That meant he had time to think about what was bothering him. That's when the demons would whisper to him insecurity and doubt.

So, he covered those problems the way a lot of us cover problems. He tried not to think about them, and once he found out that sports helped him not think about the problems, well, forget it. Sports it was.

But sports could only do so much. Kevin's world shook, again, during his

Photo courtesy of Kevin Berthia

As a kid, Kevin Berthia played many sports, but soccer was his favorite. He threw himself into sports in order to battle his demons.

seventh grade year. Looking back, he sees this as the point where his life took a really bad turn. Knowing what he knows now, it's obvious why.

His parents divorced, and like many children of divorce, Kevin blamed himself. This opened a lot of wounds and issues that he never knew existed. He was very close with his father, but now, his dad wasn't around as much. This started a battle of sorts between his parents over everything from how much time Kevin spent with each to what the rules would be.

His mom was the stricter one, his dad laid back. That meant two very different experiences, no consistent structure, and some fights between his parents.

Kevin put those fights on himself, figuring that since he was adopted, maybe *he* was really the problem in all of this. Maybe *he* was really the reason they were no longer married. His parents already had two kids, after all, so maybe the third was too much of a burden, the last straw. His dad had a gambling problem, but Kevin wondered if he wouldn't have felt the need to gamble if he'd only had two kids. Kevin started to see himself more as a drag than a child in his family, more of a headache than a joy.

Of course, he never talked to anyone about any of this. Kevin kept it bottled in, always, an unknowing time bomb ticking away.

• • • •

By the time he got to high school, he was, in his own words, "just existing." He felt passionless. Saw school as stagnant. He still played sports and smiled with his friends and made people laugh, but inside, Kevin began to feel empty, hollow.

The bad thoughts came at night, always late at night. No distractions. It's just you and your thoughts when you're lying in bed trying desperately to fall asleep, and for Kevin, this was a dangerous thing. These toughts depressed him, constantly, incessantly. Feeling bad meant telling himself he shouldn't feel bad, that he should be over whatever issues he was complaining about, which just made him feel worse. He was putting so much into sports and his friends that he didn't put nearly enough into himself.

This is also around the time he became curious about his biological parents, and with his emptiness grew his curiosity. There is a government program where adopted kids can seek out their biological parents. So, when he was 16, Kevin met his birth mother.

He thought that would help, but it didn't. Meeting her only opened up more wounds.

He went into it with all of these high expectations. The mom who raised him was great: loving, smart, provided lots of guidance. The bar was set. When he met his biological mother – the one with whom he shared DNA – he thought it would be even better. Like there would be this amazing instant connection, one that would fill him up and turn off his demons. Turns out, it wasn't like that, not in the slightest. This other woman wasn't his mom, not in the ways that were important to Kevin. She was nice, but it was almost like they were just friends, and Kevin wanted it to be more. He expected it to be more.

He reached out to his biological father, too. That did give Kevin some more information, but not in a good way. Kevin never could control his temper. He'd get mad more quickly than most. It frustrated him. Turned out that was one of the few things he'd gotten from his biological father.

Meeting his parents was supposed to help. Instead, it just made Kevin feel worse. At that point, he basically decided he'd no longer talk about any of this. To anyone. Not even hints, nothing. Thinking about his problems made him feel overwhelmed, and Kevin didn't like to feel overwhelmed. So, he'd act like nothing happened and put on a happy face.

That continued to work well enough into college. He played soccer at City College in San Francisco and enjoyed his first year. Had a successful freshman season on the soccer team. But he got in a bad relationship. His girlfriend had some issues, and sticking with the pattern, her issues became Kevin's issues. He didn't know how damaging this pattern was to him, that the real problems he had and wasn't dealing with were being pushed back and back and back with every argument he had with his girlfriend.

The next year, he lost interest in soccer. This should've been the first major red flag. Soccer had always been such a big part of Kevin's life. He loved soccer. He called the sport "my soul." But, after a year of playing in college, he gave it up, dropped out of school, in fact, and decided to go to work. A job replaced soccer, both as the thing taking up most of Kevin's time and as his most convenient coping mechanism.

At one point, Kevin was working two full-time jobs, 18 hours on some days. He still wanted to be with his girlfriend, but with the relationship being long distance, the geography was tough. He was paying for hotel rooms and taking on more responsibility than he should have been. This was not a normal life for a man his age – bills, two jobs, a bad relationship.

A year after he dropped out, in 2002, came Kevin's first true mental breakdown. It shocked everyone around him. Shocked him, too. It started with another argument with his girlfriend. Kevin went to the kitchen, opened a drawer, and grabbed the biggest knife he saw. He put the blade to his neck and screamed that he was going to kill himself. His sister was there and called the police.

Even in that moment, Kevin says he wasn't sure why he was there, in front of people who loved him, a knife to his carotid artery, promising to kill himself. He was yelling at his girlfriend, but really, in that moment, she was just a stand-in for him to scream his anger and pain.

Oakland police came. They told him to drop the knife. He didn't, and he was tazed. The police admitted him to John George Psychiatric Hospital. He was there for four days.

"That was the first time I was 5150'd," he recalls. "I didn't even know what a 5150 was."

Upon release, Kevin graduated to an outpatient program, which at least forced him to talk about and acknowledge his problems.

That helped, for a while, but eventually things only got worse.

· · · ·

The doctors initially diagnosed Kevin with depression and a genetically inherited mental illness exacerbated by abandonment issues. So, as it turns out, his mom gave him a mental illness, in a manner of speaking, and gave him up, which compounded everything.

He bounced around between three or four therapists. Nothing helped. Kevin says what he heard from the therapists was basically just giving voice and credibility to the worst things he told himself on those lonely nights.

You should be over this.

You're 21 years old. You shouldn't still have these feelings from childhood. You should be over your parents' divorce, over finding out you were adopted. What's wrong with you?

The doctors gave him medications, which turned out to be a bad idea. They made his Zoloft dosage too high, which ripped up his system and set him back. The whole experience just left another scar on him. He'd been the guy who never talked to anyone about his problems, and then the guy who swore he'd never talk to anyone about his problems again.

Being 5150'd meant he had to open up, at least a little bit, and what did that get him? Judgments, an even lower self-esteem, and the wrong medication. Screw that. Kevin decided, again, against all evidence, that he wasn't the one with the problems. That's what he told himself, anyway.

The time in John George cost Kevin his job. His girlfriend moved to Texas, which was good that she was gone, but bad because he hurt. Kevin tried to move on, and there were good signs buried beneath the bad. He went back to school in 2003, re-joined the soccer team, and was even voted team captain. He had some offers to play professionally after college but by then, he'd gotten a new girlfriend – an old friend from high school – and she became pregnant.

Kevin decided he wanted to be a family man. He wanted to make this work. Family had always been a source of confusion in Kevin's life, and he wanted to turn that around. This would be his new life.

He didn't know how difficult that would be.

His daughter was supposed to be born June 23, 2004. She arrived on April 6 – two and a half months early. She weighed one pound, two ounces, and spent the first weeks of her life in an incubator, hooked up to tubes and wires.

Kevin blamed himself. Doctors couldn't tell him or the mother why their daughter came so early, but Kevin convinced himself it was his fault.

He and his girlfriend were arguing during the pregnancy, so maybe that stress somehow triggered a premature birth.

Once his daughter was able to come home, Kevin was hit with another tough blow: $250,000 in medical bills. They were uninsured. They planned on getting insurance before the baby was born and thought they had at least another month or two. He wanted to transfer his job so he could help with the baby more, but he didn't qualify and was eventually laid off. He called a dozen insurance companies, and they all told him he was responsible for at least 66 percent of the bill, which was way too much for him to afford. On top of all that, his daughter needed a hernia surgery, which added to the expenses and the stress.

All of those familiar, confusing, frightening feelings of being overwhelmed were coming back, fast. The mind can be a dangerous thing.

Everything about Kevin had changed, and none of it in a good way. He had no job, enormous debt, a daughter he felt incapable of caring for, he wasn't playing sports, and he sure wasn't talking to anyone. He had no outlet. With no way to cope, every issue that he never dealt with was rushing back to him.

He met a woman and inadvertently used her to ignore his problems. She lived about an hour outside of town, and he'd go there for months at a time. He'd turn off his phone and not talk to anybody. No friends, no family, nothing. He thought he was escaping, but really, all he was doing was growing an even stronger hatred for himself.

By this point, he was completely distraught. He stopped eating. Wasn't sleeping much. Wasn't in touch with his family, or really anyone for that matter. He wasn't seeing his daughter like he wanted to see her.

All things considered, what happened on March 11, 2005 wasn't rash as much as it was inevitable.

• • • •

He woke up that morning overwhelmed. He hadn't been dealing with any of his issues, and things were closing on him much more than they ever had before. He didn't see a way out. He was tired of his pain, so he headed to the Bridge.

He'd never thought too much about the Bridge, never fantasized about killing himself there. He didn't know it was a suicide destination. He hadn't ever seriously thought about suicide, either, because thinking about suicide would've meant accepting or at least recognizing that he might have a mental illness.

That morning, he got in an argument with his girlfriend and got in his car.

He didn't even know how to get to the Bridge. He had to ask directions. He was in such a fog he didn't realize that he had to drive over the Bay Bridge on his way to his spot of choice.

He left no note. He made one phone call and doesn't even remember who he dialed. There was still this small part of him that wanted to live, which he was acknowledging with that phone call. But a much larger part of him dictated that the call was placed to someone he knew wouldn't answer.

At some point, his girlfriend called him.

"Leave me alone," he snarled. "I'm on the Bridge doing what I need to do."

She called the police, which is where I got involved. Dispatch contacted me immediately with a description of a fit, young black man in shorts and a t-shirt. There was probably five minutes between the call and me finding Kevin.

The first thing I saw was him jumping over the rail.

I yelled toward him, and from my vantage point, I thought that was it. I thought we'd lost him. He was too close to the South Tower. At that part of the Bridge, the track runs directly under the platform. There was no place for him to land other than the water.

I rushed over there, expecting to see nothing as he would have already hit the water, but when I was approximately 15 feet away, I could see that he was standing on a 12-inch pipe at street level, a couple feet below the sidewalk. As it turns out, he heard my voice as he was jumping, and something clicked in his mind which caused him to turn to his left and grab the railing.

When I got there, he was standing on the pipe, facing the Bridge. He weighed about 135 pounds at the time, and a strong gust of wind could have easily blown him off balance and into the water below. Fortunately, the wind was blowing at his back, so if anything, it was acting as a tiny bit of help for us in this tenuous position.

Kevin was in basketball shorts, a t-shirt, and sneakers. He was dressed for a pickup game or for a lazy day around the house. Instead, he ended up here, on the edge of death, shivering in the cold. I leaned over the railing to see him, and he spoke first.

"Don't come too close," he said.

"I'm not going to grab you," I told him. "I just want to talk. If you don't want to hear me talk, I'll just stay here and listen."

Helicopters hovered overhead, anticipating his jump. The Coast Guard had a boat below. By coincidence, a lot of photographers were there, too, because that same day, the Bridge directors were debating whether to seek outside funding to study the costs and effectiveness of "a suicide barrier." There was always going to be extra attention on the Bridge that day, but now the debate took on even more meaning. The photographers had their picture, and face, to put with the story.

Neither Kevin nor I thought much about the debate, of course. I was trying to help Kevin decide to live, and he was deciding whether to die. He looked down as he spoke, not to the water below but to hide his face. Shame is almost always a part of these situations, especially with men. I bent down, looking through the barrier, trying to get at his eye level so he might feel more comfortable talking.

Fortunately, Kevin was ready to talk.

I had no way of knowing exactly what brought him to that moment on the Bridge, of course, or that part of his problem had been in never talking to anyone ever about what was eating him up. Maybe it was the emotion of the moment or the reality of what he was doing up there, but so much of what was bothering him spilled out to me on the Bridge that day.

We were up there for 92 minutes, and for most of that time, I just listened. That's it. Just listened. Kevin told me so much, about the adoption, about his parents' divorce, about the memory of being six years old and looking out the window for his dad to pick him up and eventually realizing he wasn't coming. Kevin had been let down by so many people, even by those who professed to love him and care for him, and he never allowed himself to be angry about it. He ignored those feelings, either because that was the code of where he grew up or maybe because he didn't want to burden anyone else. Instead, he blamed himself.

Kevin was telling me things he'd never told anyone, things he wasn't even sure he was feeling until the words came out of his mouth. It was all very, very emotional.

You don't get to that point on the Bridge without part of you wanting to die. Part of you is giving up. Something has to bring you back from that place, though, and I've found that the most effective way is to let people know there is a human being here who cares, who's willing to listen without judgment. I had no way of knowing that was precisely what Kevin needed, but I've done this enough and educated myself enough to know that making someone feel this way is the best chance of helping them decide to stop a tragedy.

Like I said, we were up there for 92 minutes, but I know for Kevin it must've felt much longer than that. People tend to think that when someone gets to the point where they want to kill themselves, they must be in a state of panic, they must be frantic. That's true on a macro level, but on a smaller scale, the way they interact, that's not always the case.

And it wasn't like that with Kevin. He'd come to peace with his decision, at least with the part of him that wanted to die. There was a contentment. The more he talked, the calmer he became. I think it helped a lot to just get all of those feelings out of his mind and out of his soul.

He'd lost his hope and courage, and what was left in their wake was a tired young man who just wanted the pain to end. He didn't have any fight left in him. Throughout our entire conversation, he was very down on himself and still blamed himself for all of his troubles because he had yet to find out the extent of his mental illness.

I don't know that what I do is the absolute best way to approach these situations. I just know it's what I've found to have the most success, saved the most lives. You want the person to feel comfortable – listened to but not judged. You want to remind them of everything good in their lives, and for Kevin, I focused on his daughter.

That was the most important part. I had to turn it around in his mind, from thinking about the doctors' bills and his feelings of inadequacy as a parent to the love and guidance he could provide his child. Once we got to that point, Kevin understood how much he had in front of him.

That's about the time Kevin agreed to let us help him back up. There was no big emotional moment there, just a question from us and a nod from him and we pulled him back over the railing.

Once we had him back, we walked him to the patrol car. You heard the *click-click-click* of the news photographers.

Kevin has never really understood what took him to the Bridge to end his life when he didn't even know how to get there. Over time, he's come to realize that there was a bigger purpose.

After his attempt, the Bridge directors decided to pursue funding for the rail. Today, that project is becoming a reality. Who knows if Kevin being on the railing that day swayed any minds, but it couldn't have hurt.

Kevin didn't know then, but he may have helped save some lives that day.

And it wouldn't be the last time.

• • • •

The story you might expect about the guy who needed to be talked off the railing is that the low moment would wake him up to his struggles, force him to deal with issues that had been dragging on him for so long, that he would think about his daughter and family and friends and use such a scary moment to turn his life around.

That is not Kevin's story.

Nothing much changed after the Bridge. He went to Fremont Medical Center and stayed there seven days for evaluation. The doctors diagnosed him with a borderline personality disorder on top of abandonment and trust issues.

This made sense to Kevin. He'd always wondered why he felt this need to get out of situations before the situations changed. He was always terrified of people leaving him, which meant he tended to leave them first or, perhaps, even choose people in his life he might expect to leave him.

Kevin became a master of not dealing with things. In his mind, he thought that made him strong. He didn't know it made him vulnerable.

He got home from the hospital and saw a picture that was already famous. *The San Francisco Chronicle* – one of the most respected newspapers in the country – put it on the front page. It's of him, on the edge of the Bridge, his hands tucked into his shirt to deal with the cold. You can see me leaning over the railing, trying to talk him back.

Seeing that picture and knowing that seemingly everyone in the world had also seen it, shook Kevin. Instead of opening his eyes to what was really going on, it actually put him further into denial. Kevin could no longer hide, not after being on the front page of *The Chronicle* – an image that was sent all around the world – but he could run. So, Kevin did a lot of running.

For eight years, he ran. He went to therapy sessions, only because his doctors made him, and he got by with telling them as little as possible, continuing to hide from what was really going on.

This was another dangerous time for Kevin. He never made another attempt on his life, but he was close a few times, the problems that put him on the Bridge and on the cover of *The Chronicle* always bubbling just beneath the surface. On a one to ten scale, if ten is an attempted suicide, Kevin spent the next eight years drifting between a six and an eight. He probably got to nine a few times. He was unstable, felt unaccepted, and the notoriety made him hate himself even more for going to the Bridge in the first place.

Then, in May 2013, I was supposed to receive an award from the American Foundation for Suicide Prevention (AFSP). The banquet was in New York, and AFSP asked that I reach out to a survivor or a survivor's parent to present the award.

I thought of Kevin. His mother had written me a nice letter years before, and I kept it, like I keep everything I receive from people I meet and am able to help. I wrote to her, asking if she would be willing to come to the banquet.

A few years before, she had a stroke and didn't feel comfortable flying by herself. But she did have an idea. She knew it would take some doing, but she wondered if she could talk Kevin into making it for the presentation.

Eventually, she succeeded, even though Kevin still hadn't accepted much of anything that was going on. He agreed to do the presentation, mostly for his mom, but I hoped there was part of him that did it for himself, too.

Either way, he had no way of knowing what going to that banquet would end up doing for him. Looking back, I think it forced him to confront and acknowledge what he'd been through. He'd spent eight years since the Bridge running and didn't know he'd run right into an intervention.

He'd never dealt with these issues, but I think seeing my face took him back to that day he'd fought so hard to forget. He saw the picture from *The Chronicle* again, this time projected onto a movie theater-sized screen in an enormous ballroom. Perhaps, most of all, he saw an audience full of people who looked at him without judgment – and with admiration.

I don't think he'd ever felt that before. You could see it that night, the way he carried himself, the way he talked and smiled – it was like a heavy weight had been lifted off his chest. Later, he'd tell me he felt like he could breathe again for the first time in as long as he could remember.

A video played about Kevin's story, something he'd never seen before. He felt a purpose after seeing it, and feeling the support from the crowd, he saw – *really* saw – how important a story like his could be for those suffering in the darkness.

The other thing that night gave him was confidence, a sense of worth. The night was about him, and I'm not sure he'd ever really felt like that before. He'd spent his whole life hiding his own issues and taking on the issues of others. But, for this one night, it was about him. You could see the change in him after the presentation, too, when people he'd never met before were coming up to him to shake his hand or give him a hug or just tell him thank you. They told him he gave them hope, and that's the most powerful thing, which inspired him.

"I never felt the worst day of my life could ever give anybody else hope," he explains. "The day I lost hope, how can that give you hope? But that's how it was. To know my story made people feel a certain way, it just changed me."

When he got back home after the ceremony, he made a commitment to make a real change in his life. He got rid of anything and anybody who didn't contribute to or help with his happiness. That was hard at first, but something he had to do. He changed jobs, living situations, friends, everything.

He's a numbers freak and figured out that it took him 2,977 days to accept what was happening with him. That's the time between his day on the Bridge and speaking in front of all those people at the banquet in New York. Now, Kevin keeps track of exactly how many days since his commitment. I've heard from his family that they see a new life in him, a new clarity, which is so great to hear.

"I always say that Officer Briggs saved my life twice," he reflects. "If I never went to that dinner, I'd be doing the same things, and I don't think I would've lasted to 2014. No way. I'd have been in a hospital or worse."

Kevin has now dedicated his life to telling his story and helping others. He's found that he feels better every time he tells his story and that he learns something new from every experience.

He's active on social media and takes pride in hearing how his experience can help others. Once, he heard from a woman who said her son heard Kevin's story and saw his face and was struck by how much they look alike. After seeing Kevin talk, her son brought her a suicide note he'd written.

Kevin and me at an awards banquet put on by the American Foundation for Suicide Prevention in May 2013 at the Lincoln Center in New York City. I'll never forget how happy Kevin was that night. Later, he would say it was the first time he ever felt like the center of attention. It did wonders for his self-esteem.

"Mom," he admitted, "I need help."

Experiences like that have helped Kevin. It's nice for any of us to hear that we've helped people, to know that something we said or something we've done – especially the difficult times – can help someone else.

I know that's a huge part of why I liked being an officer all of those years and why I enjoy what I do now. There are so many people out there struggling, who need assistance and may not even know it.

I'm proud to be that assistance, and I'm so thrilled that Kevin has found his place now, too.

We both know there are many, many more people out there who can be saved – all they need is a little help and, perhaps, a listening ear.

11
A Struggle Toward Healing

This is the story of Megan Guerrero, a woman I did not meet until we were together on the Bridge during her darkest hour. She grew up in Davis, California, the daughter of a womanizing, alcoholic, and physically abusive father and a mother who had no coping skills. This was the 1960s when women didn't leave their husbands and certainly didn't turn them in to the police, especially immigrant, Catholic women like her mother who felt she had nowhere else to go.

Megan graduated from high school in 1973 and joined the Navy, which she loved. It was there that she began to drink. This is neither unusual nor particularly dangerous in most cases. A lot of men and women either start drinking or increase their drinking when in the service, seeing it as not only a release from the inherent stress of their lives, but also a way to make friends. For many, a drink at the end of a hard workday is a form of camaraderie, not a sign of alarm or addiction.

But, for Megan, the more she drank, the more she found herself needing the escapism she found in a bottle. Drinking's a quick fix and, when used too much, can easily turn into addiction. This is what happened with Megan.

After six years in the service, she got out with no job and few prospects. She drifted for a while, becoming a circus clown with Ringling Brothers. She really liked it there, the act of making people laugh and traveling the country, seeing different things. But the circus community is notorious as a place for people getting away from something, and Megan quickly got caught up in unhealthy relationships and more unhealthy behaviors.

She married a few times, all of her spouses losers who were looking for a party and little else. It was her second husband who introduced her to heroin, and that was the moment her life started to crumble, when her descent into hell became a free-fall.

Megan worked hard, so she never had trouble finding a job. Her addiction always came first, and she was fired more times than she could count. The one constant she had were those chemical escapes, sometimes through alcohol and far too often through heroin.

Eventually, she was living in her car with two dogs, going to the VA hospital in San Francisco for methadone treatments, and still using. She found a church, but even that involvement turned negative. She was sponging, not contributing.

She hated herself and what she had done with her life. Lost and alone, her breaking point came when she was so desperate for a hit that she stole a keyboard from the church – robbing the people who had fed and clothed her for months. After pawning it for enough cash to get a day's worth of heroin, she sat in her car and wept.

Megan wasn't the only one at her church in trouble. She was one of several who were receiving assistance there, which made it tempting and easy to take something. That keyboard wasn't the only thing that went "missing" at the church, though that didn't make Megan feel any better.

• • • •

It's a dangerous thing when someone finds themselves feeling hopeless, worthless, and unsupported. Through factors of her own doing and otherwise, Megan didn't have a support system at all. She couldn't reach out to her parents and felt too ashamed to talk to any friends or other family members about her problems.

"I couldn't support myself, I didn't have contact with my family, I could barely keep my poor dogs alive, and I was living in my car," Megan says. "I thought, *What am I doing?* That's when I realized that if I weren't here, it would be a relief. Somebody would take care of my dogs; somebody would clean up the mess; some people would be relieved that I wasn't burdening them anymore, and I would be relieved because there was no way to bring me back from what I'd done, from where I'd gone."

So, she went to the Bridge with a dejected decisiveness that, unfortunately, is not uncommon.

She wrote a lengthy, rambling suicide note that she left in her car in the east lot on the south side of the Bridge. The note spoke about her feelings of self-worthlessness, shame, and embarrassment of how she had turned out. She also left food and water for her dogs, a passenger seat heaping with heroin paraphernalia, and a duffle bag filled with all her earthly belongings.

I was on my motorcycle when the call came in.

"34-20M we have a subject over the rail..."

That was my call. Light pole No. 109. I responded to Dispatch that I was on my way, kept my ears open in case there were updates, and headed to light pole 109.

Megan was 46 years old at the time. A cold north wind gnawed through the Bay that evening and hit my face like a whip. Megan was on the chord, shivering and pale by the time we got to her. She was looking down at the water when she spoke.

"I feel like my head is one big flame, and I've got to put it out," she quivered. "Everything's gone. I've destroyed everything."

The first instinct when someone tells you their life is worthless is to say, "No, no it's not." That feels like empathy to you, but to the person you're talking to, on the edge of suicide, it can feel like one more rebuke, one more argument – one more stranger saying, "You're wrong." It can feel condescending, not empathetic.

That's what people on the chord expect you to say. That's what they've heard from others already, either friends or therapists or maybe just a random bartender.

But, mostly through past experience and speaking with other officers who do what I do, I've come to believe that when you don't challenge them on that point, they tend to listen to you more closely. They tend to hear what you're actually saying. So, I tried to speak calmly, directly, and compassionately in response to what she said.

"You think it's bad, and I'm sure it is," I offered. "Whatever it is, whatever you've done, whatever you're feeling, I believe there are other ways than this to handle it."

I always try to speak slowly. Megan was quite emotional, even by the standards of someone over the railing. She listened to me, which was a good sign. But there was some ambivalence in her words, a general sense of loss of care that could be dangerous.

Time was on my side here. The calmer I could make things feel and the longer we could stretch out the conversation, the better chance I had of getting her to decide to come back over.

"We can start with right now," I told her. "I can help you tonight. If you come back over, there are many people and organizations to help you get through many, many more nights."

She continued to stare at the water, but I got the sense that I was getting through to her. Something about her body language started to change, though she still needed some convincing.

"They told me that if you jump off the Bridge, you don't feel anything," she mumbled, still looking down.

"Oh, that's not true," I countered. "You're going to feel it. And, if you survive, you're never going to forget how much it hurts. Everyone who has jumped and lived talks about how much it hurts and how the second they let go of the rail, they wish that they hadn't done it."

The numbers are small. They are the ones who enter the water feet first and at a slight angle, the ones who somehow remain conscious and can push themselves back to the surface before drowning. There are almost always broken legs and other trauma, but afterward, these survivors are generally thrilled and thankful to be alive.

As it turns out, nearly everyone wants to live in the seconds before they die.

"Come back over, Megan," I coaxed. "You're not in trouble. We're here to help. We can help."

"I have drug stuff in my car," she said flatly.

"Don't worry about that," I reassured her. "Let's take care of you right now."

Megan looked down at the water again for a moment and then looked up at the city. After several seconds of complete silence, she reached out and asked for our help. Another officer and I assisted her back over the rail and put a jacket around her shivering shoulders.

A female CHP officer took her to our small office at the east lot where we got her a cup of coffee and started her on the road back to life. We generally try to have a female officer on the scene when we detain or arrest a woman. We are required to search people before they get into our patrol cars, and that's especially true if we're taking them to a jail or hospital for a psychological exam. In these situations, it's much better to have someone of the same gender do these searches. Women don't have to feel like they're being groped, and for the male officers, it takes away a possible claim of misconduct.

We took Megan to a satellite office near the Bridge, like we do with anyone we help back over. It's important here to do at least two things: to recognize that their life has value and to not give them any grand illusions that life will be better from that day forward.

• • • •

"Looking back on it, it wasn't so much what I'd done, but what I had become," Megan now realizes. "Once, in my own mind, I went from being a good person who did bad things to being a bad person, then it was easy to decide to head to the Bridge. You feel like if you disappear the world will be a better place.

"That's why the Bridge is so appealing. There's a sense that you can jump off and just vanish, be swallowed up by the sea and washed away. I never thought I would be cleansed of impurity, but I felt that the world would be cleansed of me."

Megan didn't get better right away. There was no light that came on after she came back over the rail. As I tell many of the people I encounter, the problems she had when she chose to go over the rail were still there when she came back. Addiction doesn't vanish because you choose life over death. The habits you've developed over the years still dominate your thinking. Megan stayed clean and sober for a while, but relapses came, as did another suicide attempt.

The next time, she drew a warm bath, wrote another note, and shot up enough heroin to kill an elephant. When she didn't die, she went back to the VA and tried to reconnect with her brother. After another failed attempt at getting clean, her brother put her in a three-month addiction center for women in Marin County. It was there that Megan's conversion took place.

Rehabs are only as effective as the patient's willingness to get better. Someone who has spent a lifetime conning her way from one hit to the next has no trouble telling others what she thinks they want to hear.

Megan had lied to so many people for so long that she hardly knew the truth herself, especially when it was coming out of her own mouth. But one morning in her second month at Marin County was different.

She had gotten up as always, combed her hair, and threw on some sweatpants. But the person staring at her in the mirror was somehow different, somehow cleaner and brighter than the vacant hull she had grown accustomed to seeing. There was color and purpose in her eyes, a clearness that hadn't been present in decades, perhaps since high school before she had ever tasted alcohol, a time when she had sworn that she would never be the person that her father had become, the person whose malevolence she had hated but whose terrible actions she had long ago surpassed.

The person she saw that morning was not a tired addict. The woman she saw was a rejuvenated spirit who wanted nothing to do with her past. The shift felt instant and real.

"During the group meeting, I felt a warmth come over me, and it changed me from the inside out," she recalls. "I'd never known what the presence of God felt like until that day. I'd talked about it, and prayed about it, but that was all bullshit, another way to con my way to the next fix. That morning, everything I'd ever done was laid out in front of me, not in a judgmental way, but in a way that said: 'That is the person I was. I am not that person anymore.'"

She spent the next several hours on her knees in the prayer room. When she came out, Megan had transformed her life and found purpose. She would spend whatever days she had left telling her story to others, letting the world know that no hole is too deep, no cavern too dark for the healing power of faith.

12
Turning Point

The winter rain feels like pebbles attacking my skin.

This is part of the job, of course, but it does change the way you do the job. We highway patrolmen and women are a proud bunch. Ego is part of the package for some of us. I always liked to ride the motorcycle on patrol because of the flexibility it provided. But, in that kind of rain – cold, hard, and stubborn – I didn't get anything out of it.

Some don't want to be seen as weak, so they'll be on the motor no matter what. Me, I'm more practical than proud, or at least I'd like to think so. When the weather is telling me to leave the motor and take a car, I listen. And, on this night, the weather tells even more than that, which is why I hear the call from a local coffee shop in San Francisco toward the end of my shift.

"34-20M, be on the lookout for a possible 10-31. White adult male, 5-foot-10, 150 pounds wearing jeans and a dark jacket on the east sidewalk of the Bridge. He is walking northbound from the south gate."

Right away, I know this one is bad. The sidewalks are closed. The rain is coming down in sheets. You know there are very few reasons someone would be out walking in this weather, and none of those reasons are good. Heck, I'm a tough-guy highway patrolman, and I didn't want any part of this weather.

We know that with calls like this, every second can be critical. But, as much as we want to get to the scene immediately, we have to be smart. Our training is very clear: If we don't get there, we can't help. Too many times, cops end up having to respond to other emergencies.

We don't like to talk about it, but it's not as rare as it should be for a paramedic, fireman, police officer, or other first responder to rush faster than conditions allow. Too often, they end up crashing or having problems of their own. It's so important to respond responsibly, so we can respond at all. If we were to crash, that just makes the situation worse and more complicated since there would be resources committed to us that should be with someone else.

So, I make my way to the Bridge. It seems like the rain is coming down even heavier now. I slow down and put my emergency lights on. This is a difficult thing because we want to get to the person in trouble and we want them to know we're here, but the last thing we want to do is startle them. Unfortunately, in this kind of rain and fog, it's hard to see much past a hundred yards. I turn my directional light on to help me navigate.

By this time, I'm going slow. Very slow. Probably five miles per hour.

I'm squinting through the wet windshield and the night, and finally, I see a man on the sidewalk on the other side. He's walking briskly. My first instinct here is to rush out as fast as I can, but I really don't want to alarm someone in this situation. So, I take the microphone and activate the PA speaker that all of our cars have.

Over the years, I learned a technique that I think helps in these delicate times. In what people might think of as traditional police work, cops tend to speak loudly, with a hard cadence. That projects authority, exudes power. But I don't want to project here. I don't want this person to feel like I'm

As you can see, it's impossible to see much of anything when the fog rolls in. I wanted to give you a taste of what that haze looks like. It's even worse at night.

Courtesy of Associated Press

giving orders. So, I hold the microphone away from my mouth and speak softly. With the pouring rain and the traffic, my voice isn't going to carry too much anyway. And, in situations like this, I can't be too careful.

So, into the microphone, trying my best to project calm, I say: "Sir, can I speak with you, please?" I do this again. A third time. The man doesn't even flinch, let alone look back. At that point, I drive slightly ahead of him to make direct contact.

Turns out, I'm the only officer responding. In bad weather like this, our resources are spread very thin because rain causes a lot of wrecks with people continuing to drive like it's a warm, sunny day.

I step out of the car, which is when I realize I've forgotten my rain jacket. Of course. Typical me. That's when I feel those rain pellets hitting my skin. Body language is so important here, so I can't even let the discomfort enter my mind. My entire focus has to be on this man I'm about to meet, this man who must be going through the worst time of his life.

I go to the sidewalk, about 75 feet ahead of the man. Instantly, I'm soaking wet. I know he must be worse. Colder, wetter. He's been out here for a while now. At first, I wonder if he sees me. He continues walking, eventually stopping about 20 feet from me. I ask if he's okay.

"Anything I can do to help?"

He looks up, doesn't say a word.

And then he jumps – right over the guardrail.

In the moment, my thoughts are more practical than emotional. I have a job to do, and that's to protect this man's safety. Plus, we hadn't interacted yet. There's no connection, only the task. My thoughts go to the chord: It's hard to see in the night and in the rain how far he jumped. If he's just over the railing, he's going to hit the chord. If he jumped out three feet or so, he's already in the water.

I rush over to the railing and am relieved to see him on the chord. Honestly, though, I am a bit surprised to see him there, too. He's lying on his side, I'm sure in a state of shock. These are especially critical seconds, and fearing he would roll over and off the chord, my instincts take over and I yell: "STOP RIGHT NOW!"

This is not what we want to do in this situation. Just like with the speaker system, we don't want to be projecting anything that might be taken with fear. We want to be compassionate, flexible. In this moment, I revert back to my training as a police officer. Rigid. Don't allow chaos. This is what our instincts tell us to do.

To my amazement, though, the command works. The man stops, sits up, and for the first time, he looks at me. I figure I have three seconds before he completes what he set out to do. But he's beyond my reach, so what can I say? I've found that, sometimes, the stranger the things I can think of to say in a moment like this, the better. Snap them out of their immediate situation. Break the ice. Buy some time.

"Hi, I'm Kevin," I say in my friendliest voice. "Nice day, huh?"

I think it's important to give him my first name, not my rank and last name. I've done it the other way, but I think this works better. They see the squad car, the emergency lights, the uniform, and the Badge. They know what I am. You're seeing people in their darkest times, so you want to be as human as possible. Cops are authority figures. The last thing these people want to see in this moment is an authority figure. So, I try to put myself on their level as best I can.

That's part of why I make the joke. I had to break the immediate context of our situation however I could. We're both soaked and freezing, making do on adrenaline and not much else – an awful environment to negotiate in.

My joke does the trick. Hey, sometimes it works. I get their attention, and then once I have it, I surprise them. The man smiles back at me, and that was the first sign I might have a chance here. *Okay, let's work on it*, I think. I ask if I can come a little closer, so he can hear me better and I can hear him. He nods, then warns me.

"You try and grab me, and I'm gone. Get it?"

I assure him we have a deal. This is another small positive sign. Now, he's willing, possibly, to speak to me.

I ask his name. "Edmond," he answers.

Okay, progress. I ask if I can speak with him before he makes any more decisions. He agrees. This is already going better than a lot of cases.

I sense that he wants someone to talk to. As he starts out, I hear a story that's not so typical on this Bridge, but one that resonates with anyone suffering with mental illness.

Edmond is battling depression. He has endured years of ups and downs. This is common. He thought the last year or so had really been going well. He was feeling better, holding a job as a gas station manager. His relationships with his wife and their young daughter are in a good place. He is proud of what he truly thought was a loving family.

As he speaks, Edmond keeps staring down at the water. I ask a question, and he takes a minute or two to answer. Often, he sobs through every word. He tries to hide it from me, but I can see, even through the rain.

We encounter every emotion that humans are capable of out on the Bridge. I always try to focus on the positive. With Edmond, there are better times, too, so I focus on those. He tells me about his daughter's laugh, and the games they play. He tells me about a vacation they all took to Lake Tahoe. Those memories make him smile.

With Edmond, I can see parts of him holding onto the life that could bring him back. I can see other parts of him that seemed to say, "No, I've had enough." I want to stretch out the time, if I can. Generally, it helps them calm down and think more rationally. The more I can help slow down a moment of chaos, the better I'm going to do.

In the best situations, we make it like two people talking. We want them to forget that we're wearing a uniform. We strive to make it feel like we're friends having a conversation, rather than a cop talking a stranger off a bridge.

One of the things I keep going back to is a simple thought: *If I were on the other end of this conversation, what would help me? What would help get my mind where it needed to be? What would come off as genuine and not bullshit?*

If I were Edmond, what would I be thinking?

I don't know if that's the best way to do it, but I've found it helps me. After some time, I think we have enough of a rapport that I can ask the big question. I want to get at the heart of why Edmond is here, on this Bridge, inches from ending his life.

"Edmond," I ask, "what really caused you to come out here tonight?"

He hangs his head even lower, and I tense up, fearing the worst. I have the power to direct the conversation where I want it to go, and the decision of when to start the real conversation. This is difficult to do, and there's no science to it. Wait too long and I might allow too much time for the bad thoughts to arise. Push too quickly, before I've earned the right to ask such a personal question, and I might lose the person.

Edmond takes what seems like five minutes to answer. I wonder if I may have gone in too soon. But then, he starts explaining. He came home from work that night, and his wife told him they needed to talk. At first, Edmond thought it was good news. Everything had been going so well. Maybe she had a surprise for him, a trip she wanted to take.

Instead, she told him she wasn't happy. She wanted out of the marriage. A divorce. Edmond was shocked. Paralyzed with emotion. He couldn't even speak, he tells me. This is the love of his life, the person from whom he got the most joy. He's battling depression, and she's the one he's battling for. Worse, she's going to take their daughter. I can see that Edmond was caught totally off guard.

He says that his hands trembled, and whatever pain he had been fighting flooded back stronger and deeper than ever before. He isn't angry or disappointed at his wife. At least, not as much as he's angry and disappointed with himself. Questions fill his mind: *What could he have done differently? What should he have done differently?* Like a lot of folks I meet on the Bridge, Edmond's self-image is very poor. He assumes everything was his fault.

Mental illness takes a heavy toll on self-image. There is so much shame associated with it, particularly with men. They digest shame as weakness, and that can be a dangerous thing.

In his darkest moment, Edmond admits he doesn't really want to die, but he just can't see another way. His marriage is over, and his wife's desire to take their only child away has broken his will to live. But, even here, amidst the darkness, I see a good sign.

He tells me he does not want to die. That's my hook. That is what negotiations are all about in law enforcement. Gathering good information – hooks – that may help create a positive outcome, or at least prolong the conversation.

You see, when people are in a "crisis state," they have lost their coping abilities. Sometimes, they see suicide as their only way out. In these situations, family members can be great hooks, children even better. This is delicate ground, though, because those same family members are often part of why the individual is on the Bridge in the first place.

I ask Edmond if he was prescribed medication for his illness. He says he was but felt like it hadn't been working, so he stopped taking it a few weeks back. This is very typical of people I've encountered on the Bridge. Most have been prescribed medication that they don't continue to take.

So, for the next 45 minutes or so, Edmond and I talk about his daughter. Her smile. Her laughter. How happy he is when he's with her. If he brings up a camping trip, I ask if they built a fire, and if so, how big. You want the entire focus to be on the good. His daughter turns out to be just the hook I need.

As time passes, we get colder and wetter, but things also get better. Edmond calms down. Reality begins to set in. I explain to him how his daughter needs to have him in her life – children who lose parents to suicide are much more likely to end their own lives. I also explain to him that his marriage may or may not be over – no decision had been made. They could still go to counseling, work on their differences – but his relationship with his daughter is certainly not over. Kids are the most important things in a lot of our lives, and this is what really turns Edmond around.

He looks up at me and smiles.

"Let's get the hell out of here."

You can imagine the relief when I hear those words, but I also know it's not over. Sometimes, that's the last thing someone says before jumping. I'm never comfortable until I have the person in my car. I never know for sure that the person isn't trying to fool me.

So, I reach over the railing to Edmond and help him up. I smile. Pat him on the back. I tell him my usual saying to folks who are detained for a mental health evaluation.

"You are not under arrest," I explain. "Only detained. I have to place you in handcuffs because it's CHP policy. You're not going to jail, just to a hospital for a mental health evaluation."

He nods, and I drive him to San Francisco General Hospital. He's admitted to the Mental Health Unit. Each and every time I do this, I wonder what will happen with the person. Will they get the assistance they need? Or will they be shuffled back into society with a bottle of pills, never to be seen again?

On purpose, I don't follow up with people I've detained for mental health evaluations. I need to respect their privacy. For some, seeing me again may mean reliving experiences they want to forget. This is, by definition, one of if not the worst moment of their lives. Seeing me or talking to me – even hearing my name – can mean a lot of bad memories.

In the moment I help them off the Bridge, I can be a symbol of hope for them. But, outside of that moment, I can be a symbol of shame – a reminder of the worst time of their life.

So, like everyone else I've detained for a mental health evaluation, I tell Edmond he can contact the Marin Area CHP Office if he'd like to get in touch with me. I welcome the calls if they come, but very, very few ever do. I respect that and wish them the best.

Edmond, as it turns out, was one of the few to contact me.

• • • •

TED Talks have earned a tremendous reputation and now enjoy a tremendous reach. I was so excited to go and be able to use the platform there to spread the word about mental illness and suicide prevention. A couple months after my TED Talk, Edmond reached out to me.

I didn't know what to think of his email at first. It was very brief, didn't say much, but included his phone number. I read the email several times, then made the call. It was a wonderful reunion. We needed some time to get the ball rolling, so to speak, as we both had forgotten certain things from that day on the Bridge. As we talked, what he remembered helped me recall some details and, in turn, what I remembered helped him.

I was so happy to hear his voice and also what he told me. I was surprised and delighted to hear that he had moved to Colorado, remarried, and had another child. Another girl. He still sees his first daughter fairly often, traveling back to California for visits and video-chatting on Skype nearly every day. Their relationship is good. Instead of working at a gas station, he now owns three. He is happy and well, both physically and mentally. He takes medication for his depression and now has many more good days than bad.

One thing that stuck out was how Edmond now viewed the events that pushed him to the brink. When we were out there in the cold and the rain, part of what shook him so much was the feeling that everything was going so well. He was truly taken off guard by hearing that his then-wife wasn't happy. That shock was so hard for him to process and immediately turned into shame.

Now, he looks back and understands there were many more bad days than he realized at the time. This is common with the people I meet for mental health evaluations. It's hard to see in the moment when things are going badly and they're living through the malaise. But, once they're out of it, when they're on their medication and doing the work necessary to battle their depression, they tend to see that old life in a new light.

"Thank you, Kevin," he said. "You literally saved my life, and I am forever indebted to you."

Edmond is still fighting, just like everyone who suffers through depression. It's a disease, and even if you can never be recovered, you can be recovering. Edmond, like most of the people I talk to on the Bridge, wants to fight his battle in private. The ones who chose to speak out are rare, and that's fine. He was kind enough to allow me to use his story in this book since it could help someone else fighting this same battle. He knows there are far too many in his situation and hopes his experience can help.

It warms my heart to hear stories like Edmond's. This is the way I always hope those encounters on the Bridge end, that they are turning points instead of end points.

13
My Next Assignment

This is not how I envisioned spending my time in retirement from law enforcement. Going on radio and television, talking to reporters, the TED Talk, and a similar event in Mexico called La Ciudad de las Ideas. My longtime friends know I'm a natural introvert and sometimes joke about all this attention. I wonder along with them sometimes: *How did this all get started? Why me?*

I never graduated college. I don't consider myself particularly charismatic. That's not me. But I do believe that opportunities come along for all of us, and what you do in those moments is what's really important. What you do defines you. I've been fortunate to have more than my share of those moments, fortunate to recognize and take full advantage of them.

Over the course of my career, I've talked to reporters from many magazines, newspapers, and radio stations, and have grown quite comfortable with the process. The number of requests for such interviews has increased steadily. So it makes sense that during my last couple years with the CHP, I had unknowingly become the "spokesman" for mental illness and suicides on the Golden Gate Bridge. Other officers perform the same work as I do and work the same beat, but for whatever reason the press seemed to focus on me.

. . . .

In 2007, *The New Yorker* magazine did an article about the Golden Gate Bridge. I was interviewed for it. If I remember correctly, my sergeant asked me to do it because of my working knowledge of the Bridge and the good relationships I have with those we've helped back over the rail. I thought the reporter did a great job with the piece, and – I have to say – it was fun to be in the magazine. My name had never been in a publication like that before.

Jump to November of 2012, when *Yahoo! News* called the Department. I was asked to do the interview, again, not knowing what all it would entail. Most of these things take a half-hour or so, but this one took five hours. We did interviews at the office and around the Bridge. They even put GoPro cameras on my motorcycle and had me drive up and down the Bridge. The people I worked with on that piece were really nice. Thorough, respectful, easy to deal with. Sarah Parsons was the lead person, and a few months after the piece ran, she called to tell me it had won a prestigious award. Good editing can make even an old traffic cop look good, I guess.

I had no way of knowing that the *Yahoo!* piece would be the start of so much more.

The interview was in November. I generally have a lot of vacation time built up, so I'm able to take Decembers off. It's my favorite time of the year. So, when I got back to work after the New Year, I returned to a lot of voicemails and emails, requests for more interviews from reporters who saw the *Yahoo!* piece.

I was a bit overwhelmed but called the reporters back and went through with the interviews as requested. Suicide prevention is such an important issue. It was an honor to help spread the message. That said, every time I talked to a reporter, I was sure to mention that I was not the only person doing this type of work on the Bridge. Hell, law enforcement officers worldwide do this type of work. Despite my efforts to widen the scope of credit, I quickly became sort of the face of suicide prevention on the Bridge, at least in the media's eyes.

Full disclosure: It's not that I didn't like the interviews – I did. But, like I said, I'm an introvert at heart, so I began asking reporters if they wanted to talk to other officers. I'd had enough spotlight and wanted others to have recognition as well. We do our best work as a team, after all. It was too late. The reporters had identified me as the one to talk to, so I just went along with it because I wanted the message to get out there. And, sooner than I expected,

I even began to find a comfort zone with doing these interviews.

Eventually, publications like *People* and *Men's Health* magazines called.

• • • •

Around that same time, law enforcement agencies from outside California began calling. In January of 2013, the AFSP invited me to New York to receive an award for my work on the Bridge to be held in May.

This opportunity needed to be cleared by CHP management. That's just how it works. Management approved the trip, so I went with my commander, my best friend Jim, and my girlfriend Mary.

The event was spectacular, held in the Jazz Room at the Lincoln Center. Mariel Hemingway hosted. What a night. The room has multiple levels, all facing toward a floor-to-ceiling window which looks out over Central Park. This was the banquet I went to with Kevin Berthia, the night he credits for turning is life around. Kevin presented me with the award, which I accepted on behalf of the CHP because, as I've always said, it's much more than just me out there.

Looking back, this was the tipping point in how the rest of the Department viewed these media opportunities. Something changed. People I considered friends began ignoring me.

Other friends at work told me some were disgruntled about the attention, and I made it a point to approach each and every person I heard was upset. I wanted to know what was going on, why they were talking behind my back. These were friends, people I'd gone to coffee with, even been to their homes.

I didn't ask for all this attention, and I certainly didn't think it would cause a rift with people I considered friends. Sometimes, you see the worst in people when the spotlight shines brightest. One person said: "Why not me? I've saved at least the same amount of people you have, maybe even more."

This is their way of saying, "Acknowledge me, acknowledge me, I'm a hero!" I have even seen some officers post their "saves," along with a photo, on Facebook.

The way I see it, this "attention-seeking" is dangerous. If you're doing this type of work for recognition, you are in it for all the wrong reasons.

You might even get someone hurt or worse by trying to be the hero. The majority of us in both the CHP and Golden Gate Bridge Patrol believe as I do – that we don't "save" anyone on the Bridge. We can only be a positive contact, someone who helps them through a tough time, someone who ultimately helps them save themselves.

Anyway, requests for interviews and presentations continued to come in, and each had to be cleared through CHP management, like the banquet in New York. Some just required approval at the local level, while others needed to be OK'd by the Commissioner's office.

There are some within CHP management with egos that would fill a circus tent, just as there are in any law enforcement office. We have some great leaders who truly care about people and set a fantastic example for everyone. But I suppose there are a few in every organization who are in it for the wrong reasons.

It's a shame. Egos destroy relationships. Egos breed discontent and foster nothing but negativity in the workplace. Since I was just a sergeant, it soon became clear the requests for me to travel out of state would not be easily granted.

The reason I was given was the limited number of times that members of the CHP can leave the state – how ridiculous is that? Police departments were asking for me to present my experience relating to mental illness and suicide in order to save lives. The trips cost CHP nothing and presented an opportunity to build good working relationships with other departments. These were chances to share skills and knowledge.

As things became more tense, I was relieved to know I was getting closer to retirement. We are lucky to have a great retirement program in the CHP, and I had always thought that 25 years would be a good point to retire. Counting my time in state corrections, I reached that mark in December of 2012, when I turned 50. So, I figured the time was near.

In October of 2013, I got a call that would change my life, even if I didn't know it at the time. It came from the *Steve Harvey Show*. They wanted me to fly out to Chicago in November and be on the show.

I went through the normal steps and waited for a response from management. After a couple of weeks passed, I still hadn't heard anything. I

Going on The Steve Harvey Show *was an unforgettable experience. It was wonderful to reconnect with Kevin Berthia and a total surprise to be named one of "Harvey's Heroes."*

asked again and was told my request would probably be denied. I couldn't believe it. Every time I do a presentation, I wear my uniform and speak on behalf of the CHP, being sure to give credit where credit is due. I thought this would be great publicity for the Department, but here I was being shut down.

At the same time, there were some publishers and production companies calling, and I knew nothing of that sort would be possible while I still worked at the CHP. So, the wheels of retirement really began to turn.

The folks at the *Steve Harvey Show* wanted me to fly out on a Tuesday, do the show on Wednesday, and then fly home later that day. They would cover all costs. Well, I had Monday through Thursday off. The CHP could not control what I did with my days off, so I told management I was going to do the show.

This was on a Friday, and I was to leave for the show the following Tuesday. If I wasn't given official clearance from the CHP to do the show, I wasn't going to wear the uniform. Management was, to say the least, not pleased.

I worked the weekend and then had my days off. Monday afternoon, the day before I was to leave, I got a call from my commander – a great guy, by the way – who told me management had decided it was okay for me to go. I just laughed at that one.

I flew to Chicago, and when my turn was up, the staff led me to the stage where I met Steve Harvey. What a genuinely nice man he is. We began filming, and after several minutes, he said there was someone here who wanted to thank me.

All of a sudden, Kevin Berthia popped up from the audience and walked on stage. I was really surprised – as it turns out, it was actually Kevin's mother who had written to the show.

So, the three of us talked for a few minutes about that day, March 11, 2005, when Kevin drove to the Bridge. It was really a great moment to be on that stage with Kevin. He was smiling the whole time. I didn't know it, but another surprise was waiting for me. Mr. Harvey announced I was to be one of "Harvey's Heroes." He presented me with a letterman's style jacket, a very cool honor. What a wonderful day that was.

• • • •

I retired from the CHP in late November of 2013 in order to start and run an organization called Pivotal Points. I thought this name would be appropriate since my work involved many people at a pivotal point in their lives. This new chapter involved travel and invitations to share experiences and teach other agencies.

Eventually, this progressed to very large events and some of the biggest negotiations conferences in the United States. Prior to retiring from the CHP, I had the opportunity to go through Peace Officer Standards and Training instructor school. I was also fortunate to be one of the few CHP personnel to be trained in crisis negotiation by the FBI. Since my training, I have been asked on occasion by the FBI to speak about my experiences on the Bridge when they've had other crisis negotiation classes in the Bay Area. Along with the FBI, many other agencies, colleges, and corporate entities see the benefit of the work we are doing at Pivotal Points, which in part motivates me to continue.

In January of 2014, I was contacted by the Marin Area Public Affairs Officer. He asked if I could go to Sacramento to receive an award from Assembly member Marc Levine.

On January 17, I drove the two hours to Sacramento and met Levine. During the Assembly Session, I was presented with an Assembly Resolution for my work. My area commander, Capt. Shon Harris, was present. He was the same man who went with me to New York for the AFSP event and has always supported me as well

November 15, 2013. Capt. Shon Harris presenting me with my retirement certificate. It was a pleasure working with him.

as this important work. A high-ranking manager from the CHP also showed up.

Since my retirement from the CHP, I have been traveling and speaking about mental illness, suicide prevention, communication skills, and employee relations. I have been to Canada, Mexico, New Zealand, Australia, and all over the United States.

The stigma of mental illness is still alive and kicking for sure, but more and more, we are winning the battle and people are coming to see mental illness for what it really is: an illness that requires treatment. Spreading that message is my mission now.

• • • •

When Kathryn Schulz contacted me on behalf of TED (Technology, Entertainment, Design), I quickly learned that was, in fact, a *big* deal. For a speaker or author, TED is like making it to the top of Everest. The talks are amazing. You learn so much in a very short time.

She invited me to speak at TED2014, which was the first TED conference held in Vancouver, where it is now based. Of course, I gladly accepted the invite. What an organization. Top notch. I can't recommend it enough to anyone who can attend. It is a week of opening your mind to new ideas, to things you either never thought about or never thought possible. By the end of the conference, you've made many new friends and leave generally exhausted from everything you've seen and experienced. I was mentally drained but so motivated.

Speaking at the TED conference was a special honor. Prior to TED, I had given just a few talks to audiences of 30 or fewer – all law enforcement folks. The people at TED were great in working with me, giving me some feedback, and I have a friend in the radio business who helped me with my content and presentation style.

Fortunately, they scheduled me for the last day of the conference, which gave me the week to sit in on some talks and get an idea of how others presented. I had to be one of the least experienced presenters there, so I took particular care to make sure I had my speech just right. Come to think of it, I probably missed half the talks while I was up in my room practicing.

I felt ready but also nervous by the time my turn came. As I began speaking and walking a few feet in either direction being sure to make eye contact, various thoughts were racing through my head.

Oh my God, I'm doing a TED!

Stand up straight!
Look at people!
Now look at different people!
Hey, this is going okay!
Don't trip!
Look at people!
Oh my God, I'm doing a TED!

All the while, the words were streaming out of my mouth. It was a surreal experience. When I was done, I noticed people standing up. I figured they were leaving, off to their next talk. Turns out, they were giving me a standing ovation. What an honor.

Speaking at the TED conference in March 2014 was one of the great thrills of my professional life. It was such an amazing chance to meet so many smart and passionate people, to share ideas, and to learn. If you ever have the chance to go to one of these events, I can't recommend it highly enough.

14
Too Close to Home

I had no way of knowing that voicemail would be a nightmare.

I'd just turned on my cell phone after my flight landed in San Francisco; I'd been gone a few days, delivering presentations in a few different places. There was a voicemail from my youngest son, Travis, and I figured it would be a "welcome home" sort of call.

My heart sank when I heard how wrong I was.

"Hurry home." He was in tears and sounded obviously panicked.

Kevin, his older brother, was very angry. He'd punched an iPad, shattering the screen, said bad things to his mother, my ex-wife, and was now in the backyard, by himself.

Then came a text message from Travis, "Try and hurry, he said he's gonna kill himself tonight."

My heart sank further. Then another text.

"When you talk to him stay calm, don't yell, and use nice words." This from an 11 year old.

I called Travis. It was a short phone call. I wanted to make sure I could get there, but in the meantime, I needed to see if Kevin was okay. Did I even have time to make the hour or so drive? Did I need to call the police?

I deal with suicide prevention every day, but it's so different when it's your own family, when it's your own son.

I have to admit I sped on the drive to my ex-wife's house, where this was all happening. I was trying to keep calm and cool, as best I could. I knew I had some time in the car, and I wanted to use it to plan the best way to approach this nightmare. If not for that mindset and my law enforcement background, I would have driven much faster.

My youngest son had given me a general idea, but I still did not know what I was stepping into. Kevin said he was going to kill himself, but what was the context? I didn't know what he would say when I got there, whether he would be calm after the time alone or spun into more anger. I wasn't wasting any time driving there. But, just like a call at work, I had to get safely and go into it with an open mind before making any assumptions.

I had about an hour from the time I heard the voicemail to the time I walked into the house, seeing my ex-wife, sister, and youngest son in the living room. Everyone was silent.

Kevin was in the backyard, pacing, in the darkness.

I walked out toward him. I greeted him with a soft tone, for the same reasons I hold the microphone a certain way to project calm and comfort on the Bridge. I'd dealt with people going through suicidal thoughts hundreds of times, but there is no way to prepare yourself for going through it with a loved one. There's a reason doctors aren't allowed to operate on family members, one I now understand.

Kevin was facing away from the door. His back was to me. I made enough noise that he could hear me, though. He knew I was there. I walked to him, put my hand on his shoulder.

"Hey, baby boy," I said softly. "What's going on?"

Immediately, he began to cry.

We sat down in the darkness, and I started asking questions to see what was happening in his life. He was a straight-A student and told me he was beginning to feel a lot of pressure to keep that up. He was also feeling pressure from some peers at school who were doing drugs.

He was great about opening up. I started to see this night as the release of an accumulation of stressors that we hadn't talked about – stressors I didn't know about or had even failed to discuss with him, like the divorce.

I talked to him like any parent would talk to their child in that situation. I told him that he and his brother were the best things in his mother's and my life. That he mentioned suicide shook me, and if nothing else, that was the point I most wanted to make.

I just wanted him to know how I felt, how his mother felt, how his entire family felt. How much we care about him. How important he is to all of us. How even the thought of losing him shook everyone. There was no judgment, just love. This seemed to calm him down. When he talked about grades, I told him I'd much rather him come in with C's or D's or F's and be around and happy than to struggle keeping up his straight-A's and have a hard time with these dark thoughts.

Kevin is an achiever. He puts a lot of pressure on himself and wants to do his best. He likes to excel, likes getting good grades, and studies hard. He knows how important it is to do well in school. But it was important for me to tell him that if he needed any kind of help, like tutoring, that we could do that for him and that he shouldn't put so much pressure on himself. I told him that grades are important, but as long as he tries as hard as he can, that's all we can ask, which comforted him.

About the drugs, I tried to let him know I understood he had a lot going on. He was 13 years old, which can be a stressful time for a boy. He felt pressure from some peers who were doing drugs and also felt bad for them because he knew what those drugs can lead to.

"You can't control what they do," I told him. "But you can control what you do. You can control your choices."

I didn't dig too deep on any particular subject. That was on purpose. I wanted our conversation to be comforting rather than feel like an interrogation. He didn't need me to be an authority figure here. He needed comfort and understanding. He needed his dad.

We were out there for about 45 minutes. Sometimes, we just sat there in silence. Silence can be good. I wanted him to have a lot of time to calm down before we went back into the house. I knew he was embarrassed. I knew he thought he was in trouble for breaking the iPad, which I never brought up other than a way to get into the scale of the night. I never told him he was in trouble for it or that he had to pay for it. Nothing like that. In this type of situation, I knew there was more going on. So, I wanted to focus more on the real issues, making sure he felt comfortable, not embarrassed.

Once he was calm, we went inside and he knew it would be okay. Nobody in that living room judged him. We all love him.

• • • •

After that night, we decided it would be appropriate to see a clinician. I made the appointment, and I told the clinician about my previous work with the CHP and what I do now. I wanted him to know about my work and experience in suicide prevention and that I had been in the media quite a bit as I thought my experience and exposure may have been a factor in my son's suicide ideation.

The doctor and my son both agreed to have me in the room during the initial visit. From what I gathered, this was the norm, at least for the first appointment. I don't think this had anything to do with my background.

The session began with about 20 minutes of personal history. We talked a lot about the divorce and Kevin's home life. About school life and sports. The doctor asked Kevin if anything about me, his mom, his aunt, his little brother, anything about all the people in his family he sees on a regular basis was bothering him.

This was informative for me. I found out the divorce affected him in ways I didn't fully recognize. I wish I'd had a better understanding for how he felt about the divorce much earlier. After learning how he felt, his mother and I have each tried to consciously acknowledge his feelings and keep them in mind. It's normal for kids to blame themselves for their parents being divorced, but in Kevin's situation, I think he was just sad that he didn't have both parents together all the time. I think he misses having us around as a couple.

Let's face it, I'm not there as a father figure every day when he comes home. I'm there *for* him, but I'm not always *with* him. He sees other families that travel together, and that's not the case with ours. He gets to travel with his parents, just not with both of them on the same trip.

Kevin told the truth and was quite candid. We talked about stress and coping mechanisms, and Kevin said that he actually cut himself once – on the left forearm, on his wrist. It wasn't a slash, but you can still see a small mark there.

This was a total, heart-stopping shock to me. I tried not to have a physical reaction because I didn't want him to feel like I was disappointed in him. No judgment. But, immediately, I began to tear up. This was the first I'd known about it, my own son cutting himself.

My reaction was the reaction I believe any parent would have. *No way. Not in my family. Not my son.* I've dealt with hundreds of people contemplating suicide, but nothing hits your heart like your own child saying something like this.

Through research and speaking with those who have cut themselves, I have learned there are lots of reasons teens result to self harm. Most often, it's a release from intense pressure, strong emotions, or relationship problems – it temporarily relieves their pain. In one way or another, Kevin was dealing with all of these things. There are also cases of people cutting themselves out of nothing more than desperation. They can't think of another way to free themselves from emotional pain or pressure. For others, it can be a way to express rage, rejection, longing, or emptiness.

One of the reasons it happens with teens is that their coping mechanisms aren't fully developed and their emotions can be so strong that they have no other way to deal with them. Some teens who've cut themselves have said it seemed like a way to feel in control of something, anything in a life where they often felt control over nothing.

Beyond obvious physical consequences like infection or stitches or scarring, there are a lot of other consequences and dangers associated with cutting. It can become a habit. The more someone cuts themselves, the more they may feel the need to do it. If a person truly feels relief from it, their brain often craves the same relief the next time there's a lot of stress or pressure. It can build into an addiction and become very difficult to stop. A teenager may begin cutting to feel control, but it can quickly turn the entire way around: The need to cut can start controlling the teenager.

Cutting isn't always tied with suicide, though. In fact, because it's sometimes seen as a release from pain, it's not always a path toward ending it all. Still, there are many cases of people who cut themselves and eventually attempt suicide.

In Kevin's case, he had cut himself and thought about suicide. He told the clinician that he had thought about killing himself and knew how he'd do it – he'd use a gun.

This was my second heart-stopping shock of the session, another major development that I wasn't aware of, and it made me so disappointed. Not disappointed in Kevin, of course, but in myself. I literally talk people back from the ledge for a living, so you'd think I should be able to communicate with those closest to me a lot better than those I don't know.

Just another example of how you have to watch what's underneath your nose.

Hearing about Kevin's thoughts on suicide shocked me. I have a pretty large gun safe, so I'm not sure if that's why he thought about using a gun. All my weapons are in the safe, locked up; the only people who know the combination are my sister and me. The weapons also have trigger locks on them, and the ammunition is in a whole different locker, so it would take quite a bit of effort and time to break in.

Logistics aside, hearing Kevin talk about this, I thought, *Somebody's going to find this little guy in the house or the backyard with his head blown off.* It shook me.

The clinician asked Kevin how he thought his mother and I might feel about all of this if he really did go through with suicide.

"They will probably be sad for five to seven years, then they'll be okay."

Oh my gosh. You can imagine how that hit me.

But, then, the clinician responded with a completely inappropriate question.

"You're not suicidal now, are you?"

I was shocked, again. How could a trained clinician ask a question about suicide in such a leading manner? By phrasing it that way, he had answered the question for my son without giving him a chance to respond.

I thought that was as bad as it could get, but then he turned to me and asked: "Did I cover all the bases?"

Talk about losing rapport. When talking to people who may be suicidal, rapport is the most important thing you can have on your side. It builds trust and allows the person to feel they can open up to you. Without rapport, you have nothing. I went from feeling sad about my son's pain to feeling angry with this guy's questions in one heartbeat.

Why the hell is he talking to me? Is this guy for real? Is he causing more emotional damage?

When the session ended, I asked the clinician if I could speak with him privately for a minute. I explained I thought his approach in asking if my son was suicidal was not very good and that he actually had answered the question for him. I said, "When an adult tells a little kid something like, 'You're not going to throw that snowball at your sister, are you?' Of course the kid is going to say, 'No.'"

To his credit, he took what I said with grace. He didn't have an ego and was willing to listen to me. I appreciated that, and that's why we decided to stay with him.

• • • •

There was so much from that session that I needed to talk to Kevin about, but at the top of that list was his idea of what his mother's and my reaction would be if he went through with suicide: that we'd only be sad for "five to seven years" and then be okay.

The impact that losing him would have on our family, on his mother and me specifically, was the point I tried hardest to make in the backyard, in the darkness that first night, but obviously, I needed to make that case even harder.

I looked him right in the eye and told him that if this ever happened, if he ever went through with suicide, the only thing keeping me alive would be his little brother. That's it. Those boys are everything to me, and they need to know that. Other than them, I don't really need to be here. Losing even one of them would be devastating. I told Kevin that and made sure he heard me. He didn't say anything back, just looked down.

Kevin Jr. is doing really well now. This is him at 14, a picture we took in his room after he was named MVP of his soccer league. I'm so proud of him. We have much more open communication now than we did a few years back.

We've had a lot of conversations since, Kevin and me. We have talked about that night in the backyard and about that appointment with the clinician. We've talked about everything we talked about then, and more. One topic brings up another, which brings up something else. There are a lot more conversations to have, too. But I do think it's important to do this little by little, so each step makes an impact and isn't too overwhelming.

I've seen signs that things have been improving, that Kevin is getting better at using and developing his coping skills. There's been some good that has come of this experience, too, because it's given his mother and me more reason and urgency to have the kinds of deeper conversations that all parents know they need to have with their children but are sometimes hard to start. In that way, I hope this can improve the relationship Kevin has with both his mother and me as he continues to grow up.

Thoughts of suicide, to whatever degree they occur, are the kinds of things we have to stay on top of, but I've been encouraged by what I've seen since that night in the backyard. A while back, I found a something Kevin left behind on the printer. He didn't know he left it. I think it was a school project where the teacher assigned the kids to write about their greatest day. Anyway, I read it.

I'd just come back from a trip. This was over the summer. I'd been gone about a week. I was with my girlfriend on our way to pick up Kevin. When we got to the house, I asked Mary if she'd sit in the back seat. I wanted to catch up with Kevin.

Well, when we got to the house and picked him up, Kevin, of course, headed toward the back seat.

"Hey, baby boy," I said. "Can you sit in the front seat with me?"

His face kind of lit up. He looked at Mary, who nodded, and he hopped in the front seat. We talked about his week, mostly me asking questions and him recounting all the cool stuff he'd done, a week in the life of a happy boy.

Honestly, I'd forgotten about that day and that conversation when I picked up the piece of paper from the printer. I had no idea the impact and impression it made on him, just one father to son conversation. Reading what he'd written made me glow inside.

I put that letter in my safe, the one with the guns in it. It's under lock and key, so to speak, so I never have to wonder where it is.

Sometimes, when life looks darkest, it's the little things, the small joys that bring back the light.

15
Rock Bottom Recovery

You never know when rock bottom will come. You never know when someone will finally decide that they've had enough. You never know when a person's mind and soul will give up trying to navigate the complexities of life, no longer able or willing to steer in a straight line. This is that scary time when all coping skills have been exhausted.

Teresa Jones' day was hot. Very hot. She hitchhiked from her home in Vallejo, California, to Novato, where she begged for money from strangers. Eventually, she found her way to a bus station, scanned the schedules, and bought a ticket for San Francisco. She was headed to the Bridge, hell-bent on the only decision that made sense to her in that moment.

The bus ride from Novato to San Francisco is less than an hour south on Highway 101 through Marinwood, San Rafael, Corte Madera, and Mill Valley. That's a lot of stops and enough time for a wounded mind to wander. Every time the bus stopped, Teresa looked at the people getting on and off and imagined what those other lives must be like. They didn't have her problems or her struggles. Teresa imagined them all going home to happy marriages, lots of friends, and none of the worries that were shaking her to her core.

Why couldn't she be like them?

Why were they so happy, and she had to beg money from strangers just to go kill herself?

Teresa is about 5 feet 8 inches, slender, with short black hair. She stays in good shape and, when her mind is right, can be engaging and funny. But Teresa's mind was often not right. She'd struggled with bipolar disorder for nearly half of her life, and the nasty disease was driving a hard wedge right through the middle of her world.

The depression and mania had worn her out, like a corrosive rust that wouldn't stop eating away. Teresa's parents split up when she was very young. Dad was a mechanic; she couldn't remember the last time she saw him. Mom was a drug addict and barely in her life.

As is so often the case with the children of drug addicts, Teresa had her own struggles with drugs. Her sister and two brothers were all doing well in life, holding steady jobs and on paths of improvement. Maybe they figured it was up to Teresa to conquer the same demons they faced. Most of the time, they had no time for her.

She could stay with a sibling every once in a while, but mostly, Teresa bounced around. House to house. Apartment to apartment. Couch to couch. Teresa thought her siblings saw laziness more than a debilitating disease: *They had the same genetics she had, so why was she the only one struggling?*

Teresa tried to do right by her disease. She had seen several doctors over the years and been prescribed medication, but when she lost a job, she would run out of insurance and money for her pills. The cycle fed on itself.

On some level, Teresa could understand where her siblings were coming from. She didn't make it easy. Her friends were mostly drug addicts, so when her siblings invited her to stay with them, they were also inviting other addicts. On occassion, Teresa's sister and brothers would find drugs in their homes. Things would get messy, and sometimes, Teresa's friends would steal.

There's a fine line there. I'm sure her siblings wanted to help, but if you're being robbed by your own family or their friends, how far can you let that go?

Usually, it was crack cocaine. When Teresa's mind was right and she found the motivation, she would go to rehab. She wanted to do better and, when sober, was actually a strong advocate against drug use. She knew the damage it could cause.

Out of rehab, she didn't know how to stay straight. Her friends offered little support, struggling with addiction themselves. No matter how much they may have told themselves they wanted a better way, it didn't take long for old habits to reemerge. This is where the cycle would start again.

Teresa had no job, no money, and no place to go. Nobody she knew who would listen to her except other drug addicts, and that never ended well. With no health insurance, she couldn't get the help she needed and wanted. There were some public programs, but those were relatively minimal. It was clear to Teresa that the county felt it had many more important issues to take care of besides her mental health.

When Teresa had money, she spent it quickly. She sometimes bought drugs, sometimes just clothes. When the money was gone, the depression and self-criticism started up again. *Why couldn't she be more responsible?* Her self-esteem plummeted, so she did what she had to do – "unmentionables," she called them – to get money for drugs that would temporarily make her feel better before letting her down again and making everything worse.

It was at the bottom of one of these cycles that she felt the need to go to the bus station to beg. Once on that bus, she watched all those other supposedly happy people on what she thought would be the last day of her life. When the bus approached the Golden Gate Bridge, Teresa asked the driver to stop.

She wanted off.

The bus driver told her there were no stops in the area because it was dangerous for him to stop at this point in the route. Teresa felt a desperation to get off the bus before it crossed the Bridge. She lost control. She rushed toward the front of the bus and started kicking the door.

"Let me off!" she screamed. "LET ME OFF!"

The bus driver was unsure what Teresa would do. Would she hurt someone on that bus? So the driver let Teresa off, and as she jumped off the bus, she could see the driver on his radio asking for assistance.

Everything that happened next was a blur for Teresa. She ran down a hill on the northwest side of the Bridge. The bus driver's call was transferred to the CHP Dispatch, and within a few minutes, to me.

• • • •

I heard the call and headed into the problem. There is a routine we have to follow even during hectic moments, to keep our heads and make sure we're always thinking and doing what we need to be doing.

For most traffic cops, it's the traffic that kills us most often. In law enforcement in general, domestic violence calls are the No. 1 reason officers are killed in the line of duty. Traffic collisions are second. As a cop, we never know what our day will be like. We don't always know when we'll be going home that night or if we'll be going home at all.

I showed up at nearly the same time as a U.S. Park Police Officer, both of us arriving as quickly as we could. We knew the general location but had no idea where Teresa was until we heard the swearing.

The side of that hill was steep and covered with a very heavy brush. That's how we tracked Teresa. We could hear her moving through that crackly brush.

The brush is so thick, we could barely walk through it. It's nasty. We tried to move through it, and we were breaking branches and snapping twigs, loudly. We were audible from quite a distance away even with the traffic from the Bridge.

Teresa had gone about halfway down the hill and stopped, hiding in the brush. There was a little opening in the middle of the mess, maybe 15 feet, a circle. That's where she stopped.

We called out to Teresa several times to come down the hill to us. She would yell back, "Don't come up here! I have a gun!" This was actually helpful to us because she was telling us where she is. We continued to plead with Teresa to come down. The hill was so full of brush it was going to be a nightmare to go up and get her. Regardless, after about twenty minutes of this back and forth, we decided it was time to go get her. We started through the brush.

We had our guns out as we approached, just in case. We had a good idea where she was by now, so we positioned ourselves on a dirt road near the bottom of the hill and started calling to Teresa.

In law enforcement, we want to empower people in these situations. Usually, they find themselves in this dark place in large part because they feel stripped of power, hope, and purpose. They don't feel any control over their lives, and that alone can drive a person to the edge. We don't want to give them false hope, but we do want to bring them upbeat a little if we can.

After about a half hour of pleading with Teresa, we had to try to move in and make contact with her directly. The brush was so thick that half the time we were stepping on the brush and not dirt. Teresa could hear us crackling through the brush, of course, which didn't help. She constantly warned to us not to approach her.

"Don't come up here!" she yelled again. "I have a gun!"

Her voice was sort of expressionless. Although she was shouting, it wasn't panicked and wasn't angry. It sounded more like a mom yelling to her son. Deliberate. Calculating. I didn't think she had a gun on her, but you can never be too sure in these situations. The first time we assume something is safe and don't take the precautions we should, that's when we're going to pay for it.

We finally made our way to within 15 feet of her. Our hearts were pounding. We were covered in ticks and sweat. What we saw next took us completely by surprise.

Teresa was sitting on the ground, completely naked.

We approached cautiously and ordered her not to stand up. She did as we asked and began crying. This is an important time to show compassion, not flaunt authority, so we told her we were there to help her, not arrest her. She didn't put up a fight. I just remember her being very sad. It's almost like she went limp, like all the energy and angst and mania and depression took all the energy out of her. She just sort of gave up, like her body language was saying, "Okay, you got to me, thank you, now help me."

We asked her about the gun. She told us there was no gun. She dressed herself, and we escorted her down the hill. I made small talk with her and, after some time, asked why she got off the bus. I wanted to know her intentions.

Teresa told me she was contemplating suicide but probably would not have been able to go through with it. She actually seemed relieved to be talking to someone, like she was finally getting the help she knew she needed but didn't know how to ask for.

I drove her to Marin General Hospital for evaluation. On the way, I asked why she had taken off all her clothes.

"I thought it would scare you away."

The way she was, the way her mind was working that day, she thought being naked would scare people away. In her thinking, that was the right thing to do. There was no other option. No other choice.

• • • •

Teresa was quite talkative on the ride to the hospital. She asked about me and was freely talking about her childhood and issues at home. She mentioned that she quit taking medication for a mental illness a few months ago because she didn't think it was working. She was really just dissatisfied with her entire life, and I think there was a sense that this was her worst moment but also, potentially, a life-changing one.

"You are on a rough road, Teresa," I responded gently. "I've had the misfortune of seeing many people on this road. I've listened to what you have told me, and I have to tell you that I, for one, believe you can get off this road. I'm just a beat cop, not a clinician, but I believe I can read people pretty well. I see a spark in you. Ignite that spark into a fire. Take small steps to achieve larger goals. Keep those goals in your pocket and look at them as often as you can. Be proud of who you are. I believe in you, Teresa."

She doesn't remember a lot about that day, which is entirely normal. I believe there's something in the human brain that turns off at a certain point. Our brains know that certain memories are best forgotten. There is too much shame, too much embarrassment. We would rather forget the worst and move on. Sometimes, that's good.

I got her into the hospital, in the mental health evaluation unit, and I took off. I felt sweaty, dirty, itchy – all the while happy for her. I always want the person to leave on a good note whenever possible. I want the contact point to end with that person believing in their hearts that law enforcement cares about them. The only way I can do that is to make them know that I care about them.

Incidentally, it wasn't long before I saw exactly why I felt itchy. I went back to the office and changed clothes, which is when I found that quite a few ticks were now calling me "home." Oh my God, it was horrible. I don't know how all those ticks got onto my chest. Maybe it had something to do with how hot it was that summer day. I don't know. But I couldn't work.

That walk up and down that brushy hillside turned into a nightmare for me. I didn't notice it at the time, but there was poison oak on that hill and it was also attacking my chest with a vengeance.

Wearing any sort of long-sleeve shirt, especially with the bullet resistant vest we wear, was just too much. I could not afford to be that distracted all day. In fact, I had to take several days off work. I stayed at home, unable to wear a shirt without attacking myself with scratches.

I had remembered the rash but forgotten some of the details until several years later when I heard from Teresa. She'd seen a piece about me in *People* magazine and all the memories flooded back to her. She called the CHP to reach out to me, and we got together on the phone and talked for quite some time.

She's in Florida now and has been for several years. Her life is so much different, so much better. She married a man who works as a welder for a boat repair company. They actually met in California, at a support group. Her husband's brother owns the company and offered him a job. Family support can be so very important.

More often than not, mental illness isn't something you can master and defeat as much as it's something to be managed and dealt with. Teresa still suffers from this disease, but she is now well-equipped to handle it.

She has great coping skills, which are enhanced by her strong religious beliefs. Her family is now a huge part of her life in a very positive way. She has great support from them as well as from an entirely different group of friends. That's so important. Teresa has a strong set of people to bounce things off of, to share both the good and the bad. A lot of times, that can be the difference between someone who's able to manage mental illness and someone who's just between bad cycles.

It was so nice to hear she's doing well. Teresa and her husband have a child, and she's a stay-a-home mom. She also volunteers every week at a local crisis hotline center. That's important to her because she knows many are out there suffering from the same problems that drove her to the edge.

She knows what it's like on both sides of a mental crisis and has learned that, in those moments, it has to be all about the person who is suffering on the other end of that call. It can't be about her. It was so gratifying to hear that she uses some of what we talked about on that hillside when she's talking to others in need. Mental health problems can often be managed through support, accepting that things might be tough, and by setting goals toward recovery.

All the problems and insecurities that led Teresa to the Bridge that day – undeniably hitting rock bottom on that hillside and the years of recovery since – have formed a toolset of strength, belief, and coping. She uses her experiences every day in her life, in raising her child, and in her work at the crisis call center.

We know that the risks of depression can be related to genetics, that parents who have suffered from depression are more likely to have children who suffer from depression. It's probably only human nature that we blame ourselves when we see our kids battling the same problems we have battled. But I believe that those of us who acknowledge our own depression and look at our battles honestly can better see it in our kids and can thus be better equipped and positioned to help.

Teresa is lucky. Her husband knows these same battles firsthand, and together, they are diligent about working toward a better life, not just for themselves but for their child. Teresa serves as a model for how others might deal with their own depression. She made major changes after her rock bottom moment, moving across the country and developing a new support system to help her through what she understands and accepts will always be a tough road.

She is a shining symbol that, even in our darkest hours, if we embrace the challenge and fully understand what's in front of us, we can make sure those shadows are indeed behind us. Teresa represents hope.

That said, the important thing is to make that decision – that choice to go on – and give yourself to that decision fully. You have to do more than just say you're going to give yourself to recovery. You have to truly surrender yourself to that recovery.

Teresa is now grateful for those dark hours. She knows the struggle that took her to that bus station to beg for money, the ride toward the Bridge seeing all those people she imagined to be happier than she was, and the afternoon spent on that hot, brushy, poison oak-infested hillside ended up as the keys to unlocking a much brighter future.

That's the great thing about rock bottom. As awful as the moment is, it can be an opportunity. You can get your life back. One of the last things Teresa said to me on the phone was that she's grateful for that awful day and glad that we met because it helped her recover. If she didn't hit that low, hit it in the way that she did, and accept that she had to make major changes for a different path, who knows where she'd be right now?

16
A Lost Soul, A Wonderful Life

Kurt Thomet is in his 50s, though he prefers you know he is 55 years *young*. He has blue eyes, a grey mustache, is barrel chested and wide shouldered. He works out every day, either going for a four-mile run through the woods or a bike ride on the hills around his house.

He met his wife after a bit of a blind date snafu. They were set up, but the wrong roommate showed up the first time. Kurt and the roommate went out. It didn't last, so he asked out Karen. They've been married 30 years and live in a home they custom built about a mile from where Kurt grew up in Eugene, Oregon.

They have two great kids. Chase was a state champion tennis player in high school and went on to be a 4.0 student at Santa Clara University. He now works for a private equity firm in La Jolla. Kayla is in high school, where she plays tennis and runs cross country. She's a gifted writer, involved in her church, and is going through the college application process.

Kurt opened his first computer store in Eugene in 1983, and grew it into a large educational dealer. He now runs a multi-million dollar company that does mobile computing and barcode integration. They just went public.

Kurt has a wonderful life.

One day, Kurt ran across my TED Talk online. He watches a lot of TED Talks and had no particular expectations for mine. But, by the time it was over, he was in tears, sobbing so hard he went to the floor to recover.

There wasn't anything special about my presentation, mind you. It was the content, the act of breaking open a topic that is too often hidden in the shadows, Kurt's shadows.

Kurt shared the talk on Facebook and then emailed me.

"Thank you for your talk and for helping others to choose life," he wrote.

Chances are, you are acquainted with someone who has contemplated or attempted suicide. You may not know who they are exactly, but mathematically speaking, it's much more likely than not that someone you are friendly with has been driven to the edge. Chances are, you may even know more than one person who is all too familiar with the darkness.

It's also likely that at least one of these people is someone you would never guess. They may appear to have everything in order, to have great and happy lives. They may appear as though they have never and will never have a reason to think about ending it all.

They may, in other words, be a lot like Kurt Thomet.

• • • •

When he looks back on it, the problems started his freshman year at Arizona State University.

Freshman year is a critical time for anyone who goes off to college: the first time away from home, the first break from being taken care of by your parents, teachers, and coaches in high school, the first chance to really be independent. College is such a fun time for most people, but the beginning can definitely be scary.

There's a gap between the comfort of being at home with your parents and the friends you've known your whole life and then being in this big place with all these new faces. Arizona State is a very big school, and despite being surrounded by thousands upon thousands of would-be friends, Kurt felt lonely. He didn't have a significant relationship with anyone at the school, which made things even worse.

This is a common and often dangerous situation because it's so easy for loved ones to miss: You're with more people than ever before, but you're also lonelier than ever before.

For Kurt, it wasn't any particular thing. It was a combination of things, a thousand subtle paper cuts that opened a big wound that only he could feel.

Back home, he had this beautiful, green Alfa Romeo Spider sports car. They didn't make many of them, usually fewer than 5,000 per year. Kurt always wanted one and worked hard in high school doing landscape work and selling vacuums door to door. It took him a few years to save up for the car, but he bought it and cared for it like a child.

Well, that child was left at home in Oregon. Kurt didn't have a job lined up at college, so he wouldn't have the money (or time) to keep up the car. Besides, where would he park it out of the sun? Maybe that feels like a small thing – it's just a car – but to Kurt it came to represent something more. Freedom. Responsibility. Diligence. A tangible accomplishment that he could point to, something he'd earned through hard work.

It wasn't just the car. He had no money, no real friends, and for the first time, wasn't playing organized sports other than intramural volleyball. That meant no natural way to meet and become close with anyone. It meant no practices, no big games, no structure in place with a common goal to work toward.

College in general provides a first real taste of freedom, and Arizona State in particular offers that as well as a beautiful setting – some of the best hiking in the United States is a relatively short drive from the campus in Tempe – full of vibrant, healthy students. It's the last place you'd think someone could get lonely, but it takes time to build relationships. It takes time to build good relationships, anyway, the kind where others truly care for and look out for one another.

Kurt never thought much about any of that until it was nearly too late, until he was looking back on a time when he didn't have the kind of relationships that are important to all of us.

• • • •

Feeling lonely was a new thing for Kurt.

He'd always been a happy kid growing up, always surrounded by a lot of friends and a lot of different things to do. That changed immediately at Arizona State. From the very first day, he felt surrounded by what he perceived as crazy kids who were so different from him and what he was used to. All he wanted was a roommate who wasn't named Star, didn't dress in "look at me" chic, or didn't spend his time making fun of athletes.

Kurt thought the Greek system might help. After all, he wasn't the only one who started college looking for friends and feeling a bit out of place. Fraternities and sororities are a great place to build meaningful relationships. So, Kurt went through rush and felt the best connection with the Phi Delts, who had a house on Alpha Drive.

It was a gorgeous house, built by Frank Lloyd Wright. There were two hallways, upstairs and downstairs, and sleeping porches that were converted to individual rooms. They had a front room with a fireplace, a grand dining room, and a kitchen. Off of the front, there was a separate room, next to the House Mother's room. Everybody wanted that room because it had its own private bathroom and shower. All the hallway rooms shared a shower and bathroom.

That room became Kurt's for doing dish duty in their kitchen, which he did to earn some of his housing costs. It was supposed to be a prize and was seen by most of the fraternity as such. In reality, it added to his feeling of loneliness and separation from the rest of the house.

And, like most fraternities, joining meant going through hazing: Hell Week for pledges.

He was among about 15 pledges, initiated only if they could survive Hell Week. It was the typical fraternity stuff: physical exercise, cleaning toilets with toothbrushes, showering while sitting on ice blocks, and mental mind bending. A sort of boot camp that included screaming and intimidation from existing members of the fraternity.

They also had to chug beer, the class draining a keg in a very short time. Ever seen *Animal House*? Remember the scene where Dean Wormer is yelling at Flounder? They had a replication of this at the Phi Delt house on beer chugging night, pledge Kurt projectile vomiting all over brother Curt. If you know anything about fraternities, you know that incident would be used against Kurt.

Pledge Kurt's moment of reckoning came in a secret ceremony where the leaders of the house wore hoods. Sacred vows and candles added to the drama. This was the day the pledges were to be initiated. They didn't know that, though, and part of the routine involved telling each pledge that they didn't make it. They'd failed, and not just that, they failed because of something specific. Kurt's, of course, involved vomiting on Curt. Disrespect, the fraternity leaders called it. They told him he was a good guy, but it just wasn't going to work and that they would try to help find him a new place to live. Kurt believed them.

The pledges were then led out of the room, where existing members all screamed WELCOME! The whole thing was a hoax, just a play on the pledges' emotions. It was meant to bring everyone closer together, but to Kurt, he was left in disbelief that the members did this to the pledges and felt good about it. He vowed to never be involved in that kind of thing – to never mentally harm anyone, especially as a form of admission, acceptance, or entertainment.

What a strange feeling. He'd gone through all that craziness of Hell Week and everything else, but once he got through it – once he was at the finish line – he didn't want it anymore. Here he had all these guys he knew with a common bond of going through the same thing together, but the whole thing just left him empty and unhappy and – worse of all – lonely.

Kurt went to classes, parties, and other fraternity functions. It was fine, as far as that goes, but he always felt a bit out of his league, looking around at others in the Greek system with cars, money, friends from their hometown, and trips home every holiday. He was isolated in that room of his – the prized room – and everything added together in a feeling of overwhelming sadness. The only phone he could use was a payphone in the hallway, with no expectation of privacy.

It was then that Kurt began thinking about killing himself.

• • • •

Suicide dominates his family history. His mother's mom, Kurt's grandmother, tried to kill herself in a car crash. When she got out of the hospital, she shot her husband and then herself, not wanting either one of them to live with the shame of her illness. Both died.

Her father, Kurt's great-grandfather, likely killed himself during the Great Depression by turning on a gas heater and not lighting it; Kurt's grandmother was 13 at the time.

Kurt's uncle, Jack Danley, was a charismatic livestock auctioneer and owner of a stockyard in a small Michigan town called Saint Johns. Jack killed himself the day he learned they were going to close the livestock auction business. No note. No warning. No nothing. Kurt was young and didn't go to the funeral or truly comprehend what had happened.

As he grew up, Kurt learned that suicide in his family was something they just didn't talk about.

All of those thoughts and images were in his head. Life experience had shown him that suicide was an option, something people he loved and knew chose to do. Thoughts of suicide still scared him though, particularly with the family history.

One day, Kurt went to the campus health clinic and met with a doctor. Kurt believed those thoughts to be poison in his mind, and he wanted help. The doctor listened – kind of – and gave him some anti-depressants.

In the middle of this enormous school and a fraternity house full of "brothers," Kurt just couldn't shake the feeling of isolation. He thought about the seriousness of what was happening.

He tried to combat this with visualization and goal setting, a mechanism he'd come to rely upon. He wanted to be positive. He had great weather, a good school, a nice family. Really, he thought, maybe the only bad thing was his own thoughts. Maybe he was the problem.

The doctor told him that one of the side effects of the pills could be more awful thoughts of suicide. The whole thing scared him. Just the thought of suicide entering his mind was terrifying. He knew what that could do, what it looked like.

Although Kurt didn't know what he wanted to do with his life, he felt sure that those pills – a danger in themselves if not used properly – were not going to help. That much was simple. He decided the problem was that he wasn't working out enough, not feeling engaged enough, and that the only thing wrong was his own attitude.

Kurt left the clinic and headed back to the fraternity house, his mind racing to the conclusion that these thoughts – *his* thoughts – were his worst enemy. These thoughts were there because of him, nobody else.

He flushed those pills down the toilet in that private bathroom of his. He went for a run, convinced the endorphins from exercise would give him a healthy mindset. It would, but he would find the help to only be temporary. The real demons were still in there.

The worst part about it was that Kurt was convinced that nobody knew and nobody cared.

· · · ·

Kurt started working out regularly, and that did help some. He felt better, had more energy. But that didn't help with his loneliness or his desire to be more like his "brothers."

Those feelings never went away. They never got better but didn't get bad enough for rock bottom until his third year at Arizona State.

Kurt never stopped missing his car. When he was back home during the summers, he loved the feeling of freedom that driving gave him. So, one night during his junior year after a party, he and a pledge brother went to a used car lot. They picked out a gorgeous brown Fiat 124 Spider convertible. The keys were in the car. The boys snuck it off the lot and went for a joy ride.

When it came time to take the car back or abandon it, Kurt instead decided to drive it around as his own. He'd find some shady character to get plates made for it. Only he didn't know any shady characters and never changed the plates. The cops soon found him and took him to the Tempe city jail. Some guys from the house bailed him out, and he was given the fraternity's big-shot lawyer to represent him in court.

Any feeling of comfort in his legal representation evaporated quickly when he learned that no lawyer could get him off for stealing a car like that. He went to court in the morning and then straight to jail. Nobody knew where he was, and nobody cared. It got worse from there.

His cellmate was big and angry and, as it turned out, horny. The first night, Kurt's cellmate climbed on the upper bunk and tried to make Kurt his lady. One of the common threads in a lot of stories about depression and suicidal thoughts is that hitting rock bottom can be a good thing. Once you're there, you have nowhere to go but up. It can be liberating, this fight-or-flight instinct, though it's not always as literal as the fight-or-flight situation of having a cellmate trying to rape you.

Kurt fought like hell and, in spite of the size difference, beat up the bigger man pretty good. That earned Kurt an isolation cell, which was fine with him. Away from others, and with nobody to harass him, he quietly did his calisthenics with nothing to blur his thoughts.

Kurt spent his 30-day sentence in isolation. That's a lot of time to think about what he'd done and, more importantly, how he'd gotten to that place of desperation. This wasn't the person he wanted to be. He decided that he needed a hard goal, something with a number, something achievable.

He came up with a clear objective: Pay back the $12,000 debt for the car, attorney fees, and court costs, then get back to school.

Eventually, Kurt came to think of his time in jail, as well as the debt it left him with, as one of the best things that could have happened to him. He saw it as a just punishment and honored the opportunity to pay back the money. He looked forward to the sense of accomplishment that it would give him. That was the way he would wash away the guilt and overcome those feelings of inadequacy and of being lost.

Now, instead of feeling buried in loneliness and isolation, he saw his life as very simple. Work hard to pay back his debt, exercise to stay healthy, and sleep and eat to keep it all going.

His life had a purpose again.

• • • •

Kurt absorbed his punishment. He welcomed it. In fact, he took it to the extreme. If he was going to pay back that debt as fast as possible, wouldn't it help to strip his expenses, too?

So, since no one seemed to be looking for him anyway, Kurt went homeless instead of returning to school. By choice. He took to thinking of it like camping, like recreation, like something he had to do to give himself guidance. He started, literally, in a cardboard box in a field. One night, it rained so hard his box turned to mush.

Kurt started working. His first job was at a steel mill doing nasty clean up under the steel-casting wheel in hot, wet, stinking, casting sand. This was a job for the desperate, and Kurt was desperate. There aren't many circumstances where doing hard, demanding physical labor around burning hot and dangerous machinery is a good thing. Kurt's was one.

He did well enough on the clean up that he was trusted with pouring hot, molten steel. They gave him a fire suit, gloves, a mask, and protective boots. This was the kind of work where even a momentary lapse in focus could have life-altering consequences because hot metal would bubble out of an opening atop a ladle used to pour the melted metal.

His was a critical job. He had to pour the metal at exactly the right speed. Any mistakes would cost the company money and create problems for others at different parts of the job. And, no matter how careful he was, once in a while, balls of burning hot metal would roll into the gap between his glove and coat sleeve. His skin would sear against the molten metal.

The work was hard and humbling. Kurt was around grown and calloused men who ridiculed him for being a college kid. The way he dressed, the way he talked, even his soft hands – it was made very clear to him that he didn't belong. The older guys took great joy in watching him do the dirtiest jobs. They probably made him do more than his fair share.

Kurt was determined, though. They had to give him that. He quickly learned his way around the large manufacturing wheel used to cast tractor treads. The wheel moved slowly around; compressed sand molds were put in and clay was hand packed between them so the liquid metal could be poured from a giant ladle.

The metal cooled as it flowed into the molds. As the wheel turned further after curing, the molds were opened up and were blasted off with water. The finished pieces were dropped onto a conveyor and moved to a tall cylinder that banged the pieces around and separated them into smaller pieces. The smaller pieces were later assembled into tractor treads.

Each day was a cuss of a challenge.

But it did have a start, a break, and a finish. Kurt found some comfort in the schedule. The difficulty of the work allowed him to count it as his workout for the day. And, after a few weeks, he moved up the totem pole when the mill hired a newbie and someone above him quit.

Kurt had the night shift, which was great because in the Valley of the Sun daytime temperatures are routinely above 100 degrees.

Eventually, the older guys started to respect Kurt. He worked hard and, even through the jokes, always listened to the men who knew what they were doing.

The good side of doing this type of work is that it pays well. You don't get – and you wouldn't trust – this kind of work done at minimum wage. And, not just the pay, but they also had showers. You can imagine how much a job with decent wages and showers would appeal to a man focused on repaying debt and living in self-imposed homelessness.

Kurt made enough from his first paycheck to buy a moped to get around. He parked it next to his box while he slept, but the bike was quickly stolen. After that, he bought a small, used Honda 350 motorcycle.

He moved from the cardboard box to sleeping in an orange grove and, after that, a storage unit that he rented. Storage facilities have rules against these types of things – nobody wants to store their stuff around a bunch of homeless guys – so Kurt had to sneak in every night and then out early the next morning after just a couple hours of sleep.

Working at the mill was a good fit for what Kurt wanted to accomplish, but it wasn't enough. He got a second job at a steakhouse, busing tables on the lunch shift. That's definitely the entry level, low-man job. The waitresses treated him terribly. Even the dishwashers didn't respect him. Managers never looked him in the eye. They only barked orders his direction.

After a month or so, he earned a spot as a waiter and took pride that he had the highest ticket average and had developed regular customers who wanted only him to wait on them.

The second job left some time between his lunch shift at the steakhouse and his night shift at the mill. So, Kurt got a third job as an oyster bar manager at the Great American Seafood Company on Indian School Road in Scottsdale.

Wearing a tux and black slacks, he shucked oysters. He'd make oyster stew behind a gorgeous mahogany bar. Customers tipped him, and he'd chat with the servers and customers. A bonus of working at two restaurants, of course, is that it meant two free meals every day, which allowed him to save even more of what he earned.

Kurt didn't think about this before starting this new life, but each of those jobs required a different personality.

At the mill, it was all about the work, maintaining focus, and doing his part of a much bigger operation in which each man depended on the other. It was a very regimented life. Kurt had to be on time, stay out of the way, and not waste time talking or anything else. It was a job of isolation and self-dependence.

Before he was promoted to waiter, busing tables meant accepting that he was the least valuable and most expendable part of the restaurant. Kurt was treated with no respect because he hadn't earned it, and the only way to get by was to keep his mouth shut and do as he was told.

The oyster bar was more fun, more of a showman type thing. Along with the job as a waiter, it was about smiling and telling jokes and making people feel good. There was no time to be tired, even in a life that consisted of showering and shaving at the mill, sleeping in a field or storage unit for a few hours at a time, and riding that Honda between jobs.

It was like he was living three lives at once, each of them independent – and each of them secret from pretty much everyone he knew.

Kurt saw the people he worked with every day, of course, and a parole officer once a month. That was it. He didn't tell many of his brothers at the fraternity that he'd taken a self-imposed leave of absence. He assumed people would figure he'd just taken some time off. He never told his parents about any of this, either.

It wasn't that he was purposefully hiding something, it was more that he was so immersed in this new life. Where he felt chased by these demons before, he now felt like he was chasing goals. That's a liberating feeling.

Not telling his parents felt normal, actually. He was away at college without an easy way to communicate, so he and his parents had become used to not speaking for months. His dad owned and managed a clothing store and a bookstore. His mom had gone back to school and eventually became a nurse for an OB/GYN center. They were busy, too.

Kurt was on his own, which by now, he had come to see as a good thing.

• • • •

Kurt eventually went back to school, though he didn't have much to do with the fraternity. He ended up leaving school one semester short of his degree to start a career. An insurance company had given him an opportunity to sell computers, using the Commodore PET (one of the first full-featured, personal computers) to print finance and insurance documents for car dealerships.

Kurt and his family at the Thomet house in Eugene during the summer of 2014. That's his wife of 30 years, Karen, and their kids, Chase and Kayla. Kurt is sharing his story in hopes that it serves as an example of overcoming both suicidal thoughts and a family history of suicide.

He partnered with a man named Ron Isaacs, who Kurt began to see as a truly positive force in his life. Together, they grew the Commodore business into the first computer store in Eugene, eventually introducing personal computing to the public in the area.

There have been downs in the years since, but mostly ups. Kurt's wife battled thyroid cancer. Kurt had a tumor on his back and melanoma. Both of his children have had unrelated brain tumors.

Business hasn't always been great, either. He was fired five days before the end of a contract that included more than a million dollars in stock options. A business partner stole $2 million, which Kurt and his other partners had to repay to banks and vendors. He did that with a bit of a retrofitted approach to his first debt, taking no salary from his business until he was square.

But the ups have been significant, too. He started a technology integration company called Quest Solution in his garage and built it over 20 years into a publicly traded business with revenues over $65 million. He has other business interests that keep him busy as well.

There are still marks of his old life in his new life. Exercise is still very important. He bikes and sails with friends and family when he can.

Kurt hasn't thought about killing himself since that dark time in college, even after one of his business acquaintances killed himself after losing his business and struggling with side effects of anti-depressants.

But that doesn't mean Kurt hasn't continued to think about suicide. He's involved with an organization called Team Rubicon that helps support returning military members who are challenged with suicidal thoughts and actions. His daughter has cared for a young girl who lost her father, a police officer, to suicide.

Kurt has come to see his recovery from those demons not as an accomplishment, but as an ongoing process requiring maintenance, respect, and care.

He starts each day being grateful, posting one positive thought on Facebook. Kurt considers this an important part of that maintenance, remembering the positive things in life and focusing on those at the start of a new day's challenges. Before he goes to sleep each night, he stops and thinks about small, incremental steps he's made toward goals he's set for himself.

Recovery isn't a destination – it's a goal you never stop reaching for.

• • • •

Stories like Kurt's give me so much joy and so much hope for others. Dark times can feel like they'll never end, but if we can help people through the worst moments of their lives, there is often so much happiness on the other side.

Kurt's story is an example of that.

17

Stories from the Road

I probably see business trips like most people who travel a lot for work.

They can be the best and worst part of the job. They can be a way to visit places and experience things that you otherwise never would, limited by time or money or both.

They can also take you away from your family, your friends, your home, and the life you've worked to build for yourself. I've found that airports can sometimes be the worst places around.

You can have a delicious dinner at an amazing restaurant, and you can be stuck eating out of vending machines for days. Like I said, good and bad. A lot like life in general when you think about it.

Helping to spread the importance of mental health awareness and suicide prevention is both my duty and privilege. That part of my life takes me on the road two or three times a month, across the country and overseas.

My presentations have been in front of thousands across the United States as well as in Mexico and in the Outback of Eastern Australia.

At one of my first presentations for a law enforcement liaison committee, an elderly woman approached when no one was around.

"Do you make personal house calls?" she asked. "Like tonight?" She sort of winked at me.

This was not a plea for a mental health evaluation, so I wormed my way out of that one. I don't make *those* kinds of house calls.

Of course, the message of suicide prevention is not mine to carry alone. There are a lot of us trying to spread the word, and we need all the help we

They call this "The Gap." It's near Sydney and, unfortunately, has become one of the most popular suicide destinations in Australia. A man named Don Ritchie is credited for helping save 164 people who came here to kill themselves. He was nicknamed "the Angel of the Gap." He passed away in May 2012. I came here to pay homage to him.

can get. For someone dealing with mental illness or suicidal thoughts, it is often most effective for the conversation to be brought to them. We are making progress on shaving down the stigma of mental illness, but it's still very real for many people.

In some of those cases, seeing a person talk about these things with confidence and compassion can change lives. It can break the ice, and start an honest conversation or effective treatment for a problem that too often goes unchecked.

Being able to look people in the eyes and help them come to terms with a silent killer is what keeps me going, keeps me traveling. You never know who you can reach or how you can reach them.

Sometimes, you don't know until months later.

For instance, here is an email I received in June of 2014 from a high school student in New Hampshire:

> I am one of your Freshman Health students writing you using my online alias. The only reason that I'm doing this is because

I wish to remain anonymous. This email is regarding the video we watched last Thursday regarding the topic of suicide and the Golden Gate Bridge.

Before I even begin, I have to inform you that I am getting help. My family is aware of my situation and of the severity. There is no need to be concerned or even to reply to this email. You don't even have to read this if you don't want to or don't have the time. This is not a cry for help. This is a thank you.

When you showed it to us, you told us that it was just a cool video to see, but to me it was much more than that. I sat in your classroom and tried to keep myself from crying in your classroom as I listened to the words spoken. Those words may have saved my life.

I suffer from depression. In the past year, it has gotten so bad that most days, I struggle just to get out of bed. Many days, I wonder if life is really worth living at all.

Thursday, June 12, I had a plan. I planned to get through the day at school then go home and die.

Of course, nobody knew about that plan. Most people don't even know that part of me exists. As you can probably tell, I didn't go through with it. Your decision to show us a TED talk about suicide is the reason for that.

I'm used to hearing that "it gets better." That's one of the most difficult parts of depression: you have to keep it hidden or else you're mocked by an onslaught of meaningless encouragements and it-gets-better's and I-know-how-you-feel's. For me, hearing those things just makes it easier to dig myself into a hole.

I never would have seen that talk unless you had decided to show it in class. I would have gone home and probably killed myself without ever thinking of the collateral damage. Now I have that reason to live: the people who would have found me, my family.

Even now, it's hard to say that I want to live. I have no interest in living. However, I do have an interest in not hurting my family. The Bridge Between Suicide and Life was the first time I'd ever heard anyone even mention the effect suicide has on other people. I don't know if it would be the same in my case, but I love my family and that is not a risk that I'm willing to take.

So, I beseech you to show The Bridge Between Suicide and Life every year. Most students may think that it's boring and a waste of time, but I guarantee you that there will almost always be a student whose life it may save. It may seem like a small action, but sometimes metaphorical pebbles make tidal waves.

There are signs of suicide: losing interest in things, what I call moodiness, tying up loose ends, etc., but some people, myself included, keep all of those things hidden very far from where others can see them and worry. My point is that you never know what your students are truly thinking or how these little things may affect them.

Thank you for what you unknowingly did for me.

I wrote back to the teacher, asking if he had any way to follow up with the student. He told me that he and the student had written back and forth a few times and that the student was seeking treatment, along with the family. The teacher believes the student is doing much better.

I use this story in my presentations from time to time, not to promote my TED talk as some grand fix, but to illustrate that by talking about mental illness and suicide *out loud* we can really break down barriers and help those who are suffering.

This is why I travel so much. Hearing a story like this makes the time away from my family, the airport meals, the long layovers worth it.

• • • •

Once, I was asked by a crisis negotiation association in the Midwest to do a presentation on suicide prevention, engaging possible suicide subjects, and officer welfare concerns after an incident.

Two negotiators picked me up at the airport, and from our conversation on the ride back, it was so encouraging to hear the amount of time their department spent on training for negotiations. I certainly wish all departments could do the same, including my own.

Too often, we see a reaction instead of preparation. Reactivity as opposed to proactivity. I think of it like a busy, four-way intersection that residents and officers familiar with the area know is dangerous. Citizens complain and officers make the case to their superiors, but there are no accidents, so no action is taken.

Then one day, a little girl is hit by a car and dies. Watch how fast they react then. Immediately, you will see stop signs and lowered speed limits and constant police attention. But why did it have to take tragedy to move toward action? If those in power had listened earlier, they could have saved a life.

It's a lot like that with mental illness and suicide prevention. The best way to help someone off the Bridge is to stop them before they ever get there, before they have the opportunity to climb over the rail.

Anyway, for this presentation, I arrived a day early to settle in, see the room where I would present, and meet the people in charge. That night, I was in my room, relaxing, going over my presentation one last time before bed. It was about 10 p.m., and just when I started thinking of turning in for the night, I heard this awful noise.

At first, I thought it was an earthquake. Then, I looked out my sixth floor window, out to a parking lot, and saw a young man with two women standing by a Harley Davidson motorcycle. This knucklehead was out there making noise, revving the engine as loud as he could, showing off for the ladies. I swear the motorcycle had no muffler because I've owned three Harleys and none made the wall-shaking noise of that machine did.

That guy didn't just raise hell for a minute or two, either. It was the better part of a half hour, never getting on to ride the motorcycle, just revving it there in the parking lot. *The hotel is filled with cops for this conference, so how the hell could this be happening?* I wondered.

I thought for sure that someone would come out and slap that guy, but nope, he just kept revving that damn engine. If my hotel window could open, I swear I'd have thrown a bottle at him. I was so mad that even after he stopped, it took me two hours to calm down and fall asleep.

There were approximately 300 law enforcement members at the conference, most of them negotiators. These conferences are a great way to keep up to date with current trends, learn new skills, and make some new friends. Most of these folks have been to these events before and know one another.

Being new to these conferences, I didn't know anyone. But that wouldn't be the case for long. When it was my turn to speak, I walked to the middle of the stage and stared at the audience for a few seconds.

"Did any of you hear that earthquake last night?" I said.

Some people looked back, stumped. Others knew exactly what I was talking about.

"Who the hell was on that Harley last night showing off to the girls?"

Almost immediately, about ten people in the front row all began yelling out "Jacob," pointing at a young correctional officer who was already turning beet red. A round of mocking applause followed. I guess there were quite a few people angry with Jacob.

After the presentation, I walked out of the room to get some coffee when Jacob came up to me with his supervisor. Jacob apologized for the noise, and I could tell he was embarrassed. I then talked with Jacob's supervisor, a man named Steve, who apologized for what happened. He was embarrassed for his department and said that's definitely not the way they wanted to start the conference or be remembered.

Correctional officers are sometimes looked down upon by "real cops," Jacob's actions did nothing to improve their image. I told Steve it's like that with the CHP sometimes, also. I have heard CHP means "Can't Handle Police work," or "Triple A with a gun."

I guess that's what you get when you specialize in a particular area of law enforcement. All things considered, I loved working the road and wouldn't have changed a thing.

Steve approached me several times during the conference, still apologizing for Jacob's actions. I highly doubt Jacob was invited to the next convention.

Anyway, at the end of the presentations, I went to dinner and then back to my room for a bit. But it was still early, around 9 p.m., so I decided to go down to the hotel bar and celebrate what I thought was a good presentation with a drink. You know, I didn't swear, fall off the stage, or throw-up. Pretty good, indeed.

Not too long after I got to the bar, a bunch of folks from the conference started pouring in. It went from maybe five of us to 75 in a matter of about 15 minutes. I'm not complaining, though, because I didn't ever buy a drink. People from the conference made sure I knew my money was no good there.

Law enforcement people generally hang out with law enforcement people. That's just the way it is. And, when I was on stage, they got to see who I was, what I did, and where I worked. We were no longer strangers. We were friends.

• • • •

When I do these presentations, one question comes up over and over. Being in law enforcement, it's actually something I've never thought too much about until I was asked.

The question is about handcuffing people we detain for mental health evaluations. This is a sensitive subject, obviously, and I'd like to explain what are generally two different views – those of law enforcement and those of mental health professionals.

We are speaking in generalities here, but officers often find themselves responding to a call that might involve mental illness. How we deal with people battling mental illness, ongoing stress, or trauma can affect their lives and requires a different mindset for officers.

Police officers are taught to directly manage every situation we are involved in. We have to be the ones in control making the decisions. We are trained to be direct, decisive, and fair. If things get out of hand, that's when injuries happen – to us, and to others.

Officer safety is always number one, and generally, that line of thinking works. But, when it comes to any sort of hostage event or negotiation, we need to change our thinking a bit. Trained negotiators are usually very good at this.

Beat cops, who usually don't have that training, can struggle. Mental illness calls require an officer to take a more gentle, low-key, patient, and flexible approach. How you speak to someone is critical in how the call will go. Your tone, rate, and volume are all extremely important.

When I worked with someone who was over the rail on the Bridge, I would do my best to establish rapport, using their name as often as possible – really personalizing the situation.

In those situations, people are often scared or embarrassed to come back over. They feel like they have done something wrong, and the thought of going to jail can be frightening.

I'll tell you how I worked around this. It is quite simple, but highly effective. Let's say the person on the Bridge is named Joe:

"Joe, I understand you're scared to come back over the rail. It takes a tremendous amount of courage to come back, to face everything again. I will tell you this, however; you will not be placed under arrest or taken to jail. That is my promise to you. You have done nothing wrong, Joe. What will happen is this: I will help you in getting back over the rail, and once over, I have to place you in handcuffs. This is my Department's policy. You will not be mistreated, thrown to the ground, or in any way abused. Joe, like I said, you will not be arrested or taken to jail. I do, however, have to take you to a local hospital for an evaluation."

If Joe decides to come back over, I assist him back, shake his hand, and reassure him his decision was the right thing to do.

I have never had an issue or complaint about handcuffing someone under these circumstances. I believe that's because I explain what's happening, and I keep my word.

But, after I retired and began traveling and speaking, I have heard resistance to this part of the call. I certainly understand the other side, that handcuffing can be seen as a scary or demeaning thing and can bring to mind images of straightjackets.

I have heard from civilians and mental health professionals alike that handcuffing leaves a person angry and confused – two things you don't want someone who is suffering mental illness to be, especially if they have just considered harming themselves.

But, handcuffing is the right thing to do. It is the policy of most departments, and I believe it should be.

Let me give you an example. Most of the time, we in the CHP are working alone. Many of our cars do not have barriers inside, and when we arrest or detain someone, they are often placed in the front seat so we can watch them. If that person is handcuffed and seat belted properly, there is very little chance something bad can happen.

But, if they are not handcuffed, what happens if they change their mind halfway to the hospital? What happens if they hear voices telling them to jump from the car or to hurt the officer? Driving 65 miles per hour down the freeway is no spot to have that kind of confrontation. It's a danger – not just to the officer, but to everyone else on the road. Safety has to be our top priority.

I do understand the concerns about handcuffing those we believe to be suffering from mental illness, which is why I think it's so important to treat these subjects with care and respect. If the process of detention is thoroughly explained by an officer, it is in the best interests of everyone involved.

• • • •

I get nervous every time I speak, but this particular presentation was worse.

This was July 2014, at the Gaylord National Convention Center in Maryland for a mental health care symposium with two thousand professionals in the field. In attendance were psychiatrists, psychologists, social workers, school counselors, and everyone in between.

An hour or so before I went on, I felt like running away. What an intimidating crowd. The thought that kept me there was that the presentation was for everyone who has lost his or her life to suicide. I

Final prep before speaking at a mental health convention in Maryland in front of two thousand people in the summer of 2014. Man, I was nervous.

needed to be strong for them, so that maybe my stories could be used to help someone else.

This is why we all attend events like this, so we can share knowledge and keep our mental toolbox full of options we can use to help someone else. My turn came to go onstage.

If I can remember the first few sentences of my presentation, it usually it goes smoothly and my nerves ease a bit. I thought the speech went well, actually, but then came an issue I hadn't anticipated.

Ever see two thousand people all try to get out of a room at the same time? It's a fiasco. Add in that I was the one who had just presented and there were a lot of nice people coming up for a handshake or a hug or a question or a story.

That's always my favorite part of presentations, but on this particular day, I was supposed to do a live radio show in 15 minutes. I shouldn't have scheduled it like that.

I have to say, the mental health crowd is such a fine group. It is difficult for me to get on stage and spill my guts to people I don't even know. Hell, it's difficult to get on the stage with folks you do know. But, after I spoke, it felt like I was surrounded by friends and family I'd not seen in years.

Some were in tears, some were smiling, some wanted to take a picture. I'll never be one of those speakers who show up, talk for an hour, grab their check, and head out the door.

Speaking to folks after my presentation is therapy for me. I meet wonderful people and we bond.

So, I was a bit frustrated with myself for scheduling this radio show so soon after my presentation, but, hey, live and learn.

The radio interview was with Dr. Pamela Brewer. We talked about the need for more access for folks to get proper care, especially considering that one in four Americans are affected by mental illness. When we were finished, I headed back downstairs to a large room adjacent to where I had just spoken.

The room was set up with many booths, all relating in some form or another to mental health. As I walked around, people came up to me

This is the bracelet that Liz Sweet gave me after that talk in Maryland. Her son T.J. lost his life to suicide while in the Army.

and introduced themselves, took photos with me, and just chatted. Some thanked me for my story and wanted to share their own.

I saw a woman standing by herself, waiting for the crowd to thin. When it did, she walked over and introduced herself as Liz Sweet.

She removed an aluminum bracelet from her arm.

"I want you to have this," she said, handing it to me.

The bracelet was red and engraved with the words: "Sgt. Thomas J Sweet II, Bismarck, ND Army 11/27/03."

Her son, T.J., had died of an apparent suicide while in the Army. She had been wearing the bracelet ever since. T.J. was her only son and, from a very early age, wanted to be in the Army. But he had health issues growing up, so she really did not want him to go into the Army.

He was born with pulmonary stenosis, which is a fixed obstruction near the heart and pyloric stenosis that causes difficulty keeping food down. As he grew up, he also had ADD and a learning disability that doctors traced to his father's exposure to Agent Orange in the Vietnam War.

His junior year of high school, T.J. asked his mom to take him to the Army recruiting office. With T.J.'s permission, Liz mentioned her son's health issues. The truth is, she was hoping this would make him unfit for duty, but the recruiter said he could get waivers.

Fifteen months and five waivers later, T.J. was in the Army. He did his training at Fort Still in Oklahoma, and excelled. He even loved boot camp and felt like he'd found a home in the Army.

His first duty station assignment was in Fort Riley, Kansas, working on Paladin tanks. T.J. rose to the rank of Specialist Four in his first enlistment period, which lasted four years. After that, he re-enlisted, was deployed to Iraq, and was on the E-5 (Sergeant) promotion list.

One day, he argued with his supervisor and was told he would be recommended to be removed from the promotion list and was to move back to the enlisted barracks. The supervisor gave T.J. some time to move his belongings and told him to get to it.

T.J. walked away. About five minutes later, a gunshot was heard. They found T.J. in a stairwell. He was pronounced dead a short time later at the base hospital. An Army investigation determined T.J. killed himself.

Liz was very proud of her son and told me T.J. loved the Army. "He was a good soldier," she said. He would've done well if there had not been a personality conflict with his Staff Sergeant. This belief was substantiated by many emails from others who served with T.J.

"It's not that he shouldn't have served. It's that the chain of command should have been better trained to use his skills," his mother explained.

Liz works at a center for mental health services and is an instrumental figure for adolescents who are suffering. But, ever since her son's death, it's Liz who has been suffering. The day of T.J.'s death is as fresh now as when it happened.

Her giving me that bracelet was such an honor. She wore it on her own arm for so many years. I could barely speak, my eyes welling up so much I could hardly see. That bracelet will have a place of honor in my home, and my heart.

Most of us cannot even begin to imagine how Liz must feel, losing T.J. Unfortunately, the loss of a child occurs all too often. Moving on from that is one of the hardest things I can imagine.

I once heard a woman at a conference speak about losing her child to suicide at a young age and her sister to suicide a short time later.

"Suicide can be very toxic," she said, and she is so right.

Suicide is not a ripple effect, but a tsunami. We all have a part to play in suicide prevention to keep these tragedies from occurring.

18
A Survivor's Mission

I've mentioned that survival of a jump off the Bridge is extremely rare, believed to be just two percent. But now, I want you to hear from one of the fortunate few.

I worked Kevin Hines' case, though I can't say I really got to know him until after he jumped. Kevin will live the rest of his life with some physical pain and difficulties from the injuries he suffered that day. He has dedicated his second chance to promoting suicide awareness in general and in erecting a barrier on the Bridge to help prevent deaths.

I've mentioned the barrier but not in detail because I was not as involved in its inception as many others have been. Kevin helped lead that charge, and he can explain how it came to be better than I can.

Here, then, is that story in Kevin Hines' own words.

• • • •

I consider Kevin Briggs to be a true friend, a brother. He is a gifted storyteller, a patriot, and a sort of a logistical genius.

Kevin may not privately (or publicly) concur, but he has truly lived up to the title of being the "guardian" of the Bridge. More accurately, Kev was guarding those who came to the Bridge. He guarded each individual from themselves.

What you don't know, and what you may not be able to deduce from Kevin's many media appearances, is that he deals with his own personal and ongoing darkness on a daily basis. His inner turmoil has led and leads to terrible periods of depression, relationship struggles, and all-out emotional damage. Kevin is a suicide loss survivor and has dealt with close family members who have thought about killing themselves. He's been married and divorced, has two beautiful sons, and he lives and loves every day like it could be his last. In living through those harrowing times, Kevin has always maintained resolve and a powerful resiliency. He is his own breed of survivor. KB has always, and will always, pick himself up, dust himself off, and begin all over again.

He is full of a clear and earned bravado and is quick with a joke (often off-color). If you know him well, you realize it is part of his charm. He has what many people deem to be a very attractive quality. People are drawn to him, his handsome face, diligent fitness, and a grin you can spot from across the room. Some ladies have even made a point to tell me that he's got a twinkle in his eye. If you've ever had the pleasure of sitting beside him

Kevin Hines and me at an event at the University of Oklahoma where we were both speaking. Hines is a good friend. His work, story, and passion were instrumental in convincing the powers-that-be to construct a barrier that will save lives on the Bridge.

in conversation, you would immediately recognize his quick wit, charming tone, and obvious natural intelligence.

Kevin made his big break into public speaking after being invited to the TED2014 conference in Vancouver. His TED video has been watched nearly two million times. I have grown to know Kevy-Kev (as I call him) as a kindhearted man and a very methodical goofball. He never misses a chance to make fun of me or of himself.

· · · ·

As I write this, our latest journey was to eastern Australia. Australia as a whole has nearly 2,500 suicides a year. It is a place where the police officers are dealing with many forms of suicide, a place where construction workers are battling their inner critical thoughts, often leading to their self-demise.

We speak together about our connection to the Golden Gate Bridge and our connection to one another. Kevin happened to be the officer who handled my case when I jumped from the Golden Gate in an attempt to end my life due to my own mental illness.

Kevin was there in the hospital soon after I was wheeled in – strapped down, neck brace on with three shattered vertebrae, a sprained right ankle, and splinters of those shattered vertebrae lacerating my insides.

I was battered and mangled. My body was broken.

When he came to the hospital, Kevin was sure I would be in a body bag, zipped up, and ready for the morgue. Jumping off the Bridge is almost never survivable. My father was on his way to the hospital, too, and like Kevin, thought I was dead.

They found me limp, distorted, and heavily medicated. But they also found a fighting spirit, regained some time after my jump.

When Briggs walked in, he introduced himself to my father, who turned to me.

"Kevin," he told me, "shake this man's hand."

That's my good ol' dad. Tough exterior, serious as a heart attack, always pragmatic and proper. Gotta love him.

The medication still clouds my memory, but I'm told I reached my hand out and gave Briggs a surprisingly firm handshake. He spoke with my father, took some notes, and left the hospital. I would go on with my healing, and of course, KB would continue his work as a conduit that has beautifully altered the path of so many forever.

We would not meet again until a San Francisco State Senate Hearing on Mental Health. It was the first of its kind in San Francisco. Briggs received a proclamation from the California Assembly that day.

As I took the stage and began to speak, I caught Briggs, out of the corner of my eye, heading to the very back row of the theater. He sat alone. He was overpowered with emotion. Tears flowed from his eyes. Still in the CHP, that day he donned his uniform browns and bright blue bow tie. Even in it, the man remained stylish – the guy's got swag. When he came down after the speech, we shook hands, I said thank you and went in for a bear hug. Kev's not a natural hugger, but he was as moved as I was to finally reunite.

I am forever grateful to KB. His role in saving so many and his role in saving my life are two things I will hold onto forever.

Traveling with Kevin, I have come to be a victim of his ridiculous pranks, and often. I don't have many comebacks either, but I know that if I pull one on him, I better be prepared for ten in return. The man has come to know how much I am fascinated with, and equally terrified of, arachnids. Kev capitalizes on that fear on a regular basis. Actually, "regular" doesn't begin to describe it. More like as often as humanly possible.

The truth is that he does have an amazing way with people. Kev allows those who are in the depths of pain to experience a true release. When he spoke to people on the Bridge, he utilized active listening skills.

He and I both realize that we are so blessed to be given the opportunity to hear others shed such internal pain. We hear stories from so many around the world who to tell us, often for the first time, the things they are "really" going through. We've found that being strangers to these people while also sharing our souls with them provides a comfort. We hear things people haven't been able to tell their best friends, their parents, even their husbands or wives.

These interactions shine light on our natural instincts. Human beings are funny creatures. We are sadly so conformed to bullshitting ourselves, and each other. On a daily basis, people we know and love ask us the question, or a variation of the question: "How are you?"

This occurs at work, school, home, and elsewhere. Yet, we have molded it in our heads that we must go at this great big world alone. We tell ourselves that we are burdening those around us. We feel that letting them into our internal mental struggles and inner critical strife alienates us from them.

We tend to answer such inquiries with more politeness than honesty.

"I'm good."

"Fine."

"Can't complain."

In reality, a great deal of us sit in denial of our unstable mental reality. High levels of insecurity and immense feelings of shame and guilt follow us around from the moment we can comprehend what they are. The kind of guilt and shame a person experiences when a mild, moderate, or serious mental instability is present can be crippling. This self doubt is the deepest internal war people go through. But still we remain quiet. We stay silent. We are constantly lying to ourselves.

The people asking us how we are may honestly care and want a real answer, but this façade is so ingrained in all of us that people are usually ill-prepared for a truthful or even difficult answer.

• • • •

Kevin Briggs used to believe that a net or railing to prevent suicides on the Bridge was unnecessary. One fateful day, someone put it in terms he could understand: a net or a life. Upon that moment, his beliefs about the suicides from the Golden Gate Bridge changed forever.

He became an integral piece of the massive puzzle of dialogue in pushing for and approving a net. The net that would make stopping death at the Golden Gate Bridge a reality.

Yet, with all of the reporting on the topic of suicides at the Golden Gate Bridge, there are a few things missing from public reports on Kevin's life's work and the life of the Bridge. I explore the discrepancies in my documentary, titled *The Net: A City Divided.*

The film digs down and reveals a lot of mysteries. It explores the void in this tale. Over the period of the last 30 years, a narrative about these suicides is purposely left out of the continuous reports and past debates about raising the "rail."

It is crucial to the story of the Golden Gate Bridge Highway and Transportation District, often referred to as the Bridge Authority. To fill the void, we must head into the lies perpetuated within the district and other related agencies.

In particular, a former Golden Gate Bridge Public Information Officer instructed the Bridge Patrol to not talk about suicides at the Bridge, fearing it would lead to more deaths. She was instructed by her superiors to keep things quiet and out of the press when it came to the people dying off of the Bridge.

The Bridge Patrol was clearly encouraged to never speak about "the problem" – that's what they called the suicides – at the Bridge unless they had been authorized or were going to put a calculated positive spin on the story. Briggs said, "If you were asked about the rail or safety net by the press, you were instructed to refer the media to your superior." The media would take the referral and reach out to those superiors, who either did not respond or deflected the issue. Thus, the patrol and the general staff stayed quiet.

Regardless of such hurdles, the families who lost their loved ones to suicide off the Bridge were fighting day and night to raise the net. The issue of installing a physical prevention to suicides at the Bridge goes back all the way to 1939, just two years after the Bridge opened, when a group asked for fencing along the rails.

In 2004, Dr. Mel Blaustein, Director of Psychiatry at St. Francis Hospital in San Francisco, founded the Psychiatric Foundation of Northern California (PFNC). One of PFNC's goals was to raise a railing at the Bridge. They made some good strides between 2004 and 2006. Then, in 2006, PFNC merged causes and the BridgeRail Foundation (BRF) was formed. The small grassroots organization was co-founded by David Hull (who lost his daughter to the Bridge), Paul Muller (a businessman and engineer by trade), and my father Patrick Kevin Hines (a banker and economist who was devastated by my suicide attempt). My father felt like he had to act and had to do what he thought to be right. For a time, my dear dad was even the president of the BRF.

The organization blossomed in the next few years. Its directors and colleagues agreed that once they began, they would never give up their fight for justice and peace at the Bridge. #NoMoreNames is one of their Twitter campaigns advocating for not one more death at the Golden Gate Bridge. #MakeTheNetReal was another.

Between 2006 and 2010, BRF worked diligently for a barrier between the Bridge and those who were suicidal. In 2006, Eric Steel's documentary film *The Bridge* opened in New York's Tribeca Film Festival and then in the San Francisco Film Festival.

Steel's *The Bridge* is about the deaths at the Golden Gate Bridge and contains footage of people who died by suicide from the Bridge. It wasn't long after the movie that people from all over the world had an opinion about what should or shouldn't be done about raising a so-called suicide barrier. Steel's film shed light on a taboo subject and started a worldwide discussion about the Golden Gate Bridge. Today, the film still captivates audiences on nearly every continent. Screenings at major universities and conferences occur regularly.

During one memorable Golden Gate Bridge public board meeting, a former board member and previous head of the bicycle coalition stood in anger. She interrupted my father's allotted three minutes of testimony. She pointed at him with her finger and said "More people die from sedentary lifestyles than die of suicide!" It was such an irrelevant thing to say in the context of our discussion, so my father replied: "I like ice cream! Do you know how to roller skate?" The individual immediately responded with "That's preposterous!" My father looked straight into her eyes, pointed back at her and said, "So are you!"

At a separate board hearing, during my three minutes of testimony, I pointed out to the board that it was able to erect a barrier to the traffic lanes after a three-month old baby tragically fell from the Bridge after the stroller hit the curb on the walkway. They sealed that gap in less than three months without any public comment, consent, or outside funding requests. They did that because it was the right thing to do. And, after pointing this out to them, I asked why they wouldn't do the same for people who live with mental illness and consistently die by suicide there.

"Because that little girl was innocent!" a board member replied.

I thought that would be the response.

"So I am guilty?" I asked.

Silence.

The animosity between those fighting for a net and those fighting against it became clear. There was one point where a former Golden Gate Bridge Public Information Officer and I stood next to one another during a media interview at the Golden Gate Bridge parking lot. This individual blurted out, "No one's gonna mess with this Bridge! This is my bridge!" She was constantly exerting an abrasive and aggressive tone. She also used what many of us felt were intimidating verbal techniques to try and instill fear or intimidation upon those of us fighting against her. She wanted us to go away, and she wasn't the only one.

A group that called themselves "The Friends of the Bridge" responded to every public statement we made. They claimed that it would be devastating to the city of San Francisco if the rail or net was raised. Their basic argument was that it would ruin the aesthetics of the Bridge. I responded to one of their attacks with an editorial in a local paper:

"What are the aesthetics of a bridge compared to just one life...your mother, your father, your brother, your sister, your fiancé, your loved one, your son?"

It took a long time for things to turn in our direction, but we never wavered. Eventually, things seemed to shift. News report after news report showed the dedication of so many driven individuals, mental health organizations, groups, and foundations. Finally, we were gaining traction. The Bridge's board of directors were slowly swayed. Many came out in favor of the barrier.

Most notably were Tom Ammiano, a former Golden Gate Bridge director turned Assembly member and amazing human being, as well as philanthropist Janet Reilly. With others, they put their hearts and stature behind this effort.

All the while, at BRF, we met champions for the cause amongst the families who lost loved ones on the Bridge. We became the collective voice for this dream. We chose to go up against an agency that for so long turned a blind eye and pushed us aside. We did this, never gave up, and we prevailed.

Meanwhile, Golden Gate Bridge board director Dennis Mulligan worked serious overtime to help further the cause. His work was instrumental in the entire process.

During this up and down struggle, John Bateson, the director of the Contra Costa Crisis Center, wrote of the Bridge's public health problem in a book titled *The Final Leap*. Bateson's book is considered to be the definitive answer to why we needed a barrier. It perfectly expresses why reduction of access to lethal means saves lives. The book includes stories from Steel as well as current and former BridgeRail members, involved politicians, suicide prevention experts, and my father, who compares a barrier-less Bridge to a loaded gun in the middle of a psychiatric ward.

John Brooks, whose daughter Casey jumped off the Bridge and died, wrote a powerful biography of his life with his daughter and how he and his wife have suffered this great and immeasurable loss. The book is called *The Girl Behind The Door*. It is eye-opening and heartbreaking.

With all of this work being done and with so many working day and night toward change, things were bound to lean in our favor. Several notable politicians – most visibly senators Darrell Steinberg, Mark Leno, and Jim Beall – believed in our cause and lent their influence. That really helped us get the final piece of the $76 million needed to build the net, which was finally approved on June 27, 2014.

The board members voted unanimously to raise the net, committing to have it built within three years. What a victory for all involved. I cried, as did everyone behind me at the public hearing. Eve Myer, executive director of San Francisco Suicide Prevention and a tireless advocate for our cause, embraced me with tears.

There was an emotional overflow for a lot of us. Finally, we could say that more than two thousand people who jumped off the Bridge over the span of nearly eight decades did not die in vain. Within the next three years while the net is being built, about 200 or more people will die as a result of jumping off the Golden Gate Bridge unless the walkway is closed. The BRF fights for that cause now.

There was an immediate glaze in the eyes of the families who had already lost their children, husbands, wives, fiancés, and loved ones to the Bridge. Huge success and epic grief simultaneously overwhelmed us all. The feeling was palpable. Some looked up to the sky in prayer, others to the ground in awful emotional turmoil. All of our faces displayed tremendous pride and simultaneously, rather unbearable pain. It was something to be seen.

Today, we all feel such loss even more immensely. We all wish this could have been done decades ago.

But, now, we finally move forward and can reach our goal of zero suicides on the Bridge. In doing so, we will set a precedent for the rest of the world. One that makes people recognize that human beings suffering mentally and fighting with their brains don't "commit" suicide. They die by it.

19
The Fight for Awareness

It was the summer of 2006. I had a craving for sushi. There's this spot not far from my beat in San Francisco that I was trying for the first time, just me and a co-worker.

On this particular night, I sat on a stool at the sushi bar. My co-worker was to my left, and I put my motorcycle helmet on the stool to my right. About twenty minutes later, a man walked in and sat on the other side of my helmet.

It was Robin Williams.

Like most everyone else, I've loved so much of his work and always admired his talent and humor. *Mrs. Doubtfire* is one of my favorite movies, especially the scene at the pool where he chucks a piece of fruit and hits Stuart (Pierce Brosnan) in the back of the head – Robin goes on about it being a terrorist attack, a run-by-fruiting. Great stuff.

I thought about saying, "Hi." I debated it in my mind, actually, pretty much until the moment he walked out of the restaurant. Just to say, "Hello," just to tell him I appreciated his talent and his movies. I never did, though.

I've always thought of him as a friendly guy. I'd see him riding his bike across the Golden Gate Bridge from time to time, and when I'd say, "Hi," he'd always say, "Hi," back with a big smile on his face. At the restaurant, he was there to get his to-go order and get out, like anyone else, so I didn't want to disturb him. If I were him, that's what I would've wanted.

Some years later, I was as shocked as I'm sure you and everyone else was when the news hit that Williams had killed himself.

None of us ever know what's going on in someone's life or someone's mind, of course, but my shock about Williams' suicide wasn't that a famous movie star would be having personal problems. It wasn't that someone so funny could be in so much inner pain – it was much more personal than that.

What if I'd said, "Hello," to him that day? What if we'd gotten into a conversation? What if he'd asked me what I did for a living, and it sparked something in him?

I know it's highly unlikely that anything would have turned out differently. Trust me, I do. But there's always that chance. There's always the possibility that you can reach someone, but in order to do that, you must first make contact. And with Robin, I didn't.

Williams' suicide hit Americans hard, and that's fairly rare. As a nation, we don't like to talk much about suicide. Every now and then, when someone famous kills themselves – Williams, Kurt Cobain, Tony Scott, and too many others to name here – we're forced to confront an otherwise largely ignored problem.

Invariably, however, we go back to our regular routines soon enough and, if we're lucky, never think about suicide again until the next famous one hits the news.

That type of dismissal, I guess you could call it, isn't at all surprising. Suicide is a tragic, sad thing, and we'd all rather not think about it.

But there is something like a self-perpetuating feedback loop here. Part of why suicide continues to affect so many people worldwide is that we so rarely talk about it. We tend to hide it and hide from it – all of us do.

Those who suffer from mental illness and suicidal thoughts often don't tell anyone or seek help until it's too late. And those who lose loved ones from suicide often don't talk about their loss or how it happened. We ignore it, like it's not there.

We all have different ways of coping. I'm not here to tell anyone how they should grieve. But I do think that the stigma surrounding mental illness and suicide is part of the problem, a stigma perpetuated by a long-standing silence.

It's like anything else: How do we fix a problem if we don't first address it? And isn't the first step to solving a problem admitting that one, in fact, exists?

How will we ever dedicate the energy, focus, and compassion needed to confront a growing killer in our country and the world if we'd rather pretend there's no problem at all?

As tragic as it is that Williams took his own life, and as tragic as it will be the next time someone else does the same, we make the problem even worse by ignoring it, by avoiding hard, honest conversations about suicide.

· · · ·

The Golden Gate Bridge is one of the top sites in the world for loss of life to suicide. Forty people plummeting to their deaths every year is an awful number. That's forty people no longer with us, forty families grieving, and forty different groups of friends wondering what they missed, what they could have done.

Forty is a lot, but there are forty *thousand* suicides around the United States every year.

On the Bridge and elsewhere, on average, someone in America ends their own life every thirteen minutes.

In fact, more than twice as many Americans die by suicide than homicide, but which is more likely to make the local news?

There is an old saying that goes: "Don't tell me what's important to you. Show me what you spend your money on, and I'll tell you what's important to you."

The amount of focus, resources, time, and energy we spend trying to curb the homicide rate dwarfs anything we do to address suicide.

That's certainly understandable – to a point. Homicides are scary, and we all want to live in a world where we don't have to worry about or fear someone inflicting physical harm on us.

But suicide is scary, too.

Suicide is a silent killer, one we far too rarely see coming. It takes the lives of grade school teachers and drug addicts, of housewives and corporate executives, of brothers, of sisters, of friends. It takes the lives of men and women, gay and straight, rich and poor, black and white and brown. Far too often, it takes the lives of those who no one realizes are struggling.

Annual Suicides versus Homicides in the United States for 2013

Total* Deaths
*Excluding deaths where age was not stated

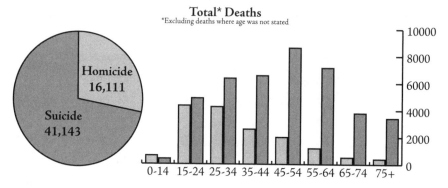

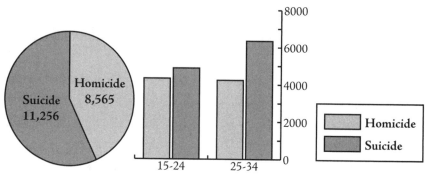

People are shocked to find out that suicide kills more Americans each year than homicide – and that it's not particularly close. In fact, the number of homicides per year decreased an average of 162 deaths from 2009-2013, where the number of suicides per year increased an average 1,084 deaths, that's 1,084 human lives lost to suicide. Something has got to change.
Data taken and compiled from the United States Centers for Disease Control 2009, 2010, 2011, 2012, and 2013 National Vital Statistics Reports; the latest available as of June 2015.

It is said that some 90 percent of those who take their own lives are suffering from some form of mental illness. The problem, of course, is that we often don't know who is suffering from mental illness until it is too late.

Research by *USA Today* finds that each suicide costs society about a million dollars in medical and lost-work expenses and emotionally victimizes an average of 10 other people.

Extrapolate that over a year, remembering there are roughly 40,000 suicides in the United States annually, and we're looking at $40 billion gone and 400,000 people trying to move on with their lives.

But, even with all that we lose, even knowing that this silent killer is around us, we do precious *little* to address this *massive* issue.

It doesn't have to be like this. At various points in the United States' history, we have decided that certain killers are worth our particular attention. And, when we do, those diseases and epidemics tend to diminish.

This has been done this with HIV/AIDS, breast cancer, and even homicide. We've never done it with suicide. Part of that is because of the misconception that if we stop someone from killing themselves today they will do it tomorrow or next week or next month instead.

But that's not true. The more we find out about suicide, the more it becomes apparent that we need to address this killer. Research shows that a significant majority of people who survive a suicide attempt never make a second attempt. Additionally, suicide disproportionately takes away our young people. It is the second leading cause of death among people ages 15 to 24.

Put those two facts together. When it comes to our teenagers and young adults, we *can* help them find decades and decades of productive life by recognizing the signs and helping them through a dark period.

There is a stigma around suicide, too, that it is what happens to drug addicts or alcoholics or soldiers with PTSD or people who "just went crazy" because of "bad things" that happened to them.

But that stigma simply isn't reality.

Thousands *upon thousands* of men and women have attempted suicide; men and women who may appear to be perfectly happy, perfectly healthy; men and women who wouldn't be around to be husbands and wives, fathers and mothers, sons and daughters, friends and colleagues had their attempt been successful.

Chances are that each of us will be affected by suicide at some point in our lives. For some, that means thinking about suicide, about going through a dark point in our lives and wondering if the world and those we love would be better off without us. For others, that means attempting suicide – some 750,000 Americans try to kill themselves every year.

For the most unfortunate, that means losing someone we love.

We can change this. We need to change this. We can save lives.

• • • •

Among those of us focused on suicide awareness and prevention, there is a hope that we are just on the cusp of an increased effort – even if the reasons are something we'd all much rather have never dealt with.

The wars in Iraq and Afghanistan have put a lot of attention on the brave men and women fighting for the United States. Americans are more sympathetic and supportive of their soldiers than ever before, specifically young men and women exposed to the brutal life-and-death stresses inherent in war.

These are true heroes. The sad truth about soldiers is that they don't always come back to us the same as when they left.

They experience the obvious and tragic physical danger – both in casualties and serious injuries. But they also often experience the mental toll that war takes from soldiers, including PTSD and a skyrocketing suicide rate.

Between 2004 and 2012, more than two thousand Army soldiers ended their own lives. More soldiers died by suicide than in combat. This is three times the previous suicide rate, and at some point in that time period, the suicide rate among soldiers surpassed the rate for civilians for what is believed to be the first time in history.

That spike in numbers has helped drive attention and resources toward tracking, learning about, understanding, and hopefully preventing future suicides. Since 2005, the military has put more than $150 million into suicide research. That the problem has impacted our soldiers so heavily has inspired others – individuals, corporations, and non-profits – to look more deeply and with more compassion at suicide as well.

This is a critical time for the fight against suicide. The Army and the National Institutes of Health (NIH) are teaming up on a $65 million study that will cover thousands of troops over several years to better understand suicidal tendencies.

Their research could be a breakthrough on many levels. For starters, it's a recognition from the NIH – the United States' biggest funder of research – that suicide is a more worthy cause than its past levels of funding would indicate.

Depending on how you calculate it and which organizations you follow, suicide research has actually been shrinking in recent years, even as research and resources for less prolific killers – vehicle accidents, for example – continue to rise. I'm obviously not advocating against efforts to make our roads safer or anything else that saves lives. What I am advocating for is raised awareness about the growing suicide problem.

The fact that an effort to support soldiers dealing with suicidal thoughts is leading to more research and understanding of suicide is very exciting for those of us working to promote suicide awareness. I hope it will help save lives in the future – maybe even someone you know.

There is just so much we can learn, and there has never been a study like this before. I hope this and future research can find out how genetics play into depression or suicidal thoughts as well as how suicidal thoughts manifest into action, and so much more.

The joint effort between the Army and the NIH may be our best hope right now. Their focus is on soldiers, and there are surely some aspects of their research that will be inapplicable to civilians, but for the most part, I think what's found will be of use to everyone.

It's frustrating that we haven't had more attention and public sentiment to address and prevent suicide, but it's starting to change now, which is all that matters.

• • • •

There is much about suicide that researchers are still trying to learn. There is even more that we want the general public to understand.

Priority one: getting people to realize just how prevalent the problem is.

Suicide's stigma makes it dangerous. It becomes easy for those who deal with it to feel alone and easier still for those who haven't dealt with it to feel like they never will. Both uniquely intimate as well as deceivingly distant, suicide's stigma is part of what has made it into such a pervasive silent killer.

Ironically, because we are selfish creatures by nature, the more we understand the scope of suicide – the more we understand that this is something we or someone we love may deal with – the more we will work to fight it.

But, until we can raise awareness, suicide will remain a major problem worldwide.

People tend to think of teenagers and soldiers when they think of suicide, but did you know that the most common victim of suicide is a white male, age 45 to 65? It used to be elderly males who were most at risk, but they've been surpassed by this younger demographic.

Research shows that suicide affects the rich and the poor and everyone in between. Women attempt more suicides, but men die by suicide more often.

Suicides account for more gun deaths than homicides and accidents combined.

"The science has been bursting at the seams the last ten to twenty years, and especially the last decade," says Christine Moutier, chief medical director for the AFSP. "I think it's at a point where the science has shown us enough that we have actionable things, but the lay understanding is way behind, and that's partially due to stigma."

There's a powerful and important book called *The Invisible Front*, written by Yochi Dreazen with the help of Mark and Carol Graham, a couple from Kentucky who lost both of their sons to tragedy.

Their oldest son, Jeff, was killed by an IED (improvised explosive device) in Iraq in 2004. The state legislature passed a resolution praising him. A packed arena cheered when his face was shown on the scoreboard at a college basketball game. His funeral procession was decorated by friends and strangers alike waving American flags.

Mark and Carol's younger son, Kevin, killed himself just the year before. His aunt didn't even want the funeral at a local church. According to the book, Mark and Carol heard from members of the community that their son was "a weakling, a coward, and even a sinner."

The book sends a powerful message about the stark contrast and double standard we have in our country. The family has said they lost their boys to different enemies, but we're still trying to get the broader public to see it that way.

Eliminating that stigma through education and understanding is so important. Hopefully, as research continues to show that suicide risk factors include biological components – as well as psychological components and past history – the public will begin to see that mental illness is a lot like physical illness, whether it presents obvious symptoms or not.

Think about it this way: You wouldn't judge someone for having the biological chemical imbalance that leads to diabetes, so why should anyone judge someone for having a biological chemical imbalance that leads to depression?

Or, perhaps, like this: Why is being overweight so much more acceptable than having a mental illness? Both are conditions often brought on by a combination of biological factors and behavior, and yet one is readily discussed and openly dealt with in public, while the other lurks in the shadows and dark corners of victims' minds.

Despite this being a "back burner" issue for much of the public, research has shown that one in four Americans will suffer from a mental health condition, either temporarily or chronically. That's more Americans suffering from a mental illness than are physically disabled and more than twice the rate of any form of cancer.

Yet, of those who suffer a mental health condition, only one in five will seek professional help for it. We have to improve that. Ninety percent of those who die by suicide have a diagnosable mental illness at the time of their death, which means that many could have been helped.

There is an interesting history of how Americans have dealt with various diseases that is relevant to suicide awareness.

Fifty years ago, people didn't talk much about cancer. Thirty years ago, people didn't talk much about HIV/AIDS. Twenty years ago, people didn't talk much about Alzheimer's. In each case, education and outreach helped the general public understand and ultimately fight these prolific killers.

With increasing research, let's hope the same can finally be done with mental illness.

"Mental health issues are the final public health crisis in the closet, so to speak," says John Madigan, vice president of public policy for AFSP.

One example of the struggle for awareness can be found in the automobile industry. Rearview cameras are much more common now and will be required in all new cars by 2018. That's the result of a wonderfully organized and powerful coalition made up largely of parents who lost young children in horrific accidents that could have been easily prevented with this type technology.

There is a similar effort to get Congress to require automatic shutoffs for cars. This would help prevent up to 800 deaths a year from people who kill themselves by running their cars in the garage. The technology would cost about $20 per car – which is about one-tenth of one percent of the average sticker price of a new car.

One of the forms of resistance to the automatic shutoff is the misconception that if we prevent someone from killing themselves with the car in the garage that they will instead kill themselves by some other means.

Research directly contradicts that assumption.

Again and again, in different ways, we find that suicide is largely an impulse. If we can help block that impulse, we can give people second chances at life. Studies that follow people who survive medically serious suicide attempts show that, even decades later, 90 percent of them are still alive.

That means that, in an overwhelming majority of cases, if we can stop someone from killing themselves today, we can help them live a productive life tomorrow.

There is a suspension bridge in the United Kingdom called the Clifton Suspension Bridge that had a high suicide rate before a barrier was installed in the late 1990s. The results were amazing. Not only did the suicide rate at that bridge drop dramatically, but there was no rise in the suicide rate of a similar bridge nearby, and no rise in suicides by other means. In fact, the suicide rate for the entire region dropped after the suicide barrier was installed.

We're hoping that the suicide barrier at the Golden Gate Bridge can have a similar affect. Think of all the good we can help create – up to 40 or more people every year given a second chance at life.

It's imperative that we're able to reach people in their darkest moments.

"There's a timing element," Moutier says. "The impulse and strong urge, the desperation, peaks and lasts on the order of minutes to a couple of hours.

That's an important message to get out there. A lot of people think suicide can't be prevented, because it's a random act, so how could you prevent it?

"Or they think that if someone wants to kill themselves, they'll find a way to do it no matter what. That's just not true. These key moments of intervening can absolutely reduce suicide rates overall in a population."

• • • •

I mentioned the military earlier, and the data collected there will be an enormous help for us.

One of the interesting findings so far is that of the soldiers who have killed themselves, many had undiagnosed and unnoticed mental health conditions when they enlisted. It wasn't the military that necessarily pushed these people. In fact, most of the soldiers who kill themselves had never been in a war zone. The research actually suggests that repeated placements in war zones may actually help with resilience.

That means the more research learns about soldiers who have suicidal thoughts or actions, the more we'll know about mental illness in general.

Like I said, there's still so much to find out. I asked Moutier what she would do if she could only do one thing to address to this complex issue. Her answer is telling.

She explains that her choice would be a way to address what we refer to as access to lethal means. People often assume that refers to firearms, and that's part of it, but it's more than that. We're talking about bridge barriers, the automatic shutoffs for cars, trigger locks on guns, and pill bottles that could help deter overdosing by making it harder to dispense potentially lethal medication in bulk.

This goes back to a fact that both goes against what many think about suicide and is at the core of what we try to do in prevention.

It's the idea of timing. That's one of the most important things that we're trying to dispel, not only to educate people, but because it can help save lives.

There are so many people who survive serious suicide attempts and then go on to lead happy, productive, long lives. It doesn't mean they don't ever get sad or depressed or ever think about attempting suicide again. But it does mean that for a lot of people, we can give them a life full of light and love.

That's one of the reasons I try to promote hope above all. Hope can get us through so much. Hope can get people through that dark time because hope means better times may be on the way.

When I'm on the Bridge, I don't try to fill people with any illusions. I don't tell them I can fix all of their problems or that coming back to my side of the Bridge will mean they'll never again have feelings of depression. But I do know – not only from the research, but also from my own experience – that if I can convince them to just give it one more day, they're highly likely to give it much more than that.

If you talk to people who've survived serious suicide attempts, you start to see this resilience in action. A lot of them don't even remember what drove them to the brink, or if they can, they don't understand why they came so close to killing themselves.

Mental illness is as real as it is misunderstood, and I'm not here to tell you that even those of us who dedicate large portions of our lives to educate ourselves know it all.

One of the problems we run into is that we rely on self-reporting way too much. Someone asks, "Are you thinking of taking your own life?" And then, depending on the answer and the interpretation from the clinician, it's categorized and addressed. This is where the science can begin to help us.

Already, we know that much of what the general population thinks of suicide just isn't true. One of the biggest challenges we have is simply promoting awareness because many of the misunderstandings people have make it harder to talk about, study, and address suicide and depression.

The research from the military and other sources will help change misconceptions and public perception. So will the unfortunate experiences of more and more people dealing with these challenges.

In the meantime, we can all continue to spread the message that those who suffer from mental illness aren't alone. The problem is often biological, not unlike many physical diseases. There is help available.

I think we're making progress breaking the stigma and raising awareness, although there's a lot more work to do. I hope this book helps.

20
Hope

September is National Suicide Prevention Month – a very busy time for those of us in the mental health field. This is also the time colleges, mental health commissions, radio and broadcast networks, as well as a host of others focus on suicide prevention. Having a month dedicated to the cause gives us an important chance to reach people each year. It is an opportunity we all try hard to take full advantage of.

During September 2014, I was traveling all across the United States doing presentations. I even did a Skype keynote from my home to a mental health commission in Australia.

You can imagine how strange that felt, sitting in the place I'm more familiar and comfortable with than anywhere in the world, talking to strangers on the other side of the planet. I remember a good friend saying to me, "If I was asked to do that, I would be in my underwear just wearing a nice shirt. How are they going to know the difference?"

I knew better. Somehow or another, I would be discovered and then embarrassed beyond belief, I'm sure, sitting there in front of strangers in my underwear. That's just how things go for me.

Anyway, one of my events was held at the University of Oklahoma. I was speaking to 400 or so college students, teachers, counselors, and really anyone in the community who wished to attend. I spoke for an hour or so and then opened the floor up for questions. I have found that very few people ask questions in this type of setting. They're nervous, or don't want to be first, or don't feel comfortable speaking up on such a sensitive topic in front of so many strangers.

After a few generic questions were asked and it seemed there would be no more, I thanked everyone for attending and announced I would be available in the lobby if anyone would like to speak with me one on one.

This is actually my favorite time. You see, when I'm on stage, I tell stories about my personal life and things that have occurred in my careers with the Army, corrections, and the CHP. I really bare my soul to folks, and the one on one time afterward allows them the opportunity to do the same if they'd like.

On stage, I talk about mental illness and how to communicate with someone who may be in crisis.

There are specific reasons I talk about myself in these settings. First, I truly believe in being an example. If I cannot talk about all that has occurred in my life, including my depression, how could I possibly expect someone else to do the same?

Second, I want to show that anyone – and I mean anyone – can have mental illness. It may appear that everything is great with me. I look healthy and am somewhat fit, but deep inside, I have suffered and still do from time to time. Seeing people who appear to have their lives together talk openly of struggling with mental illness can do wonders for a person's willingness to share.

Sometimes, people who have never talked about depression to anyone feel comfortable opening up to me after these talks. It's such an honor to hear their stories and, hopefully, give them a little help and a little hope.

Well, the lobby at OU was crowded with folks, some leaving and others forming a sort of line to see me. As I previously mentioned, this is my favorite time. It's a chance, although brief, to bond with new friends, to cement the fact that we are our brother's keeper and are here to help one another.

There was one gentleman who purposely waited to be the last one to see me – let's call him Mike. As he approached, I could see his eyes watering up. He introduced himself and asked if I had a few minutes to talk.

"Of course I do," I said.

Mike was 25 years old, clean cut, wearing jeans, a t-shirt, and a jacket. Just your normal, average guy.

As Mike began to tell me his story, he started to cry. I took my eyes off of him and scanned the area for a more private place. I asked Mike to walk with me, and I began checking doors in the auditorium, finally finding one that was unlocked. Mike and I then had privacy in a small utility room.

The first thing I told Mike was that I am not a clinician, counselor, or psychologist. Actually, there were counselors still at the event. I told Mike this and offered to introduce him. He wanted nothing to do with that. It was easy to see this was not just someone who wanted to say "Hi" or "Thank you." Mike had a lot on his mind.

He thanked me for my presentation and said he too had been in the Army, just as I was. He told me about his time in combat, about the horrible and traumatic things he'd seen firsthand. The devastation, the firefights.

I wanted to keep him talking, for him to feel comfortable unloading whatever was on his mind, so I didn't ask questions about his experience right away. He came to this auditorium and waited all this time to talk to me for a reason, so instead, I asked what steps he'd taken after his discharge regarding his own mental health.

Mike told a story that's been the topic of so many conversations recently, from the White House to rural America. His nightmares about what he had done in combat and what he had seen overseas ate at him. Mike did not come out and say it, but there are code words and terms people in the service often use. It was obvious to me that he had been forced to take lives, at least one of them a child's.

He saw the horrors of war up close, and tragically, he felt forced to be part of that horror. Kill or be killed. You have to change the way you look at things to survive in that world, and it's hard to change back. We all have a self-preservation mode, but that is for a short term "fight or flight" matter, not a constant existence. Not a way of life.

The cortisol levels that build up in the body during these extensive times of stress are quite damaging. Sustained high levels of cortisol can destroy healthy muscle and bone, can slow healing, impair mental function, and weaken the immune system.

Mike had been to VA hospitals many times, but the lines were long. When he did get to see a doctor, their meeting would last only a few minutes and he would only be prescribed medication to help him sleep and cope with his nightmares. They were not treating the disease. They were treating symptoms, which wasn't getting him *real* help. Meaningful conversations did not take place. That silence, that half-hearted, uninvested "help," can leave a man feeling empty.

Mike was living with his girlfriend, and their relationship was strained. Money was an issue, as they both had jobs that paid just minimum wage. His mother, who lived in the same town, did her best to support him, both financially and emotionally.

But then there was his stepfather, who would belittle him and tell him to get his act together. His stepfather had not been in the service, had no empathy for him, and thought Mike was faking all of this to get attention. His story was heartbreaking to hear. With all we know about mental illness – particularly all the attention given to soldiers fighting PTSD – for a family member to treat someone like that was simply appalling.

Mike was sobbing so much it became difficult to understand him at times, but I heard every word of what he was trying to tell me. I listened.

"I'm hardly ever happy anymore," he confessed. "If this is how it's going to be, I don't want to be here."

I placed my hand on his shoulder and told him to raise his head and look at me. This is something I've used with good results to get people to calm down and clear their minds.

"Listen to my breathing and follow it," I directed calmly. "Match it as you think of a time in your life when all was right. Close your eyes and think of a time in your life when you were really happy."

I began taking long breaths in through my nose and exhaling through my mouth. As he mimicked my breathing pattern, he regained his composure after several minutes. Mike opened his eyes and stared at me briefly.

"Thank you, sir," he said. "That was more than the VA ever did for me. There's one doctor there who I really like, but he was transferred to another hospital somewhere."

"There are many people out there just like me, willing to listen and help," I reassured him. "I know it doesn't seem like it all the time, with long lines at the VA and jackass stepfathers to deal with, but there is real help out there for people."

I really wanted Mike to see a counselor that evening and reiterated that I was not a trained therapist. I told him how concerned I was. I didn't think he was a risk to hurt himself that night, but this was definitely a man who could use some help. Counselors were at this auditorium, willing to speak with him. Maybe we could help him find a program or other assistance.

He asked how much it would cost. I said, "It's totally free and confidential."

He thought about it for a moment then agreed. Mike asked if we could keep in contact. We exchanged emails and now keep in touch every so often.

He seems to be doing better and is seeing a private therapist his mother is paying for. He makes a conscious effort to avoid situations that cause him direct grief, such as seeing his stepfather. He hopes that will mend some day.

His hope is what encourages me most about his progress. Hope is what brings us back.

• • • •

In my travels across the world, I am asked over and over again a myriad of questions with regard to hope and happiness.

Two examples I hear most often are "How can I be happy?" and "How can I have hope when I have nothing and no one loves me?"

For eons, humans have asked these questions of themselves and of others. As many times as these questions have been asked, there have been as many people trying to answer them. Do we have a predisposition for success, failure, happiness, sadness, good health, or madness?

Ask a hundred doctors or philosophers, and you will get a hundred different views. Our brains are amazing. We can fill chalkboards with calculations and travel to the stars, but miss the amazing colors of a butterfly in our own backyard. Each of us is unique and special in our own way.

The events, circumstances, feelings, emotions, and actions that prompt one person who loses their life to suicide may be nothing to someone else – just another day in their life. Some have seen, experienced, and felt misery so often and for so long that they are now accustomed and numb to it.

We all seem to have a "point of no return" where the wrong number of wrong circumstances occur simultaneously and continuously, creating the potential to send us spiraling downward. Whether those circumstances ever occur may or may not even be up to us. But what is certainly up to us is how we handle those circumstances.

In my ongoing quest for knowledge, I came across this beautiful quote: "Sometimes I can hear my bones straining under the weight of all the lives I'm not living." It's from an American fiction writer named Jonathan Safran Foer in his book *Extremely Loud and Incredibly Close*.

For me, I find this quote profound, and a truer statement regarding mental illness than most I have seen. In thinking about my own life, I ask myself these questions at times:

+ *Why are so many people accomplishing so much while I sit here wasting my days away?*
+ *Am I truly weak in spirit and will?*

These questions, though somewhat dark and heavy, actually fuel me forward.

I think a lot of us can relate to this, the pressure of accomplishment and the disappointment of not achieving success in a traditional or measurable way. It's easy to read or hear about others' success and assume their lives must be so fulfilling because of an award or business deal and that ours deflate in comparison. But it's important to remember that we all have successes and we all have struggles. The temptation to measure ourselves against others is both constant and dangerous, particularly when we don't know what someone else is going through.

I have been asked two extremely crucial questions, often during pivotal points in people's lives:

"What does a person do who loses all hope?" and "If there is no hope, why go on?"

The truth is, there is no one answer. All answers are unique.

The personal connection you make with someone struggling through a particularly hard time can make all the difference for them. Lead the connection with your heart and empathy. Egotistical involvement will only undermine what you are trying to accomplish. My experience has been to use my own life experiences as well as the individual's experience to develop a plan.

For instance, I once spoke to a well-to-do businessman on the Bridge, over the rail, crying and scared to his wit's end. He'd been successful for many years but had recently made some poor money management decisions that didn't go his way.

He felt ashamed and embarrassed about telling his customers and family. His wife worked, and they needed both incomes. He shared several of his "hopeless" stories with me. No longer would his children go to private schools. The family home was in foreclosure status. The new Mercedes Benz was two months delinquent in payment.

He thought suicide was his best option. In his mind, he was a failure. But this was all based on material possessions. I asked him if he thought his marriage was based on love or material objects. He replied, "Love."

With a calm voice and looking directly in his eyes, I asked, "If your wife lost her job or your child failed a class and was up here as you are, contemplating suicide, what would you say to them?"

I asked him to think about it for a few minutes before answering. He answered, "I don't have to think about it. I would tell them how much I love them, how important they are in my life, and how much I would miss them."

I didn't even have to say anything in reply. The silence sat between us for a brief time. Sometimes, all you have to do is help someone look at a situation from a different perspective.

I told him it's not about being right or wrong, it's about recognizing what life is about. Empathy and humanity are powerful in communicating with those in crisis.

Communicating with someone in distress is a multifaceted task. Is the person in fact suicidal? Or, on the other spectrum, are they anxious about an upcoming test or work-related issue and need a break to collect themselves?

I'll say it again: There are no tricks or magic here. I have seen with my own eyes those struggling with terminal cancer. When alone, they weep deeply. I did when I had cancer as a very young man. I should have been rejoicing about just graduating high school, entering the United States Army, and beginning my adult life.

The person facing death is scared. They are angry. They are confused. *Why me?* is asked over and over again in their minds.

If the person is spiritual, they may be angry at the deity they believe in. *What will happen to my family? What's really on the other side, and is there another side?*

But, the very second friends or family are around, they summon great courage to greet them, smile, and chat. Their fleeting hope for some miracle cure is fading day-by-day and hour-by-hour, as is their life, but their courage becomes stronger and undying. They have, in essence, passed the hope for themselves on to their friends and family.

This spiritually transposed hope can help create a new healthy, happy, and successful life. In essence, it is motivation to live a life for loved ones. I know my mom was petrified of her death. She would talk about it to our family priest and my father. But, to us kids, she showed no signs of despair. That's not what she wanted us to feel or what she wanted us to remember. She was protecting us, so all we saw was joy and hope.

So, with regard to the question, "If there is no hope, why go on?" I say this: I agree. It can be grueling to go on without hope. But I will then disagree with their hope being gone. My interpretation of hope is that it is our driving force – a reason to get out of bed – a chance to make our lives better, to help others, to make a difference.

We all experience bad moments in some form or another. They could last for days, weeks, or even years. Our hope is that they pass and do so quickly. I say this not as someone who has no knowledge of mental illness and the wrath it can have on a person, but rather as someone who has clinical depression and continues to struggle.

I've mentioned my depression several times. Here, I'd like to take a minute to talk about it in more detail, to provide one humble example of a flawed human being seeking his way through depression with hope.

• • • •

When I present to people, I stress the importance of expressing your honest feelings and emotions. If I cannot set the example and begin with myself, how can I possibly ask anyone else to do the same?

I want to be clear about something first, though. I want this book to help others, and I firmly believe that when you're trying to help someone you need to always remember that it is about them, not you. So, I don't bring up events in my life when engaging other people who may be struggling, unless they refer to it in some way, or ask directly.

But, in the interest of opening up, I think it is important for me to share my struggles. I've touched on my depression in bits and pieces, but I want to put it all together to provide a clear picture.

As it turns out, I was something of an easy target for depression.

We know that what causes mental illness is quite complex and can be any one or a combination of many factors.

There is a hereditary factor. If your parents have struggled with mental illness, that can raise your risk factor.

Environment plays a role, too. Major life changes such as losing a job, divorce, or death in the family. For kids, this could be changing schools, lacking friends, being bullied, being cut from a sports team, or missing an academic achievement.

Along those lines, physical health problems like cancer, diabetes, stroke, and heart disease can trigger depression. People who suffer traumatic brain injuries have been shown to have higher risks as well as people who suffer singular traumatic experiences like rape.

There are other causes, of course, but for the purposes here, let me recap some events in my own life that I believe triggered or at least made me more vulnerable to mental illness.

My grandfather lost his life to suicide. I was diagnosed with testicular cancer at age 20, requiring three surgeries and several months of chemotherapy. My mom died of cancer at 49 when I was 26. I was in a head-on motorcycle wreck at 38, which left me with a concussion and some memory loss. I had heart surgery at 45 and was divorced at 46.

Throughout all of this, I had what I came to refer to as "poor mental health days." These could be isolated or they could come in bunches. I never knew when it would hit me or, scarier for me, how long the wave of depression would last.

These are times I was not feeling like myself or, really, like anyone I wanted to be. I would isolate myself, covering my day with my own sadness. This came and went throughout my life, so much that I came to think of it as part of who I was.

It wasn't until I was 46 that I really began to feel the symptoms and realize that I might be depressed. I know that my depression started before my divorce, but I didn't really feel "down" until my wife and I split.

My depression has never been like what you might see in a movie or on TV. I could go to work or other engagements, participate, and be quite functional. I don't know why this was, really. I think it was just the understanding that I had to work, that I had bills to pay, that I had kids to take care of. I could put a good face on, in other words.

But, when I was at home, on my own time, and without the benefit of distraction, I often couldn't avoid the devastation. The best way I can think to describe it is that my body felt like lead. Everything was heavy, everything difficult.

I struggled to do even mundane, everyday tasks, like putting away dishes or mowing the lawn. It's strange when I describe this now because it all sounds so obvious. I think this is how depression often sounds to those fortunate enough to not feel it personally, but for a lot of us who struggle with the disease, it can start to feel ubiquitous and impossible to get away from – like a blanket, slowly smothering you.

Compared to my parents, grandparents, and others of their generation, my life has been a relative cakewalk. Fighting cancer was tough, sure, and the months of treatment were agonizing. My heart surgeries were scary, but relatively simple enough to get through after the initial trauma of the diagnosis. But, it wasn't like fighting your way onto the beaches of Normandy or Iwo Jima, seeing your buddies cut in half by enemy fire. It wasn't like I was living through the Depression when Americans huddled in lean-tos and starved, quite literally, to death. Why I should feel privileged enough to be depressed was a question I asked often but could not answer. And the knowledge that I should not be feeling this way only exacerbated the downward spiral.

Those thoughts aside, my depression was complicated because I was accomplishing things when I wasn't home. Out in the world, I was "normal." It was just at home that I felt so alone and inadequate.

One day, I finally had an epiphany. *Why am I feeling like this? I'm getting nothing accomplished in my life while others are checking off items on their bucket list, having family barbecues, generally living and loving life.*

This depression had gradually manifested itself and basically taken over my life. Being able to see it and realize how much of my life had been given over to this disease convinced me to finally see a doctor.

I liked this man from the start. He was open, fair, smart, and patient. Each and every time I've seen him, he's asked what concerns me, and then addresses everything I've brought up in a helpful, non-judgmental way. I know that our conversations have been for me to feel better, not for him to show off how smart he is – which isn't always the case in mental health, I've unfortunately come to learn.

So, I opened up to him about how I'd been feeling – like my body was made of lead. He asked a few questions and had me take a written test which included a dozen or so questions regarding my feelings and emotions during the past few weeks. I answered as honestly as I could and gave him back the test.

He left the room and came back a few minutes later.

"Kevin," he said. "Based on this test and your history, I believe you have depression. How do you feel about this?"

I can't say I was surprised at what he told me, but I answered with sarcasm, one of my coping mechanisms.

"Well, Doc," I quipped, "I guess it makes me feel depressed."

He went on to say he felt medication may be good in my case. We spoke for a while longer, and I left that day with a prescription.

Nothing changed for me immediately. That's not how it works with mental illness. It wasn't until about six weeks later that I began to feel the effects. That's a normal lag time for the drug I was prescribed. Sometimes, people think medication should be a quick or even instant fix, which is why they often stop taking it before it has a chance to work, but when I was fighting cancer, the chemo drugs took a month or more to kick in, so I knew I needed to be patient.

This time, with medication for my depression, it was a very subtle change. My mood improved. I found myself whistling songs as I drove my car, showered, or mowed the lawn. I can't point to a particular breakthrough moment. The change was so gradual I honestly didn't even notice at first. But, when I realized one day that I was more relaxed, it was such a nice feeling.

It wasn't like I was laughing and acting like a clown all day, just that I felt happier and not so heavy. To this day, I continue to self-monitor and have conversations with my doctor to make sure I am on the right path.

I must stress to you that medication is not for everyone. It has worked for me, but we are all different and have unique brain chemistry. Whether prescription medication is right for you or not must be a decision made in conjunction with your doctor.

With my story, what I want to stress most is that I got help – and things got better.

I understand that I will, in fact, have both good and bad times in my life. But, sometimes, in my worst moments, understanding that fact is very hard to remember and process.

As bad as my depression may get, the joy of watching my kids play sports, make the honor roll, laugh out loud at a silly joke I tell, or respond to a hug keeps me going.

• • • •

Unfortunately, it is very easy for anyone to tell you "Have patience, it's going to get better" or "Give it some time. It'll pass." When you are going through a bad time, though, these are not the words you want or are willing to hear.

Another phrase I hear often is "Suicide is a permanent solution to a temporary problem."

I don't agree with this at all.

I agree that suicide is a permanent solution, but I do not agree with "temporary problem." If a person is diagnosed with a mental illness, it may be with them for life. There are medications, therapies, and other strategies that can greatly help with the symptoms, but the illness may still lurk in the background. It can be a lifelong issue, one often requiring daily monitoring, proper nutrition, medication (if deemed appropriate by a physician), and a host of other checks and balances.

It sounds daunting, but I promise, the work put into staying mentally healthy is worth the time spent with family and friends, enjoying the beauty around you. It's also important to understand the problem and what's required to solve it. That's the only way we can win this fight.

The beauty of life always surrounds us, but occassionally, we simply fail to see it. We get caught up in trying to keep up with our neighbors, trying to make others happy, or being so busy stressing out over the day-to-day details we all face that we forget to take a "timeout" for ourselves.

It's important to remember that these "timeouts" look different for each person. Taking a walk, surfing the net, cooking, getting up for the sunrise, being still and just breathing.

For me, I believe in taking charge of myself and starting each day fresh. The mistakes I made yesterday are just that – yesterday. I learn from them and move on the best I can.

There are still some days when my depression makes me feel like I am in a deep hole. It's difficult to breathe and I'm surrounded by darkness. Yet I know in the depths of my soul that I will get out. When I'm in that hole, it is easy to forget how beautiful the world is around me. However dark, there's a ladder somewhere in that black hole. That ladder was tossed down by all my family and friends.

This is the value and importance of hope. It's there, just waiting for me to take hold and climb up. It is up to me to grab it and make that first move. When I do and make my way out of that hole, sunlight and friendly faces surround me. I smell the fresh air, scents like lavender, pine, and the burning wood of a campfire. Sounds of children playing, and a warm breeze in my face. All familiar and welcomed. Each and every breath after I grab that ladder brings back fond memories and helps me prepare for the next time darkness may fall upon me.

So – how do we approach and talk to someone we think needs help with a personal crisis? Someone who usually has a smile on their face, is friendly and outgoing, but recently has been disengaged with friends, family, and society? A person who seldom drank, but now is partying every night like a rock star? The individual who was at the top of their class in school, but now is failing in several classes?

I took the boys to Lake Tahoe for the Fourth of July 2014. If you're going to celebrate the Fourth of July, you might as well do it with hats. Moments like these are my ladder.

We need to be able to communicate with a person in distress or crisis in a manner which does not humiliate or disrespect them.

• • • •

As I've said, I had no formal training when I began working the Bridge. It was years before I actually obtained specialized training in negotiations.

But, even with that training, the ability to adapt is most important. Being prepared for atypical situations is what allows us to be more effective, more efficient in our thoughts and actions, and – consequently – more likely to achieve a positive outcome.

Take U.S. Airways flight 1549, piloted by Captain Sully

Sullenberger, for example. He piloted the AirBus A320 that left LaGuardia Airport on Jan. 15, 2009. Three minutes after takeoff, the plane struck a flock of geese, causing failure of both engines. If not for the ongoing training Capt. Sullenberger had received, I highly doubt he would have successfully landed that plane in the Hudson River, saving all 155 souls onboard. Nothing could be more dramatic than what Captain Sullenberger encountered, so it is an extreme example of the kind of adaption that's critical for those of us working in life-or-death situations.

Those are the kinds of stories that grab all of the headlines, and deservedly so, but I also feel that a critical part of getting through any crisis is hope. It can be dramatic, but much more often, it is camouflaged in people going about their lives, doing everyday tasks.

That type of hope can get us through our darkest moments and onto better days. Hope is the single most important tool for anyone struggling with depression or mental illness – it can save lives. I've seen it happen over and over again, not just on the Bridge but in my experiences talking with people around the world.

We can all find hope. Sometimes, we just need a little help when looking for it.

The RELEASE Model

Combining my years of "boots on the ground" experience, attending training courses such as Crisis Intervention Training and the Federal Bureau of Investigations Crisis Negotiation Course, and speaking with professionals in the mental health field, I have developed a model to address those in distress. The model is called RELEASE.

The RELEASE model will help you throw a lifeline in a non-threatening manner to those who are at pivotal points in their lives, reaching out for hope, empathy, and connectedness with other human beings without being judged.

> *Recognize*
>
> *Engage*
>
> *Listen*
>
> *Empathize*
>
> *Accept*
>
> *Support*
>
> *Encourage*

The RELEASE model is not clinically proven – but it worked for me when I was a CHP Officer responding to crisis incidents.

The key points to focus on are providing the person with a "way out," – a way to communicate without fear of being judged or scrutinized. This is why I never directly challenge someone on the Bridge, even when they say their life isn't worth living. They don't need another confrontation or criticism. They need help.

Up to the point of your intervention, the person may feel no one understands or cares about them. They may be embarrassed or frightened to speak out or ask for help. Using the RELEASE model will allow you to help the person in distress to release bottled up emotions and feelings that otherwise may never have been voiced and are preventing them from living their life to the fullest.

You may just save a life.

RECOGNIZE

Recognize the signs that an individual, or yourself, may need help:

+ Hopelessness – believing that things are terrible and not going to get better
+ Helplessness – believing there is nothing you can do about how you feel or your situation
+ Depression – sadness, social isolation, feelings of being a burden to others
+ Risk-taking behavior
+ Thwarted longing
+ Giving away belongings
+ Non-surgical self injury and/or a prior suicide attempt
+ Increased (or inaugural) drug or alcohol use
+ Not being able to communicate any future plans
+ Increased or decreased amounts of sleep
+ Financial stressors
+ For young adults, additional stressors may include living on their own for the first time, pressure to achieve goals in school and sports, or pressure to try alcohol or drugs.

These are just a few of the signs to look for. If you or someone you know is affected by these symptoms, or even if you think someone doesn't seem like their old self anymore, a conversation is the best place to start. Chances are the conversation won't include anything about suicide.

But what if it does?

ENGAGE

Engage the individual in a conversation, not an inquisition. Time and time again, we hear others say "I knew he had some issues, but I didn't think he'd take his own life. Were things really that bad?"

You can be the barrier between hopelessness and suicide. It is easy for depression to make us feel alone, both physically and emotionally. That's a scary place. It's important to normalize those feelings, to help someone understand that what they're facing doesn't make them weird or different.

Don't be afraid to ask the question: "Have you been having thoughts of killing yourself?" But, before you ask that question, think about how you would react if they respond, "Yes."

Don't panic. Get as much information as you can. Here are some questions that might be helpful:

+ How long have you had these thoughts?
+ Do you have a plan?
+ Have you attempted suicide before? (If they have) What stopped you from completing it?

LISTEN

Listen with the intent to understand. When the individual is speaking, do not interrupt. Use a quiet voice with minimal, short encouraging phrases – "Wow," "Oh yeah?" or "Is that so?" – to demonstrate that you are listening and interested in what you're hearing. Make eye contact. Nod.

If there's something you don't understand, or would like clarification on, paraphrase what you heard back to the individual to show you're engaged. For many people in distress, someone listening to them, without judgment or ridicule, is all they need to get them through that emotional and tumultuous point in their life.

It is best to have this conversation between just the two of you so the individual will feel less overwhelmed or pressured. Others standing around may be detrimental to your connection with the person. Turn off your cell phone and other electronic distractions. Have this conversation in a place comfortable for them, where you will have no interferences. Remember, we are our brother's keeper.

Also, leave any ego behind.

EMPATHIZE

Empathy that is genuine will be accepted and go further in allowing the individual to open up and reveal what true, deeper issues exist. Put yourself in their shoes and sincerely try and understand what is going on in their life.

Unless asked specifically, don't voluntarily compare a similar experience to what they are going through at the moment. If asked, provide a positive, but brief, personal story. Don't make promises or suggestions you know and they know you cannot keep.

ACCEPT

Accept the person for who they are and what they tell you. Getting angry, arguing, or giving false hope is detrimental to your goal. The person may be baring their soul to you, and they do not need to see or feel your surprise, disgust, judgment, or that their issues are insignificant.

Do not be sworn to secrecy. Keep the conversation moving forward in a positive direction.

SUPPORT

Support is crucial. Be ready to accompany the individual to an emergency room or other healthcare facility if needed. Don't be apprehensive about calling the police. Most officers now have training in mental illness and are a valuable asset.

Have a HelpLine/Suicide Prevention phone number with you before you engage the person. Support them in a positive manner such as going to the movies, festivals, or gathering friends for a barbecue. Please note: Taking the individual out all night on a drinking binge is not the support they need.

Here are some numbers that can be helpful:

- National Suicide Prevention Lifeline 1-800-273-8255
- Red Nacional de Prevención del Suicidio 1-888-628-9454
- Military Crisis Line 1-800-273-8255, Press 1

ENCOURAGE

Encourage the individual to seek help if immediate intervention is not required. Offer to assist them in finding professional help and follow up to be sure appointments are made and kept.

Let the person know that you really do care and are there for them. Personal visits, phone calls, and email or text messages are great, but don't be too pushy. Put yourself in their shoes. What kind of encouragement would you want or need?

It sure is great to have someone in your corner. Be someone who really listens and cares, but don't become a nag, calling or texting every couple of hours. You want to check on them, not hover over them. Communication is great, but do not offer clinical advice – leave that to professionals.

The Quality of Life Triad

In fighting my own depression, I developed what I call my Quality of Life Triad. I've shared it and been encouraged since others have found it helpful as well. Again, just like the RELEASE model, this is not a proven clinical treatment – just something that's helped me in my life, and I hope it can help you or someone you know.

On the top of the triangle is "Self-Care." There's a reason it's on top. It's up to me to recognize how I am feeling and it's up to me to take action for my own quality of life.

On the lower left of the triangle is "Professional Care." These are professionals who know me, my history, and can assist with my quality of

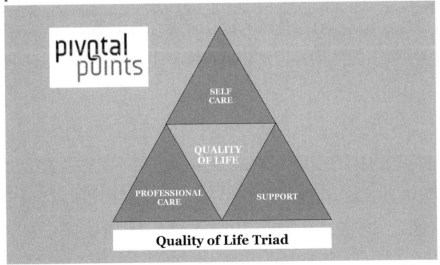

I developed this as a visual aid to help people check on their own mental health. Everyone is different, of course, but this has always worked for me, and I know others have used it with good results.

life with their guidance and evaluations of my overall health.

On the lower right is my "Support" – my right hand so to speak. These are people I can rely on day-to-day for support. Some of these people I can call day or night. They are always there for me and willing to take the time to listen.

These three elements make up the Quality of Life Triad. All three are crucial for success and quality of life. Without any one of those elements working in good health, my life isn't going to be as enjoyable or productive as I'd like. Along those same lines, each element complements the others; when one is working well, the others have less to do.

Self Care: It all begins with self. Yourself. This includes self-esteem, self-compassion, nutrition, fitness, and being honest with your feelings. I find it's helpful to keep a journal of not just how I'm feeling, but how I coped. Having a record like that can really come in handy in the future if and when new problems arise.

Professional Care: Behavioral and physical health clinicians and other professionals who assist with your well-being. This could be a life coach, a personal trainer, yoga instructor, a therapist, or any professional who makes you feel better.

Support: This is your family, your friends, colleagues, a mentor, clubs, social media, and your belief system – religious or otherwise. Basically, anyone or anything you can lean on for guidance.

Crisis Safety Plan

Finally, this book would not be complete without providing a plan for continued success in the event of a mental health crisis.

This Crisis Safety Plan is simply a note to yourself that you complete when all is going well. If you begin to feel your mental health is not as it normally is, or where you think it should be, this list may help you get back on track.

I highly emphasize that if urgent, direct professional help is required, seek it out immediately. This plan certainly does not take the place of a professional counselor, psychiatrist, or psychologist, or a plan they have developed for you, but at least you have something to work with, a starting point.

First, look through these examples and think about what you might list. Blank space has been provided for you to fill out.

1. Warning signs a crisis may be forthcoming:

    Certain thoughts, places, events, dates, moods, smells that may trigger a crisis for you. This could be an anniversary of a death or sad event in your life, an experience you know will upset you, or a person who will put you in a bad mood.

2. Self-coping strategies:

    List things you can do on your own to help mitigate a crisis. Things like deep breathing or meditation, music, crafts, puzzles, cooking, working out. Going to the park or walking your dog. Avoid using drugs or alcohol, and keep weapons locked away. Give the key or combination to someone else.

3. Places where you feel safe or might provide distractions.

    Go out with friends, go to the gym, catch a movie. Places like shopping malls, museums, coffee houses, and concerts can be good.

4. People or organizations to call for assistance.

    These are pre-designated numbers you can call for someone who is familiar with you, and you can call any time of day or night.

5. Goals yet to accomplish.

    Learning to cook, learning a language, traveling, quitting smoking, achieving a desired look or weight, volunteering (crisis hotline, retirement home, local animal shelter), anything you're looking forward to accomplishing. Daily goals are extremely helpful also, even simple ones like taking a dog for a walk or watching birds at a bird feeder.

6. What in my life do I value? What am I responsible for that keeps me going?

    This could be family members, friends, work, responsibility to others, faith, pets. Anything or anyone depending on you.

Okay, now here is a blank plan for you to fill out:

CRISIS SAFETY PLAN

1. Warning signs a crisis may be forthcoming:
    A:
    B:
    C:
    D:

2. Coping strategies I can do:
    A:
    B:
    C:
    D:

3. Places where I feel safe or that provide distractions:

    A:

    B:

    C:

    D:

4. People/Organizations I can contact for assistance:

    A:

    B:

    C:

    D:

5. What goals have I yet to accomplish:

    A:

    B:

    C:

    D:

6. What in my life do I value? What am I responsible for that keeps me going?:

    A:

    B:

    C:

    D:

For more resources on suicide prevention, or if you know someone in danger of attempting, please contact the National Suicide Prevention Lifeline: 1-800-273-8255. For detailed prevention information, please visit www.SAVE.org (Suicide Awareness Voices of Education).

Afterword by Kevin Berthia

The man who saved my life is just Kevin to me now. He is my friend, my hero, and the reason my children have a father. His spirit, kindness, and compassion gave me a second chance when I wanted to die. My life has turned 180 degrees because of this man, and I owe him almost all of the credit.

Reuniting with Kevin after that day on the Bridge has given me the courage to take complete responsibility for my happiness. When I saw him again in New York, on May 7, 2013, and had the opportunity to share my story, it was a priceless experience – I'll never forget that day. I am forever grateful for that chance, and this man. I told my complete story that night for the first time and have since committed to telling my story as much as possible. I now see my past not as a problem, but as a responsibility, something I can share with others who may be headed down the wrong path. I believe I was given this platform.

Kevin has inspired me to let everything go and to take back my peace of mind. I have three wonderful kids, and without Kevin, I would not be on this earth to be their father. Kevin's warmth has helped drive me to take full advantage of the gift of life. I'm able to do regular speaking engagements throughout the country to help others in the same kind of desperation I was experiencing when Kevin and I first met. Social media has helped me reach thousands, maybe millions.

One of those individuals told me: "Because of your story, today I have hope. Yesterday, I was ready to die."

That's exactly what Kevin has done for me. And just like Kevin and I are forever connected, I'm now connected with this beautiful individual. I work every day to keep this going, to take the hope that Kevin helped me find and give it to as many people as possible.

Thank you so much, Kevin Briggs, my friend for life.

Gatekeeper
(for Sgt. Kevin Briggs)
Lyrics by Meg Hutchinson

When the day has grown too long, the hour's standing still
When you wonder if you could, if you will
With your toes upon the edge, with your eyes upon the sky
Tell me just these things before you fly

How are you feeling?
What are your plans for tomorrow?
Will you let me make some, and after, you can do as you will

If your hand should lose the rail, if your heel should lose the chord
Will everything seem fixable that did not before?
See how the sun shines on the bay, the islands over there
You could make it through today if you dare

How are you feeling?
What are your plans for tomorrow?
Will you let me make some, and after, you can do as you will

Maybe every day in ordinary ways
We hold each other on
We keep each other here
How are you feeling?
What are your plans?

Acknowledgements

I wish to personally thank the following people and organizations for their contributions to my vision, mission, and my work. Thank you for providing the knowledge and inspiration for me to do such important work with suicide prevention, including crisis management; thank you for helping to guide me as I have worked on this book project; and most importantly, thank you for the opportunity to work with you, your clients and employees, and for the opportunity to speak to promote suicide prevention, crisis management, and mental health awareness.

My family is first and foremost in my thoughts and my day-to-day life. Certainly without them, my path would have been darker. The joy you bring keeps me going through the rough times, and I feel truly blessed because of each of you.

A hearty thank you to my beautiful family: my father, Richard; my sisters, Kim and Colleen; my sons, Kevin Jr. and Travis; their mother, Midori; my aunt, Barbara Kennedy; and my girlfriend, Mary – thank you for all your work in researching our family history, your patience with me as I wrote this book, and showing me that life has so much to offer.

To Ron and & Judy Barr, who are great friends and valuable mentors: I don't think I would have come this far without you both. Your guidance, friendship, and support have helped guide me both personally and professionally.

To Jamie S. Burton, MBA: You are a wonderful colleague who inspires and drives me to be better at my craft.

To Meg Hutchinson, singer, award-winning songwriter, and composer of the beautiful song "Gatekeeper": Thank you for helping me to realize that tenderness, compassion, and empathy are not signs of weakness, but signs of strength, humility, and true caring about our fellow man.

To Narvella Berthia, mother of Kevin Berthia: Thank you for helping Kevin and me to meet again years later. In our friendship, Kevin shared he had experienced many ups and downs, and that you were always there for him, solidifying his very existence.

To Andrés Roemer, Ph.D., Consulate General of Mexico in San Francisco and creator/curator of Ciudad de las Ideas: Thank you for your wisdom in sharing your experiences, as you have shown me the true value of an education, and that it is not only used to improve yourself, but helps improve others as well.

To Kathryn Schulz, TED speaker, author, and staff writer for *The New Yorker*: Thank you for inviting me to speak at TED2014. It was an honor to be a part of it. The conference was an experience I will never forget. Your compassion to bring suicide prevention and mental health awareness to the stage shows TED's commitment to humanity.

To Shawn Christopher Shea, MD, creator of the Chronological Assessment of Suicide Events (CASE) approach for uncovering suicide ideation and intent: Thank you for teaching me how to approach and speak to someone in crisis. Your class is of great value and should be part of every behavioral health curriculum.

To David Covington, LPC and MBA: You are a true leader and innovator in the field of suicide prevention and intervention and creator of recovery and crisis intervention programs. Thank you for assisting me with learning more about suicide prevention, helping me discover Thomas Joiner, and your enthusiasm for creating a national movement that focuses on saving lives.

To David A. Jobes, Ph.D., ABPP, creator of the Collaborative Assessment and Management of Suicidality (CAMS) approach to those struggling with suicidal thoughts: Your key philosophy of CAMS in teaching clinicians to never judge or shame their suicidal patients, but rather to understand how their suicidal thoughts and behaviors function for them is enlightening and makes sense. It is only then that clinicians can propose alternate and less life-threatening ways of coping and getting their client's needs met that conveys understanding and respect.

To Sarah Parsons, Head of Network Video Programming for *Yahoo!* and winner of the Edward R. Murrow Award for the mini-documentary "Guardian of the Golden Gate Bridge": Thank you for your brilliant work in producing the *Yahoo! News* segment. This documentary was one of the main keys to my career move that focuses on advancing suicide prevention worldwide.

To Sam Mellinger, professional writer and collaborator for this book: You have truly helped me capture the essence of what it was really like working on the Golden Gate Bridge and, sadly, the devastation suicide causes to families and the importance of breaking the stigma regarding mental illness. For helping me help others, thank you.

To Bob Snodgrass, CEO/Publisher of Ascend Books and the entire staff: Thank you for believing in this book and its message.

To the American Foundation for Suicide Prevention (AFSP): Thank you for the information you so freely provide to those who are hurting, those who are seeking hope, and those family members seeking solace.

To the National Alliance on Mental Illness: Thank you for your ongoing advocacy, strength, and focus on reducing stigmas for persons seeking assistance for behavioral health issues.

I am humbled to be connected to a wonderful family, great friends and colleagues, caring organizations, and I am so grateful to have all of you in my life. Thank you.

About the Authors

Kevin Briggs is one of the country's most active advocates for suicide awareness and prevention. Briggs has been featured in *The New Yorker*, *Men's Health*, and *People* magazines as well as several national radio and television shows. Briggs regularly travels the country helping people and businesses learn crisis management, the signs of suicidal risk, and the best steps to help prevent a tragedy that still takes the life of an American every 13 minutes. He is the father of two boys and lives in the San Francisco Bay Area.

Sam Mellinger has worked at *The Kansas City Star* since 2000, the last five years as a sports columnist. His work has been honored by the Associated Press Sports Editors, Kansas and Missouri Press Associations, and Best American Sports Writing. He lives in Kansas City with his wife, Katie, and son, Samuel. This is his second book.

Visit www.ascendbooks.com for more great titles!